"You've Changed"

Studies in Feminist Philosophy is designed to showcase cutting-edge monographs and collections that display the full range of feminist approaches to philosophy, that push feminist thought in important new directions, and that display the outstanding quality of feminist philosophical thought.

Published in the series:

Abortion and Social Responsibility: Depolarizing the Debate
Laurie Shrage

Gender in the Mirror: Confounding Imagery
Diana Tietjens Meyers

Autonomy, Gender, Politics
Marilyn Friedman

Setting the Moral Compass: Essays by Women Philosophers
Edited by Cheshire Calhoun

Burdened Virtues: Virtue Ethics for Liberatory Struggles
Lisa Tessman

On Female Body Experience: "Throwing Like a Girl" and Other Essays
Iris Marion Young

Visible Identities: Race, Gender and the Self
Linda Martín Alcoff

Women and Citizenship
Edited by Marilyn Friedman

Women's Liberation and the Sublime: Feminism, Postmodernism, Environment
Bonnie Mann

Analyzing Oppression
Ann E. Cudd

Self Transformations: Foucault, Ethics, and Normalized Bodies
Cressida J. Heyes

Family Bonds: Genealogies of Race and Gender
Ellen K. Feder

Moral Understandings: A Feminist Study in Ethics, Second Edition
Margaret Urban Walker

The Moral Skeptic
Anita M. Superson

"You've Changed": Sex Reassignment and Personal Identity
Edited by Laurie J. Shrage

"You've Changed"

Sex Reassignment and Personal Identity

EDITED BY

LAURIE J. SHRAGE

OXFORD
UNIVERSITY PRESS
2009

OXFORD
UNIVERSITY PRESS

Oxford University Press, Inc., publishes works that further
Oxford University's objective of excellence
in research, scholarship, and education.

Oxford   New York
Auckland   Cape   Town   Dar es Salaam   Hong Kong   Karachi
Kuala Lumpur   Madrid   Melbourne   Mexico City   Nairobi
New Delhi   Shanghai   Taipei   Toronto

With offices in
Argentina   Austria   Brazil   Chile   Czech Republic   France   Greece
Guatemala   Hungary   Italy   Japan   Poland   Portugal   Singapore
South Korea   Switzerland   Thailand   Turkey   Ukraine   Vietnam

Published by Oxford University Press, Inc.
198 Madison Avenue, New York, New York 10016

www.oup.com

Oxford is a registered trademark of Oxford University Press

Library of Congress Cataloging-in-Publication Data

You've changed : sex reassignment and personal identity /
edited by Laurie J. Shrage.
p. cm.
Includes index.
ISBN 978-0-19-538571-7; 978-0-19-538570-0 (pbk.)
1. Transsexualism. 2. Transgenderism. I. Shrage, Laurie, 1953–
HQ77.9.Y68 2009
306.76'8—dc22   2008047334

Printed in the United States of America
on acid-free paper

Contents

Contributors

Talia Mae Bettcher is associate professor of philosophy at California State University, Los Angeles. She is the author of several articles about transphobia and is currently co-editing a special issue of *Hypatia* titled "Transgender Studies and Feminism: Theory, Politics, and Gendered Realities" with Ann Garry. Bettcher also focuses on early modern philosophy and is the author of *Berkeley's Philosophy of Spirit* (2007).

C. Jacob Hale is currently director of the Center for Sex Research and professor of philosophy at California State University, Northridge. He is the author of "Consuming the Living, Dis(re)membering the Dead in the Butch/Ftm Borderlands" (1998), "Leatherdyke Boys and Their Daddies: How to Have Sex without Women or Men" (1997), and "Are Lesbians Women?" (1996). His teaching interests include feminist, queer, and transgender studies and the philosophy of mathematics.

Kim Q. Hall is associate professor of philosophy and a faculty member of the Women's Studies and Sustainable Development programs at Appalachian State University, Boone, North Carolina. She is currently completing a manuscript titled "Making Our Bodies Our Selves," of which this essay is a part. She is the editor of *Feminist Disability Studies* (forthcoming).

Cressida J. Heyes is Canada Research Chair in Philosophy of Gender and Sexuality at the University of Alberta, Canada. She is the author of *Line Drawings: Defining Women through Feminist Practice* (2000) and of *Self-Transformations: Foucault, Ethics, and Normalized Bodies* (Oxford University Press, 2007), as well as the editor of *The Grammar of Politics: Wittgenstein and Political Philosophy* (2003). She is currently co-editing (with Meredith Jones) a volume of essays on feminism and cosmetic surgery.

Graham Mayeda is assistant professor of law at the University of Ottawa. His current research focuses on theories of global justice, law and development, criminal law, and legal philosophy. He has written numerous articles, including "Re-Imagining Feminist Theory: Transgender Identity and the Law" (2005), "Uncommonly Common: The Nature of Common Law Judgment" (2006), and "Commentary on Fichte's 'The Illegality of the Reproduction of Books': An Essay on Intellectual Property during the Age of the Enlightenment" (2008).

Diana Tietjens Meyers is Ignacio Ellacuria Chair of Normative/Social Ethics and professor of philosophy at Loyola University, Chicago. She is the author of *Being Yourself: Identity, Action and Social Life* (2004), *Gender in the Mirror: Cultural Imagery and Women's Agency* (Oxford University Press, 2002), and *Subjection and Subjectivity: Psychoanalytic Feminism, and Moral Philosophy* (1994). Her edited books include *Feminists Rethink the Self* (1997). She has written numerous articles in the areas of moral, political, and social theory, including "Feminist Perspectives on the Self," in the online *Stanford Encyclopedia of Philosophy*.

Christine Overall is professor of philosophy and holds a University Research Chair at Queen's University, Kingston, Ontario. She is the editor or co-editor of three books and the author of five. The most recent, *Aging, Death, and Human Longevity: A Philosophical Inquiry*, won both the Canadian Philosophical Association's Book Prize (2005) and the Royal Society of Canada's Medal in Bioethics (2006). Her main teaching and research are in the areas of philosophy of religion and feminist philosophy, especially philosophy of the body.

Gayle Salamon is the Cotsen LGBT Postdoctoral Fellow at Princeton University. Her areas of specialization are phenomenology, psychoanalysis, gender theory, and queer theory, and she is currently completing a manuscript on embodiment and trans subjectivity. Recent articles include "Transfeminism and the Future of Women's Studies" in *Women's Studies on the Edge*, edited by Joan Scott (2008), " 'Boys of the Lex': Transgenderism and Rhetorics of Materiality" (2006), and "Sameness, Alterity, Flesh: Luce Irigaray and the Place of Sexual Undecidability" (forthcoming in *Luce Irigaray and "The Greeks"*).

Laurie J. Shrage is director of women's studies and professor of philosophy at Florida International University in Miami. Her books include *Abortion and Social Responsibility: Depolarizing the Debate* (Oxford University Press, 2003) and *Moral Dilemmas of Feminism: Prostitution, Adultery, and Abortion* (1994). She has written papers on ethnic identity and passing, pornography, pay equity, and feminist film theory. Her current work includes "Does the Government Need to Know Your Sex?" at http://publicreason. net/2008/10/10/ppps-does-the-government-need-to-know-your-sex/.

Georgia Warnke is currently professor of philosophy and associate dean at the University of California, Riverside. She is the author of *After Identity: Rethinking Race, Sex, and Gender* (2007), *Legitimate Differences: Interpretation in the Abortion Controversy and Other Public Debates* (1999), *Justice and Interpretation* (1993), *Gadamer: Hermeneutics, Tradition and Reason* (1987), and numerous articles in the areas of moral and political philosophy, contemporary German philosophy, and philosophy of race and gender.

Naomi Zack received her Ph.D. in philosophy from Columbia University in 1970 and, after a twenty-year absence from academia, began teaching at the University at Albany, SUNY, in 1990. She has been professor of philosophy at the University of Oregon since 2001. She is the author of *Race and Mixed Race* (1993), *Bachelors of Science* (1996), *Philosophy of Science and Race* (2002), *Inclusive Feminism* (2005), and the short textbook *Thinking about Race* (2nd edition, 2005). Zack is also the editor of *American Mixed Race* (1995), *RACE/SEX* (1997), and *Women of Color and Philosophy* (2002). Her most recent book, *Ethics for Disaster* (2009), offers philosophical reflection for troubled times.

"You've Changed"

Introduction

Not long ago at the Jazz Bakery in Los Angeles, I heard a group that included the wonderful jazz bassist Jennifer Leitham. As they began playing "You've Changed," Leitham, who once lived as a man, remarked with ironic humor, "my theme song." This is a song about preparing for change—not political change but personal transformation. A lover observes the signs of emotional distance in her beloved and dolefully proclaims, "You've changed.... You're not the angel I once knew.... No need to tell me that we're through." The lover recognizes the signs of waning affection by noting the loss of a familiar person. Profound personal and interpersonal transformations are often described in terms of a discontinuity between a present person and a past self. We often interpret such claims metaphorically rather than literally, but are there circumstances in which a claim of nonidentity between two time stages of once identical selves is literally true? In a news article about a high school principal who transitioned over a summer break, one student interviewed states, "It doesn't matter what happened, it's the person inside. It's the same person. It doesn't really matter if you change the outside."[1] The student's assertion, though, suggests that others around her do not share her conviction about the relatively superficial nature of the change that has occurred. Do some changes to the self (sex, religion, job, or age?) create discontinuities with earlier selves that are profound enough to be described as the emergence of a new self?

There is a large philosophical literature that attempts to articulate the criteria of personal identity. Sometimes questions of personal identity are practical ones. For example, family members and medical providers may need to make treatment decisions for a patient who has suffered severe memory loss. If the patient's requests contradict or are "out of character" with those the patient expressed before the memory loss occurred, which requests best represent the person who is being treated?

3

Is there a new person inhabiting this patient's body, or is it just the same person whose memories have been erased? As this question suggests, two kinds of criteria of personal identity have been discussed and debated: bodily continuity and continuity of critical mental traits. Philosophers have applied these criteria to both real and imagined cases of significant bodily and psychological change in order to settle both practical and theoretical questions regarding when someone is the same, or not, as another person.[2]

Questions about the nature of persons have also been central to debates about gender, race, and sexuality. Do these categories represent essential or accidental features of persons? Are these features grounded in biology or social norms? If I radically alter my gender, race, or sexual orientation, do I become more or less authentic, closer to or further from my "true self"? In an interview with Lucas Silveira (formerly Lillia Silveira) of the Cliks, National Public Radio reporter Renee Montagne comments: "I think most people would think that there almost couldn't be a bigger change than changing your gender…and it's mysterious…to most people."[3] Is gender typically the most unchangeable and defining aspect of a person? How can we demystify the act of changing one's gender in ways that support the civil rights struggles of people representing stigmatized and unfamiliar gender categories?

The essays in this volume bring together philosophical debates about personal identity and feminist debates about gender and sex identity with emerging debates about trans identities. How can we help people make sense of profound transformations of a person's sex or gender? Has something essential or only accidental to the person's original self changed? What does the plasticity of sex and gender attributes tell us about the categories of male and female? Does the terminology currently in use (transman, transwoman, trans, trangender, cisgender, transsexual, intersex, etc.) carve out important distinctions, or does it further mystify human difference? How are sex, gender, and sexuality related, both conceptually and concretely? If sex, like gender, is a social construct, should the informal and formal mechanisms by which we enforce particular sex identities be changed?

Understanding, supporting, and loving "women" have been central to feminist and lesbian theorizing, as well as social and political organizing. Therefore, changing how we assign sex identities to persons will have important consequences for feminist and lesbian projects. For this reason, some feminist and lesbian activists have met the claims of trans and intersex theorists with skepticism, suspicion, and even hostility. There are genuine tensions among the ideas and aims of feminist, lesbian, transsexual, transgender, and intersex activists. For example, these activists often disagree about who is to be included or excluded from single-sex institutions and events, such as schools, shelters, bathrooms, or music festivals. How do we decide who is to be recognized as a woman for the purpose of attending a women's college or festival? How do we decide who can be legitimate partners for sexual intimacy while understanding ourselves as having a particular sexual orientation? Questions such as these have become more complicated in the wake of trans and intersex activism. It is the purpose of this volume to explore some of the epistemological and metaphysical dimensions of sex and gender attributes so that we can better evaluate both our practices of assigning sex identities to persons and the meanings and rights we attach to these statuses. Trans and intersex theorizing and activism promise to enrich and illuminate ideas about sex, gender, and sexuality, just as feminist, lesbian, and queer contributions have done.

The recent debate over the book with the unfortunate title *The Man Who Would Be Queen* raises the issue of professional and scholarly responsibility when academics conduct research or write books that address the issues of marginalized communities.[4] Professors, scientists, and even humanist scholars enjoy certain privileges and opportunities not available to those they write about, and their work can be beneficial or damaging to marginalized communities. Although it is important to foster open and honest discussion of the issues, we need to ask whether our discussion promotes or discourages fair consideration of the perspectives of those who have been stigmatized and oppressed by their sex, gender, or sexual identities. If our theories and conclusions play into and revive prevalent but irrational and demeaning stereotypes, then it is somewhat arrogant and paternalistic to defend such accounts by claiming that they will ultimately serve the interests of the oppressed. The emergence of trans studies attempts to contest the ways that trans individuals have been exploited or sensationalized by others with little concern about the lives and perspectives of trans people themselves.[5]

Given current controversies within and among feminist, gay, lesbian, bisexual, queer, and trans communities, let me further clarify the aims of this collection. One of its primary aims is to subject existing accounts of what takes place when people change their gender or sex to critical and philosophical reflection. Many claims made about the nature of sex or gender self-transformations have metaphysical, epistemological, ontological, and moral dimensions. Whether "sex" is a mental or physical (subjective or objective) attribute, whether a person can have a mind of one sex and a body of another, and whether a person's wish to have healthy parts of one's body amputated is irrational–all these are questions in need of some philosophical reflection. They involve ideas about the relationship between the mind and body, the status of self-knowledge, and how we distinguish objective from merely subjective truths, or reality from illusion and the rational from the irrational. By bringing together the work of feminist philosophers who have addressed such questions, this collection critically engages and evaluates the philosophical underpinnings of claims about changing one's sex or gender.

Another primary aim here is the practical one of bridge building. While recognizing the tensions and potentially incompatible aims of different communities, it is important also to recognize our common interests and goals. Feminists, lesbians, queers, and transwomen and transmen all recognize the need to critique and resist gynephobia, homophobia, transphobia, and, in general, intolerance toward unconventional bodies, genders, and erotic orientations. We also recognize the need to fight for broad access to health care and schools and for marriage rights, employment and housing rights, and so on. Building large and diverse coalitions is important for achieving major and lasting social change. By fostering discussion among feminist, lesbian, queer, trans, and intersex theorists about the meaning of sex and gender attributes, we hope to promote the mutual understanding necessary for enlarging the movement for gender justice.

The contributors to this volume have all, in one way or another, participated in feminist debates about sex, gender, and other categories of identity. Their work has also engaged with various parts of the philosophical literature on personhood, self-knowledge, rationalism, agency, and public reason. They draw on a variety of philosophical schools and approaches, including existentialism, phenomenology, conceptual and linguistic analysis, hermeneutics, psychoanalysis, social constructivism, and realism. Their writings also draw on relatively new areas of research, such as critical race, disability, and queer theory; feminist epistemology and science studies; feminist moral and political theory; and the emerging trans studies. The authors reflect different social locations and identities, as well as degrees of social activism, both within and outside academia. The primary thing we have in common is our interest in exploring the philosophical issues that underlie debates about sex, gender, and sexual orientation.

In "Sex/Gender Transitions and Life-Changing Aspirations," Christine Overall questions whether the alternatives of *becoming* one's true sex or *masking* one's true sex exhaust the ways of understanding the transition from one sex or gender to another. Overall first explores the difficulties with the two standard pictures of sex or gender transitions. She then compares altering one's sex or gender identity to other kinds of life-changing personal transformations and projects, such as changing one's nationality or religion, acquiring an education, or becoming a musician or a parent. We don't usually regard the latter self-transformations as the realization, or masking, of a true inner person, so why should we see becoming a man or woman in this way, even when this means altering one's original identity?

In "Transsexuality and Contextual Identities," Georgia Warnke explores how a person's sex and gender can be experienced or viewed as misaligned. She argues that such situations represent interpretive challenges rather than pathological conditions. Who someone is depends on context: we may be female in one context and Methodist in another. According to Warnke, courts and medical authorities err in taking sex and gender to be somehow more fundamental, able to transcend contextual frameworks. Just as we may feel we have been born into the wrong religion and change our faith, we can feel we have been born into the wrong sex or gender and change either or both. Although such refashionings may be highly significant to the people engaged in or affected by them, Warnke contends that they do not change the contextual conditions of identity.

In "Tracing a Ghostly Memory in My Throat: Reflections on Ftm Feminist Voice and Agency," Jacob Hale explores how the category "transsexual" is constructed by nontranssexual feminist and academic theorists and how these constructions erase, delegitimize, pathologize, or even monsterize the subjects they describe. Many of these constructions fail to recognize the uniqueness of trans subjectivity and various epistemological privileges it can afford. Hale discusses the problematic relationship that ftms (females to males), in particular, have to culturally available gender and sexual categories, and he considers whether one can base notions of selfhood on political values and liberatory identities rather than on the standard distinctions of sex, gender, and sexual orientation.

In "Transsexuality and Daseia Y. Cavers-Huff," Naomi Zack observes that much public discourse about transsexuals invokes the idea that they are compelled or unfree. Zack points out that people who change their sex or gender identity need not always be imagined as passive victims but, instead, may be understood to enjoy forms of freedom and rational choice that often make people who are conventionally gendered feel less free and rational. Zack suggests that all of us might feel less stuck in our identities if we could conceive the relationship between the mind and body as a dynamic one, in which ongoing alterations could flow from one to the other, in either direction. Zack considers how the self-presentational choices of the late philosopher Daseia Cavers-Huff provided a model of this dynamic relationship, which discomfited some free thinkers in the philosophical community.

Philosophers have debated the extent to which subjectivity and mental functioning are logically independent of their physical instantiations. Feminist epistemologists have argued that the disembodied subjects of knowledge and experience typically conjured by (male) philosophers possess culturally defined male attributes and that such depictions of knowers and rational agents deny authority and agency to female subjects. In "The Sexual Schema: Transposition and Transgenderism in *Phenomenology of Perception*," Gayle Salamon explores how the ambiguous gender and sexuality of the embodied subject in Maurice Merleau-Ponty's writings can be useful for trans studies. His phenomenological method suggests that any attempt to discover the "truth" of a body's sex or sexuality must attend closely to the subjective perceptions and experiences of the embodied person rather than foreground an objective external assessment of the body's materiality as an arbiter of truth. If we are not born but become women and men, and can become so only through relations of desire, our membership in any of these categories can perhaps be thought, lived, and perceived differently. Salamon's discussion of Merleau-Ponty challenges the separation and reification of gender and sexual identities for both transgender and nontransgender subjects.

In "Trans Identities and First-Person Authority," Talia Bettcher explores the notion of first-person authority over one's gender. She observes that cultural practices have emerged in trans community contexts which depart from mainstream negotiations of gender, and she elucidates this shift in practice. Bettcher argues that, in mainstream contexts, denial of first-person authority over gender is based on sexually abusive practices and then examines how trans contexts admit an ethical version of first-person authority over gender. She rejects the view that gender is determined by the mere belief that one belongs to a particular gender. It is determined instead by one's fundamental beliefs and values. Avowals of gender can be assessed by others, using interpretive standards, such as the consistency of one's avowals with one's behavior over time. Only those familiar with the relevant practices in the resistant community contexts are in an epistemic position to make assessments. Consequently, epistemic authority over gender becomes an intersubjective matter, saturating entire community contexts rather than residing in individual first-person or third-person experts.

In a society that objectifies, sexualizes, aestheticizes, and pathologizes women's bodies, women may feel alienated from their bodies or those body parts that are the source of their stigmatization. Feminists have responded by celebrating women's bodies and bodily functions, encouraging women to embrace their sexed body parts.

In "Queer Breasted Experience," Kim Hall questions whether the need to celebrate the female body has turned into an imperative to accept one's female embodiment, regardless of one's gender identity. Hall develops a phenomenological account of female embodiment that does not assume a feminine subject, and she argues that transforming our bodies to better express ourselves does not always represent self-hatred. Moreover, refusing surgical reconstructions and other medical therapies does not necessarily signify that one valorizes the body as a natural, presocial object, congruent with one's gender.

Feminist theorists have questioned body-modification practices that appear to reflect culturally induced low self-esteem, such as breast enlargement surgery and vaginoplasty, extreme dieting, hormone-replacement therapy after menopause, and the enormous amounts of time and money women invest in nail polishing, hair dying, hair removal, make-up application, and so on. Similarly, critical race theories have questioned body modification practices that reflect culturally induced racial self-hatred, such as skin lightening, hair straightening, and eyelid and other cosmetic surgeries. In this context, some feminists have questioned whether the body-modification practices associated with transsexuals reflect and perpetuate conformity to pernicious gender stereotypes and racialized standards of beauty. Others have argued that the practices of trans individuals challenge both gender conformity and the persecution of individuals who fail to conform to our deeply ingrained expectations. In "Changing Race, Changing Sex: The Ethics of Self-Transformation," Cressida Heyes notes that criticisms of transsexual identities often employ misleading analogies linking race and sex. Heyes argues that practices involving changes in racial identity are shaped by ideas of social solidarity and class movement. Such cases are complicated by a view of race that sees it as genealogical, in a way that sex is not. Yet Heyes warns that emphasizing disanalogies with race to bolster arguments about the ethical acceptability of sex change works to sever each category from its history. Whatever ethical conclusions one draws about either race change or sex change will need to be informed by the histories of subject categories.

In "Artifice and Authenticity: Gender Technology and Agency in Two Jenny Saville Portraits," Diana Tietjens Meyers analyzes the imagery of artist Jenny Saville to explore questions about human agency, gendered selves, and the body. Meyers looks at the representational practices of Saville to guide our understanding of the meaning of gender-related body alterations and whether they represent capitulation to restrictive gender norms or expressions of human creativity in the fashioning of the self. Meyers shows how Saville's paintings draw our attention to the body as both a source of gender objectification and a source of gender subversion, and thereby help us to distinguish objectifying from liberatory body-modification practices. Meyers suggests that we think of trans body alterations not as fixes for imperfect bodies and their diminished selves but as expansions of agency and the self through extensions and transformations of the body.

In "Sex and Miscibility," I compare our ordinary criteria for sexing bodies with theories about sex differentiation emanating from evolutionary biology, genetics, medicine, and history. I first compare our criteria for sexing bodies with those we commonly employ to sort bodies by race and argue that, in both cases, our criteria are circularly defined in ways that allow socially based groupings to appear as natural ones. I then compare two strategies for making visible the social origins and inadequacies of our classificatory tools: introducing new terms for sex categories and refusing in some instances to classify people by sex. I note some of the problems with the first strategy and some advantages of the second, but overall I advocate a "partial elimitivism" with regard to sex classification.

In "Who Do You Think You Are? When Should the Law Let You Be Who You Want to Be?" Graham Mayeda considers whether the state should permit individuals to self-identify when it comes to disclosing their gender or sex. Both private and public institutions often need to have information about an individual's sex or gender in order to provide services, such as the use of a bathroom or locker room, admission to a prison or counseling facility, access to medical and employment benefits, and material redress for illicit sex-based discrimination. Mayeda questions whether the provision of such services would be disrupted if individuals were allowed to control their official sex and gender status and also whether self-identification would undermine the promotion of women's equality. Mayeda distinguishes between the moral obligations individuals have in recognizing each others' identities and the obligations of the state in protecting the rights of different groups. Mayeda concludes that, in order to balance the rights of different groups, the state should recognize an individual's self-chosen identity in some instances but not in others.

This collection of essays raises issues not only about the sex or gender identities of trans and intersex individuals but also about the sex or gender identities of those who see themselves as normally sexed and gendered. Many of the authors here contend that our sex and gender identities work like other social identities (race, religion, class, nationality, sexuality) and that each of us is capable of undertaking projects of self-transformation that could lead to altering these seemingly primary and fixed identities. So one interesting issue is why so many of us passively accept our assigned sex identity or cannot conceive of changing this identity? Although changing our sex is not practical in many cases, or socially and legally simple, we nevertheless should be able to imagine doing so, just as we can imagine changing our religion or class. When our imaginations are limited in this way, is this a problem?

Another issue is why people are often made uncomfortable when they are unable to determine a person's sex (or race). Why do we think we need this information in order to interact with someone, even superficially? Why are we reluctant to use sex-neutral (or race-neutral) descriptors when referring to people, and how does the constant use of sex-specific and race-specific language affirm the importance of these categories for organizing social life?

A different issue that could be pursued concerns the gap between current scientific understandings of race or sex and popular conceptions of race or sex. Modern biology has shown that race distinctions are not biologically significant, that the criteria for sexing bodies are multiple and complex, that these criteria have changed in the course of human history, and that the physiological mechanisms for sex differentiation have changed over the longer time span of species evolution and are still evolving, and there are more types of bodies than simply "m" or "f." Yet, this knowledge has not filtered down to public schools and is not reflected in public dialogue about the significance of race and sex distinctions. That is, scientifically outdated conceptions of race and sex persist in the public sphere. How can we change this?

Lastly, in the last few decades we have become used to thinking of ourselves as having a sexual orientation. Yet the available sexual orientations (hetero or gay) depend on people having stable sex identities. How will this change if we begin to understand our sex identities as less fixed or less either/or? Will most people start to think of themselves as "bi," will sexual orientation become less socially important, or will it be based on something other than being attracted to someone of the same or opposite sex?

NOTES

1. Quoted in Tina Kelley, "A Stir, but No Crisis, from Principal's Gender Change," *New York Times*, September 10, 2007, at http://www.nytimes.com/2007/09/10/education/10trans.html?ei=5070&en=850c5728c1b278b7&ex=1190088000&adxnnl=1&emc=eta1&adxnnlx=1189537527–97uSEY+b/tg10YtqiMrYWQ (accessed on 9/11/08).

2. Searching the online *Stanford Encyclopedia of Philosophy* by using the term "personal identity" results in several articles that provide overviews of this literature; at http://plato.stanford.edu/ (accessed on 9/11/08).

3. Renee Montague, "Cliks Lead Singer Silveira: Welcoming Change," National Public Radio, at http://www.npr.org/templates/story/story.php?storyId=13992424 (accessed on 9/11/08).

4. At http://www.nytimes.com/2007/08/21/health/psychology/21gender.html?ei=5070&en=208985e96b77d344&ex=1188964800&adxnnl=1&adxnnlx=1188843785-ufSlwpVRpgkg6BY03xwIQA (accessed on 9/11/08) and http://www.bioethics.northwestern.edu/faculty/work/dreger/controversy_tmwwbq.pdf (accessed on 9/11/08).

5. At http://sandystone.com/hale.rules.html (accessed on 9/11/08).

1

Sex/Gender Transitions and Life-Changing Aspirations

Christine Overall

The issue in which I am interested is a broad metaphysical one: how to understand the metaphysics of changing from woman to man or man to woman. Who or what is changed, and who or what remains the same? How, if at all, do these changes affect personal identity?

In this essay, I use the general term "trans" to refer to individuals who go through changes from man to woman or woman to man, deliberately glossing over the differences among transgendered and transsexual individuals. Here I am indebted to the work of Bobby Noble, who writes, "The pedantic distinction between 'transgender' and 'transsexual' cannot hold, especially for female to male transsexual men for whom surgeries are always already incomplete." Noble therefore uses "the prefix 'trans-' to signify subjectivities where bodies are at odds with gender presentation, regardless of whether that mis-alignment is self-evident in conventional ways or not" (Noble 2006, 102 n. 2).

I use the term "transition" to refer to the changes trans people undergo and the term "sex/gender" to refer to the context of what is changed. I also sometimes use the terms "gender" and "sex" on their own. As an attribute of individuals, gender is the presentation or identification (or both) of self as being a woman or a man or some permutation thereof. In this sense, gender includes femininities, masculinities, and all the variations on and revisions of them. By "sex" I mean (human) female and male, as well as (human) femaleness and (human) maleness, and I define femaleness and maleness primarily in terms of the presence of the genitalia standardly associated with each: the vulva (usually with clitoris and vagina) in the case of female, and the penis (usually with testicles) in the case of maleness. I recognize that these definitions are not parallel; that, for example, testicles are gonads whereas the clitoris and vagina are not. Moreover, my definition does not take into account the presence or absence of X and Y chromosomes or the presence or absence of specific hormones. However, in defining "sex," I am trying to capture what I think is a standard, general, nontheoretical understanding of sex—that is, femaleness and maleness—in ordinary prevailing discourse.

I assume that gender and sex are not identical but distinct, yet are equally products of social construction. While I do not have room to make that case here, I will just point out that it is by means of social processes, not biological determinism, that an individual's sex gets defined in historically specific ways and becomes almost always the most significant way of categorizing her or him (indeed, a necessary condition for personhood [Scheman 1997, 132–33, 140]), and that the genitalia are seen as representative or even determinative of who and what an individual is. As Michel Foucault memorably and ironically puts it, "it is in the area of sex that we must search for the most secret and profound truths about the individual,... it is there that we can best discover what he is and what determines him.... It is sex itself which hides the most secret parts of the individual: the structure of his fantasies, the roots of his ego, the forms of his relationship to reality" (Foucault 1980, x–xi). At the same time, trans individuals show, perhaps more than anyone else, that one's genitalia do not inevitably represent, let alone determine through biological inevitability, who or what human beings are.

In what follows I present two general and fairly common theories about sex/gender transitions and personal identity and show the problems in each one. I then go on to suggest a third way of understanding sex/gender transitions and their relationship to personal identity, a way of understanding that is, I hope, consistent with the lived experience of trans individuals as reported in their own writings.

Two Theories of Sex/Gender Transition and Personal Identity

Traditional theories of sex/gender transition have tended to understand its relationship to personal identity by means of a crude metaphor of masquerade: either (1) the "true" person is thought to be the individual manifested through and by the original sex/gender status, and the transition is, metaphorically, the donning of a mask that conceals the true sex/gender, or (2) the "true" person is thought to have been hidden behind a metaphorical mask of the wrong sex/gender, and the individual's true sex/gender is accurately revealed via the process of transition. The first version of the masquerade hypothesis is adopted by some nontrans people, usually those who are skeptical about trans individuals' credibility. The second version is adopted by some trans people. Despite being very different, what they have in common is the assumption that the real person is a reified self that constitutes the core of the individual and does not change during the ostensible transition.

I consider and evaluate each theory in turn. First, is it the case that the "true" person is the individual manifested through and by the original sex/gender status, so that transitioning is the donning of a metaphorical mask that conceals the real sex/gender?

The problem with this theory is that it means the person who goes through transition is either deluded or duplicitous. The individual must be seen as engaged in either an accidental or a deliberate misalignment between self-presentation and genitalia, in that they have, in the words of Talia Mae Bettcher, "through their gender presentation, given 'incorrect information' about what is between their legs" (Bettcher 2006, 205). That is, either the person is subject to some sort of major personality disorder and fails to understand his/her true sex/gender status, or the person, for whatever reasons, is trying to fool others. I refer to this idea as the "deluded or duplicitous" disjunct.

With respect to the first possibility, delusion, it is both condescending and patronizing in the extreme to write off all those who go through sex/gender transitions as deluded. There are too many people, of too varied backgrounds, roles, experience, and education, to permit it to be plausible that they are all subject to delusion.[1] What is more important is that the possibility of their being deluded is belied by their autobiographies and other writings, along with the evidence of their competencies. Consider, for example, people as accomplished and different from one another, as Kate Bornstein (1994), Leslie Feinberg (1996), Deirdre McCloskey (1999), Henry Rubin (2003), and Bobby Noble (2006). Certainly trans individuals suffer, and some of them may experience psychological problems. But these facts are in no way evidence of delusion, since many people who are not trans also suffer and have psychological problems, and arguably much of the suffering and many of the psychological difficulties undergone by trans individuals may be occasioned by the incessant, relentless social pressure, ridicule, discrimination, oppression, and even personal danger to which they are often subjected (e.g., Scanlon 2006). Indeed, it might be argued that it is extraordinary how healthy and strong trans people are, given the cruelty and social injustice that they routinely experience.

The second possibility is that trans individuals are deliberately duplicitous. Here one of the previous counterarguments applies: that there are too many people—of too varied backgrounds, roles, experience, and education—to make it at all plausible that every one of them is engaging in deceit. Moreover, even if they were engaged in deliberate deceit, then, arguably, many of them have failed and have indeed engaged in self-sabotage. For some trans people, like Kate Bornstein, deliberately "out" themselves as individuals who have undergone a transition from one sex/gender to another (Bornstein 1994). Moreover, even if they do not deliberately out themselves, the privacy and dignity of trans persons are all too frequently violated by individuals who inappropriately make it their business to try to discover the nature of the transition. So, if the theory attributes deliberate duplicity to trans people, then they would appear to be rather frequently unsuccessful. In that case, given the manifest rationality, competence, and dignity of trans individuals who have spoken or written about their lives, it is hard to see why they would engage in duplicity.

In addition, the hypothesis of deliberate deception raises the question, for what end? What could trans individuals possibly gain by this purported attempt at deceit? For in fact, by making the sex/gender transition they are likely also to be making themselves vulnerable to physical attack or, at the very least, open to treatment with discrimination and scorn by bigots. There would seem to be little to be gained by deception about one's sex/gender other than in some historically significant periods where, for women, passing as a man provided some advantages with respect to work (such as the military) or relationships (e.g., with another woman) (Faderman 1981).

There is, of course, the "privilege" argument. Some feminists have worried that female-to-male (ftm) trans people, for example, are seeking out so-called male privilege or that male-to-female (mtf) trans people are surreptitiously seeking to enjoy the warmth of women's communities (Raymond 1979). But a trans identity, far from being a formula for privilege or protection, is in fact a marker for oppression. As Kyle Scanlon puts it, being trans means "fighting for survival, recognition, equality, housing, employment, safety and medical care" (Scanlon 2006, 88). Scanlon adds:

> How much male privilege does a trans man actually have if he is forced to burn his old pictures, avoid old friends and make up a new history to avoid anyone discovering the truth about him. A trans man who transitions at his workplace...may never become "one of the boys," and that glass ceiling might always be there hovering just above his head. If he tries to change jobs, for the rest of his life he cannot use his old career references and will have to start from scratch. (92)

As for trans women, Scanlon remarks: "A transsexual woman can't even get a much-used mattress at an overcrowded shelter for one winter night, and...she's got privilege? What's the privilege, exactly? That she'll get to freeze outside, I guess" (92). In most circumstances in twenty-first-century North America, then, an individual could seek a sex/gender transition for the sake of privilege only if the individual is severely deluded. But that was the first disjunct, which I have already argued is false.

I conclude that trans individuals are neither deluded nor duplicitous and that the first form of the masquerade hypothesis is false. That is, it is true neither that the "real" person is the individual manifested through and by the original sex/gender status nor that transitioning is the donning of a metaphorical mask that conceals the true sex/gender.

The second version of the masquerade hypothesis is that the "true" person is hidden under a mask of the wrong sex and hence is revealed via the process of transitioning. According to this theory, trans persons' "bodies fail to express what they are inside" (Rubin 2003, 149).[2] I call this the "gender within" theory. Some trans people themselves have adopted this point of view and explain what they take to be their body's failure to reflect their core self as the result of a mistake by God, a genetic mutation, a chemical imbalance, or even, in the case of ftms, underdeveloped or hidden male anatomy (151).

For example, an anonymous interviewee in a study of transitioning says, "I don't know if it comes through, you know, different hormonal changes during pregnancy...and whether it's born or not, and there's some research on brain differences and...things like that, but...either way...it's just something that I have naturally had" (quoted in Hill 2006, 41). Similarly, writer Lesley Carter says, "I firmly believe that I was born a woman but lived in an uncomfortable denial for many years" (Carter 2006, 56). Alaina Hardie writes, "I've known all my life that I am a girl. I remember arguing enthusiastically as a child that I was not, in fact, the boy that people kept thinking I was. I have at various points in my life attempted to be the boy that everybody in my life seemed to want me to be. It never quite worked out. I came to terms with this several years ago, embraced my own identity and transitioned for the final time" (Hardie 2006, 122). An anonymous trans man is quoted as saying, in regard to his former breasts, "It's such a paradox to have to cut some parts of myself off in order to feel more like my self" (quoted in Noble 2006, 101). Another transman describes himself as the victim of "estrogen poisoning" (Rubin 2003, 100).

The idea behind this theory is that in trans persons there is a woman inside a man's body or a man inside a woman's body. Rubin describes it, in the case of ftms, as "a tension between the individual's body image and his material body" (Rubin 2003, 94) and says that transitions are "a means of making their identities visible and recognizable to the public" (145). During transition, "Who they are at heart does not change" (143). From this perspective, trans individuals prior to their transition have often been engaged in struggling for appropriate gender recognition for most of their lives; the transition finally allows them to be perceived as who they truly are. It is not a transformation (143) but an effort to repair "the link between their bodies and their gender identity" (144).

There are, however, several problems with this theory.

To begin, there is a pragmatic political problem. As a form of gender essentialism (Rubin 2003, 145) the gender-within theory has dangerous political implications. For at least three decades, feminists have been engaged in laying out the dangers of any view that sees gender as innate (e.g., Fuss 1989, Spelman 1988). If people are or can be born with a particular gender, then one is what one was born to be, and one has little or no choice about gendered characteristics, behavior, and goals. Gender change becomes impossible.

In response, it might be protested that, in fact, the theory is much more enlightened than traditional views of gender roles and identities. For this theory of sex/gender transition claims, on the evidence, that people *can* change in regard to fundamental gender characteristics. Their future is not dictated by their genitalia.

Unfortunately, however, on this theory, gender change is only apparent. Instead of destiny's being dictated by one's genitalia, destiny is dictated by one's "true" gender identity. The transitioning individual was formerly masked by an inappropriate sex and subsequently reveals and lives out his or her "true" gender identity. The theory assumes that the individual is "always already" the man or woman that was concealed and, through transition, is revealed. Hence, on this theory, gender is permanent and reified, at least for some individuals. As a member of the social grouping "women," I find this idea frightening.

Of course, the fact that the idea of gender underlying this theory is frightening for some people, and that it could have dangerous political implications, does not show that it is false; it shows only that feminists (and feminists include many trans individuals) should be worried about it. But I also want to argue that there are serious metaphysical errors incorporated within the theory.

First, on one interpretation, the theory appears to entail the adoption of a rather simple mind-body dualism, involving a woman's mind or spirit or soul in a male body, or a man's mind or spirit or soul in a female body. It is hard to make sense of this form of Cartesianism.[3] All the traditional criticisms of mind-body dualism apply: What is the relationship between the nonmaterial subject and the body? How do the body and the nonmaterial subject communicate? How does the nonmaterial subject succeed in controlling the physical body?

Second, what is even more mysterious is how a nonmaterial *woman* entity could develop inside a material male body, or how a nonmaterial *man* entity could develop inside a material female body. For trans individuals have almost always been treated by others—including parents, siblings, teachers, and neighbors—as if their gender reflected their genitalia. There appears to be no way that a gendered nonmaterial subject that fails to cohere with their sex could develop.

The response given by this theory, of course, is that it did not develop; the gendered nonmaterial subject was always present—from birth or perhaps even before. The trans person's gender is inherent in the individual. Such a claim is not an explanation but merely a refusal to give an explanation. For the problem is that gender is thoroughly social. As Simone de Beauvoir famously wrote, "One is not born, but rather becomes, a woman" (Beauvoir 1952, 249). No infant is born liking pink, or knowing how to walk and talk and dress like a girl, or preferring dolls over trucks, or wanting to wear dresses rather than trousers. All the meanings and accoutrements of gender are learned. It is literally impossible to be, as Lesley Carter claims, "born a woman" (Carter 2006, 56). One has to acquire the characteristics and accomplishments of femininity. The evidence for the social, learned nature of gender lies in the enormous variations of gender from one culture to another and from one class to another. The very meaning of "girl," "boy," "woman," and "man" is socially defined. As Marilyn Frye sardonically but accurately observes, "one can see nothing about boys or girls considered in themselves which seems to connect essentially with the distinction between wrenches and eggbeaters" (Frye 1983, 18). As a result, one cannot have a sex/gender identity without first learning, through the process of socialization, what that sex/gender is like within one's specific culture. So the notion that an individual is born as one gender or another ignores everything now known about the creation, acquisition, and development of gender knowledge, skills, and self-presentation.

Now, it might be objected to the account I have just given of the mind-body dualism inherent in the masquerade account that the inborn woman or man that is masked by the wrong genitalia is not immaterial at all, but rather solidly material, and located specifically in the brain.[4] Recall that the anonymous interviewee, quoted earlier, said, "I don't know if it comes through, you know, different hormonal changes during pregnancy...and whether it's born or not, and there's some research on brain differences and...things like that, but...either way...it's just something that I have naturally had" (quoted in Hill 2006, 41). Similarly, mtf Christine Daniels (writing as Mike Penner) says, "Recent studies have shown that such physiological factors as genetics and hormonal fluctuations during pregnancy can significantly alter how our brains are 'wired' at birth. As extensive therapy and testing have confirmed, my brain was wired female" (Penner 2007). According to this account, human brains have a sex, female or male, and trans people are individuals whose brains are sexed differently from what their genitalia or even their chromosomes may signify. It is this differently sexed brain that creates the need and motive for unmasking via sex/gender transition.

But changing the mind-body dualism of masquerade theory to a brain-body dualism does not obviate the difficulties in masquerade theory. The claim that the brain in trans individuals is sexed in a way that fails to be congruent with their genitalia or their chromosomes is, I suspect, either incoherent or false. First, if "sex" is defined (as in ordinary usage) in terms of genitalia, then it is incoherent to say that the brain is female or male, since the brain does not have genitalia. So it is a category mistake to say that the brain is sexed in that way. Second, if "sex" is defined, quasi-scientifically, in terms of chromosomes, then although chromosomes are found in the brain, those chromosomes are no different in composition (usually but not always XX or XY) than those found elsewhere in the body, including the genitalia. So it is false to say that the brain is or has a different sex than the rest of the body. Third, if "sex" is defined, somewhat anomalously, in terms of gendered characteristics and behavior, then it is also false to say the brain has an inherent sex, for, as I already pointed out, individuals must learn what constitutes the appropriate gender in the particular culture in which they grow up. The brain does not come into existence knowing the characteristics and behavior regarded as definitive of masculinity or femininity within the particular culture into which it is born.

Perhaps the claim about the alleged sexing of the brain could be interpreted in another way. Female brains are simply those that have the characteristics found in normatively female persons, and male brains are those that have the characteristics found in normatively male persons. Trans persons, then, might be claimed to have brains both unlike the brains of those with whom they share a bodily sex and like the brains of those to whose sex/gender they aspire to transition.

This claim is at least conceptually coherent. Its truth, however, would rely on the evidence for three very broad empirical claims: first, that the brains of all normatively female persons have similar characteristics; second, that those characteristics are significantly different from the characteristics of the brains of all normatively male persons, whose brains, in turn, all share significant characteristics; and third, that the characteristics of the brains of all trans persons share characteristics with the brains of the sex/gender to which they aspire to transition or have transitioned. These claims are potentially testable, but, given the huge extent of human variations, *among* female bodies and *among* male bodies, there are good reasons to be skeptical about the likelihood that they will turn out to be true.

But perhaps, it might be argued, trans persons are driven not directly by their brain structure but by their sex hormones to seek transition.

However, every human being is subject to the influence of endogenous hormones, so trans persons are not unique in that respect. Hormones do not directly determine one's sex/gender identity for three reasons. First, as biologist Anne Fausto-Sterling points out, the so-called sex hormones are misnamed: they are not specific to males or to females, they affect many organs in the bodies of persons of both sexes, and persons of each sex produce both estrogen and testosterone (Fausto-Sterling 2000, 147). She therefore rejects the label "sex hormone" altogether (193).

More generally, the problem with brain-body dualism as a way of saving the masquerade theory, is, as I said earlier, that what being a woman or a man means within a culture is highly variable and sex/gender cannot be produced without the intervention of learning and the individual's direct participation—whether conforming or resisting—in gendered culture. Moreover, to regard trans identity as reducible to a biological cause is to fail to take into account the social nature of sex/gender identities and belief formation. There is no more reason to suppose that convictions about one's sex/gender, and desires or hopes about modifying it, have just one cause than there is to suppose that any other convictions about one's identity and desires or hopes about modifying it have just one cause. Like all human beings, trans individuals are complex. To attribute trans identity to a hormonal cause is both to grossly underestimate the complexity of sex/gender identity and to trivialize the trans persons' sex/gender project.[5]

More generally, however, it is important to distinguish between the *causes* of the idea that one is a different sex/gender than is signaled by the genitalia, on the one hand, and the *epistemology* of that idea, on the other hand. There is no doubt that the convictions, desires, and hopes of any human being have causes. In no way do I deny that human beings are material entities who are who they are in part by virtue of their embodiment. I do not deny that biological factors may contribute to the development of the desire and felt need for sex/gender transition. But when trans persons make claims about their sex/gender, they are asserting their integrity, their sense of who they are as persons. They are offering an *interpretation* of their embodied being, not merely reacting, in stimulus-response fashion, to the prompting of hormones.

I therefore conclude that the second version of the masquerade hypothesis—that the "true" person is hidden behind a mask of the wrong sex/gender, and the individual's true sex/gender is accurately revealed via the process of transition—has so many problems as to be unsustainable.

An Alternative Approach

So far I have discussed two theories of sex/gender transition. Either (1) the "true" person is said to be the individual manifested through and by the original sex/gender status, and the transition is the donning of a mask that conceals the true sex/gender, or (2) the "true" person is said to have been hidden behind a mask of the wrong sex/gender, and the individual's true sex/gender is accurately revealed via the process of transition. What they have in common is the assumption that the real person is a reified self that constitutes the core of the individual and that does not change during the transition. I have argued that each theory involves insuperable philosophical problems. What, then, might be a workable theory of the metaphysics of sex/gender transition? I suggest another possible approach.

Those who undergo a sex/gender transition reveal the degree to which sex/gender in all human persons involves choice (or, rather, a series of choices) and is an ongoing life project. For human beings, sex/gender identity is neither an inborn fact nor a fait accompli imposed during childhood through socialization. Instead, it is an ongoing life project in which each of us engages in strategic decisions and actions to shape and present our sex/gender performance. The social expectations for sex/gender performance and display, which can be quite exacting, nonetheless vary, at least by race, age, sexual orientation, and socioeconomic class. Feminists, with good reason, typically argue for deliberate skepticism about and resistance to orthodox, conformist versions of sex/gender performance. But feminists and nonfeminists alike make both conscious and unconscious choices about the ways in which they will manifest their sex/gender. Moreover, everyone, to one degree or another, makes adjustments in their sex/gender performance to suit the demands of employment, family life, friends, and lovers, or for reasons of comfort and convenience, or to promote personal safety, or as a result of aesthetic or moral judgments.

The metaphysical problem of identity in sex/gender transitions arises from assuming that these transitions must necessarily be qualitatively different from other major changes in people's lives and that there are no other precedents by which to understand them. If those assumptions are false, then there is something to be learned from an examination of other major life changes. As John P. Lizza puts it, "If . . . our nature is not fixed and . . . we can create, at least in part, who we are, then personhood and personal identity should be approached more as open-ended projects than as realities determined by factors independent of the choices we make" (Lizza 2006, 49).

Sex/gender transition is best understood, I suggest, by analogy to other life-changing and life-enhancing aspirations for personal transformation and self-realization.[6] Some goals and aspirations are deeply felt and of central value to particular individuals, and it is those goals and aspirations that provide the dominant drivers of the individual. I understand these aspirations as life-changing projects undertaken by embodied human persons within specific social contexts. Such aspirations include, for example, becoming an immigrant; joining a twelve-step program in order to give up an alcohol- or drug-addicted past; leaving or joining a religious order; surviving a serious accident, illness, or near-death experience and making life-changing decisions as a result; and taking on a transformative role such as motherhood. In all these cases, the aspirant seeks to change herself (and sometimes her physical environment), to change her relationship with others, and to change others' relationship with her. Because to be a person is to be at once and inextricably both a biological entity and an individual with a mental, moral, and social life, experiences of personal transformation often have concomitant effects on one's nature as a physical being. In aspiring to transformation, a person often also aspires to be someone who changes her body or uses it in new ways. The person who undergoes a sex/gender transition is someone who seeks a radical transformation of and in her or his sex/gender project. Thus, as Anna Kirkland writes:

> Trans people are imagining life without the gender role into which they were born, of course, but many are simultaneously imagining taking up another one that is also richly described in normative stereotypes, just like ones that most nontrans men and women occupy throughout their lives. Many seek or occupy an alternative gender precisely because it is meaningful and full of content for the dignified individuality they want to construct. (Kirkland 2006, 91)[7]

In describing their trans identity, trans persons often say, "this is who I really am." What the trans individual cares about is authenticity, "a search for recognition of the innermost self" (Rubin 2003, 15). As mtf Jennifer Finney Boylan puts it, in describing her book about transitioning, "The question I'm asking is not 'How do you have a sex change?' but 'How do you live an authentic life?'" (quoted in Pozner 2004, 7). But in expressing the yearning for authenticity as a search for recognition of the innermost self (Meyerowitz 2002, 138), it is not necessary to postulate a core gendered component of the self, whether material or nonmaterial, that longs to break free.

The individual who undergoes a sex/gender transition cannot necessarily fully foresee what she will become, or the extent of the changes in her life once her aspiration for change has been realized. She cannot be sure that her aspiration will be fully realized, or realized in the way in which she anticipated.[8] But in going through the transition, she does not cease to be herself. Just as extensive international travel, several years of intensive education, undergoing a religious or moral or intellectual conversion,[9] raising children, or experiencing a severe illness or disability can transform one's life while one yet remains the same person, so also the individual who goes through a sex/gender transition undergoes continuing change, growth, development, and self-definition without losing the continuity that enables her to understand herself as one being.

In what way does the person herself persist through the sex/gender transition? She persists insofar as her way of being, after transition, is desired and actively sought by her previous self, so that the way of being after the transition grows out of the previous self, is generated by the previous self, and can be understood in terms of characteristics of the previous self.

Here I am adopting some ideas of William Wilkerson (2007b), who argues in a recent paper that all sexual orientations are subject to choice. The reason is that sexual orientations—and I would add, sex/gender identities—are no more epistemologically given than any other aspect of our self-understanding. Everything we as human beings know or believe about ourselves is known under some description and by virtue of some conceptual matrix: "Neither the desires, nor the social categories, nor the chosen responses are primary, but instead all of them are coconstitutive and coeval in the process by which sexual orientation and sexual identity fuse together" (Wilkerson 2007a, 4). He continues:

> Insofar as the meaning[s] of feelings are not given, but form in a process, and insofar as individuals actively constitute the meaning of their experiences in creating their identity, they must in some way actively constitute the meaning of their feelings and desire....Putting this point differently, choices are involved in any act of interpretation....If a person makes choices when interpreting their feelings and experiences, and *these interpretive choices partly determine these experiences themselves*, choice must be involved in the formation of the feelings and desires that make up sexual orientation. (Wilkerson 2007a, 88)

Sexual orientation and sex/gender identity are complex; they are not reducible to a single, simple feeling or even easily conceptualized as a group of simple feelings. They also involve beliefs, attitudes, and behavioral repertoires, among other items. The beliefs that any person has about her or his sexual orientation or sex/gender identity are not derived from a self-warranting feeling but come about through processes of interpretation, choice, and active performance. Similarly, the fact that a person believes she is a woman inside, despite having male genitalia, is not an uncontestable claim about an indubitable sense datum.[10] It is not a belief based solely on a feeling about which she has unimpeachable certainty. If our ideas about our sexual orientation and our gender identity were infallible—if somehow sexual orientation and sex/gender identity were immediately given—then no one could ever experience doubt or confusion about them. The fact that people do suggests that sexual orientation and sex/gender identity are not immediately given. They are not the uninterpreted deliverances of internal sensations.

This is not to say that individuals cannot be epistemic authorities concerning their sexual orientation and sex/gender identity; it is simply to say that this authority is not based on direct awareness of a datum. Instead, sexual orientation and sex/gender identity are developed by and understood through a series of interpretations.[11] These interpretations are not merely internal and private; they are formulated, usually, within the context of a community of like-minded individuals

Whatever our sexual orientation and *whatever* our sex/gender identity may be, we develop them by, in effect, creating the continuing narrative of our lives. Whereas the sex/gender identity of nontrans persons is an ongoing narrative project derived from their original sex/gender assignment, the sex/gender identity of trans persons is an ongoing narrative project that resists the original sex/gender assignment, opting instead for transition. As Naomi Scheman puts it:

> For those transsexuals who…think of themselves as women, the associations with womanhood that seem especially resonant may well be idiosyncratic, and there is no reason why they cannot pick and choose among them—why, that is, transsexuals should not have the same freedom as born women to embrace some aspects of womanhood and vehemently reject others. (Scheman 1997, 140)

Not only do mtfs have (ideally) the freedom to choose which aspects of womanhood they embrace, but the embracing of aspects of womanhood is the expression of the aspiration to be a woman, which is, I suggest, the way to understand the transition, for mtfs, from man to woman.

These claims do not, of course, mean that human beings have complete freedom of choice with respect to their sex/gender identity and self-presentation. Our freedom is rather strictly curtailed, first, because sex/gender identity and presentation are still heavily policed and there are manifold pressures that limit nonconformity and punishments for significant variations from norms. Second, our freedom with respect to choosing our sex/gender identity and self-presentation is limited because these aspects of the person go very deep, to our earliest socialization. For most people, the series of choices and decisions that constitute one's sex/gender are for the most part unexamined and not usually recognized as being potentially subject to the will. Trans persons are individuals for whom the sex/gender project is both conscious and self-conscious. They are persons in whom the aspiration for change is particularly strong. That does not mean, however, that their aspiration to transition is entirely a matter of choice, for the aspiration may well be experienced as unbidden and imposed.

Third, human beings' freedom with respect to sex/gender identity and self-presentation is severely restricted in that there are only two widely recognized, accepted, and approved sex/gender categories: female/feminine and male/masculine. Within contemporary mainstream western society, people who aspire to being outside of these two categories altogether, or who claim to create additional sex/gender categories, may fail, both conceptually and empirically. The very concept of sex/gender allows for only two such categories, each allegedly complementary to the other—indeed, each defined heteronormatively in terms of the other, as what the other is not, and as what fulfills or completes the other. There is almost no conceptual space for a third sex/gender; in order to be, and be intelligible as, a person, one must belong to one or the other of the two recognized sex/genders. As a result, any attempt to self-present as an exemplar of a third sex/gender will almost inevitably be subject to reinterpretation by others who will attempt to perceive the individual as a member of one or the other of the two "real" sex/genders.[12]

If my theory of the metaphysics of sex/gender transition is correct, it might help to explain why there appears to be an increase in individuals undergoing sex/gender transitions in the late twentieth and twenty-first centuries. Over the past fifty to a hundred years, sex/gender customs, rules, and requirements have loosened up, and there is somewhat greater freedom than hitherto. This increased liberty might seem to suggest that there would be fewer individuals actively seeking sex/gender transitions, for part of what has historically made sex/gender identity and presentation so limiting is precisely the fact that they are compulsory. With greater freedom, it might seem that there would be less of the felt aspiration to actively transition.

But the greater degree of sex/gender freedom might also make it *easier* for trans individuals to express and act on their felt aspiration to transition. While there are more ways of being a woman and being a man than previously, the requirement that there be *only* women and men—in the sense of female and male human beings—remains almost nonnegotiable.[13] Thus, the aspiration for some forms of sex/gender transition may be aided by the conceptual requirement that there be two and only two sex/gender categories.

What has still not changed is the fact that genitalia are consistently given enormous significance in defining who human beings are—whether we like it or not. Our genitalia mark our most fundamental identity. Social processes, not biological ones, make an individual's sex the most significant way of categorizing her or him, and the genitalia are seen as representative or even determinative of who and what an individual is. Every one of us is repeatedly invited, or more usually compelled, to check F or M on almost every document we ever fill out: reports of birth, marriages, and death; questionnaires and surveys; and applications for school or university, employment, health insurance, a driver's license, a pension, or a passport. In these instances, we are not being required to report our gendered behavior or feelings or our gender self-identity. A person with male genitalia, for example, who is strongly feminine in self-presentation and self-understanding, would nonetheless be documented as male on health insurance or a death certificate. Not only are genitalia treated as all-important definers of identity; they are also assumed to trump any chosen gender manifestations. A person with female genitalia who is highly masculine in her clothing and self-presentation, but who either does not want to be taken for male or does not succeed in being taken as male, is still expected and required to use the women's washroom. It is the individual's genitalia, or others' perceptions that the individual has such genitalia, that are marked as significant.

Still, the skeptic might persist: Where do the aspirations of trans persons come from? How can they be explained? Again, my point is that aspirations for sex/gender transition are not necessarily different in kind from other deeply felt and long-held aspirations. The life-changing aspirations human beings develop and express, including the aspiration for sex/gender transition, can, I suggest, be accounted for (at least in theory, however difficult in practice the explanation may be) in terms of a mixture of personal history, social environment, individual interpretation, and biological factors. In some people, this network of influences contributes to a desire to be a musician; in some, they produce an eagerness to be a parent; in some, they produce spiritual aspirations; and in some, they produce an aspiration to be a person of a different sex/gender.

Objections and Replies

I'll now consider two objections to the theory I have put forward. First, it might be argued that the personal aspiration model is open to a criticism similar to one that I leveled against the nontrans ("deluded or duplicitous") masquerade theory. That is, the personal aspiration model implies that many trans persons are deluded about the nature of their identity; they regard themselves as having a gender within, but in reality they do not. In response, I want to point out that the personal aspiration model takes seriously what trans persons say about themselves. Unlike the nontrans masquerade theory, it does not deny that trans persons are the sex/gender they say they are (or are becoming), but it respectfully accepts their accounts of their identity. The model I propose simply suggests that the metaphor used in the gender within theory is founded on an untenable metaphysics and that the personal aspiration model better captures the nature of sex/gender transition. Indeed, it is possible that trans people have ended up adopting the metaphor, to the point of even believing in it, because they have learned, either from personal experience or from advice passed on by other trans persons (Meyerowitz 2002, 161, 225), that speaking of themselves in terms of a different gender within is effective in gaining them the medical services they seek in order to realize their aspirations to transition.

The second objection to my theory is that the personal aspiration model cannot account for the experiences of those trans individuals who say they have "always" felt that they were a different sex/gender from that which others attributed to them or from what the physical evidence of their bodies might indicate. An aspiration for sex/gender transition that develops over the course of one's life does not account for the "always already" feeling of sex/gender identity experienced by trans individuals.

In response to this criticism, I have two suggestions. One possibility is that the individual who felt he was always a man inside, despite the existence of female genitalia, might be reading back into his history. This situation would be similar to the situation of some people who apparently change their sexual orientation during adulthood. They may look back on their personal history for clues to indicate that they have always been attracted to a member of the other sex. It is also similar to the situation of an individual who is ending a romantic relationship. She may survey the history of the relationship and say, "From the beginning I had reservations about him [or her], even if I couldn't quite admit them to myself." Generally speaking, then, one way of accounting for the trans individual's claim that he or she was always the person that he or she is now transitioning to is that many people's lives contain material that can be interpreted as supporting contrarian themes, themes that show rebellion against or rejection of the dominant direction that their life has taken. Douglas Mason-Schrock has documented some of the ways in which trans people "learn, from others in the transgender community, to find biographical evidence of a differently gendered 'true self' and to fashion this information into a story that leads inexorably to the identity 'transsexual'" (Mason-Schrock 1996, 176–77). This process involves, for example, the use of childhood stories of "feeling ambivalent about gender" (179), early cross-dressing stories, and stories about being "naturally inept at sports" (182). Yet, as Mason-Schrock also points out, the existence of this evidence is not a reason to suppose that another separate person always lived inside them.

My second suggestion is that many trans persons may indeed harbor what I suggest is an aspiration to be a woman or a man, in defiance of how their body ostensibly reads, that is virtually lifelong. The existence of a longstanding or even lifelong aspiration for transition does not imply that there is a person of a different sex/gender inside the individual. Many equally significant goals are longstanding and emerge early in life. Some individuals know early in life what they want to do or be for a lifetime. They may even experience this aspiration as something they were born with, or at least something that they did not consciously choose. They may be intent on being a musician, a doctor, a mother, or a priest. Yet we do not say, except perhaps poetically, that such individuals have a musician, doctor, mother, or priest inside them.[14]

All of us are inevitably and necessarily embodied selves. The nature of our bodies helps to generate our aspirations, even, or especially, when that aspiration is in revolt against some aspects of the kind of body we have. The felt desire and quest for sex/gender transition is, I suggest, best understood as being one of the many powerful life-changing aspirations that human beings experience.

NOTES

I am grateful to the audiences at St. Francis Xavier University, February 21, 2007, Queen's University, March 15, 2007, and the UK Society for Women in Philosophy, University of Stirling, April 20, 2007, as well as to an anonymous reviewer, for their feedback on earlier versions of this paper. And I deeply appreciate Laurie Shrage's stimulating comments on an earlier draft.

1. Justin Jaron Lewis objects that this argument is all too similar to the "fifty million Frenchmen can't be wrong" sort of claim, and that, indeed, large numbers of people are often wrong, even wrong about their identity (e.g., the large numbers of Americans who identify themselves as "saved" and others as damned (Lewis 2007). He makes an important point, and

as my later discussion shows, I am not assuming that trans people have an infallible insight into the nature of their transition. Nonetheless, since they are talking about something that is central to their very personhood, they are entitled to be treated not as the victims of psychological illness or hallucination but as credible reporters of an important aspect of their sex/gender identity.

2. In his book, Rubin deliberately talks only about ftms.

3. As it is to make sense of any form of Cartesianism.

4. I am grateful to both Nancy Salay and Jennifer Saul for insisting on this possibility.

5. Fausto-Sterling goes so far as to advocate that we "stop looking for universal causes of sexual behavior and gender acquisition" (Fausto-Sterling 2000, 246).

6. See Overall 2003, chapter 6.

7. Kirkland's point helps to show why it is worthwhile for trans individuals to go through transition, even when doing so may make them vulnerable to ostracism, insults, or even attacks. (Of course, for some trans individuals, a full transition is intended to make them convincing enough that they will not be targeted in these ways.)

8. Nor can she be sure that others will accept either the process of aspiring to sex/gender change or its outcome. Moreover, she will still carry the traces of who she was before transitioning. After transition, the person has not thereby made herself identical in sex/gender identity to someone who always held that identity.

9. Lewis notes that there can be similar metaphysical assumptions underlying conversion to Judaism as underlie transition: "With a nod to the teachings of the Jewish mystics about reincarnation, converts to Judaism are often told, 'You must have a Jewish soul!' On the other hand, most converts have heard a fellow Jew tell them, 'You're not really Jewish.'" Lewis points out that both reactions assume that Jewish identity is unchangeable: "You're either born Jewish or you're not" (Lewis 2007).

10. Can any of us, as trans or nontrans individuals, look within and find our gender identity? I am skeptical. People may be convinced of their gender identity but unable to point to an immediate feeling that grounds it. As Naomi Scheman puts it: "If there was something independent of social role and body that male-to-female transsexuals could recognize as their gender identity, I should be able to find whatever it was in my own sense of identity—but there simply didn't seem to be anything like that there" (Scheman 1997, 134). They are in the Humean situation of being convinced of their selfhood but unable to locate it through introspection.

11. One might be tempted to say, with Heather Battaly, that knowing one's sexual orientation requires intellectual virtues (Battaly 2007).

12. As a result of the conceptual and empirical impossibility of being anything that would be recognized as a member of a third sex/gender, my own view is that those who wish truly to transform sex/gender should be seeking to get rid of it—not on an individual level, which is impossible within a social context that requires membership in one or the other of the two as a condition of personhood, but as a matter of social transformation (Overall 2000).

13. If I am correct that sex/gender transitions are the expression of personal aspiration, and in that respect are similar to other life-changing aspirations, then it follows that sex/gender identity and self-presentation should no more be subject to social compulsion or restriction than are other life-changing aspirations. There are good reasons to regulate some such aspirations but not others. For example, there is justification for social regulations of the path to and

attainment of the goal of being a physician but fewer reasons, if any, for social regulations of the path to and the attainment of the goal of being a musician. If someone simply wants to play the drums in their local bar, it is no business of the state. Similarly, if someone wants to wear differently gendered clothes and hairstyles in their local bar, it is also a personal matter.

14. Some people speak of a thin person as "struggling to get out of a fat body," and some elderly people say they are still young inside. To the extent that these ideas are not mere expressions of stereotype and bias, they recognize that we understand ourselves both through and *against* our bodies.

REFERENCES

Battaly, Heather. 2007. "Virtue Epistemology and Knowing Our Sexual Orientations." Paper presented at the annual meeting of the American Philosophical Association, Pacific Division, San Francisco, April 7.

Beauvoir, Simone de. 1952. *The Second Sex*. New York: Bantam.

Bettcher, Talia Mae. 2006. "Understanding Transphobia: Authenticity and Sexual Violence." In *Trans/Forming Feminisms: Trans-Feminist Voices Speak Out*, edited by Krista Scott-Dixon. Toronto: Sumach Press, pp. 203–10.

Bornstein, Kate. 1994. *Gender Outlaw: On Men, Women, and the Rest of Us*. New York: Routledge.

Carter, Lesley. 2006. "Female by Surgery." In *Trans/Forming Feminisms: Trans-Feminist Voices Speak Out*, edited by Krista Scott-Dixon. Toronto: Sumach Press, pp. 53–57.

Faderman, Lillian. 1981. *Surpassing the Love of Men: Romantic Friendship and Love between Women, from the Renaissance to the Present*. New York: Morrow.

Fausto-Sterling, Anne. 2000. *Sexing the Body: Gender Politics and the Construction of Sexuality*. New York: Basic.

Feinberg, Leslie. 1996. *Transgender Warriors: Making History from Joan of Arc to Dennis Rodman*. Boston: Beacon.

Foucault, Michel. 1980. Introduction to *Herculine Barbin: Being the Recently Discovered Memoirs of a Nineteenth-Century French Hermaphrodite*. Translated by Richard McDougall. Brighton, Sussex: Harvester.

Frye, Marilyn. 1983. *The Politics of Reality: Essays in Feminist Theory*. Freedom, California: Crossing.

Fuss, Diana. 1989. *Essentially Speaking: Feminism, Nature and Difference*. New York: Routledge.

Hardie, Alaina. 2006. "It's a Long Way to the Top: Hierarchies of Legitimacy in Trans Communities." In *Trans/Forming Feminisms: Trans-Feminist Voices Speak Out*, edited by Krista Scott-Dixon. Toronto: Sumach Press, pp. 122–30.

Hill, Darryl B. 2006. "On the Origins of Gender." In *Trans/Forming Feminisms: Trans-Feminist Voices Speak Out*, edited by Krista Scott-Dixon. Toronto: Sumach Press, pp. 39–45.

Kirkland, Anna. 2006. "What's at Stake in Transgender Discrimination as Sex Discrimination?" *Signs: Journal of Women in Culture and Society* 32(1): 83–111.

Lewis, Justin Jaron. 2007. Email.

Lizza, John P. 2006. *Persons, Humanity, and the Definition of Death*. Baltimore: Johns Hopkins University Press.

Mason-Schrock, Douglas. 1996. "Transsexuals' Narrative Constructions of the 'True Self.'" *Social Psychology Quarterly* 59(3): 176–92.

McCloskey, Deirdre. 1999. *Crossing: A Memoir*. Chicago: University of Chicago Press.

Meyerowitz, Joanne. 2002. *How Sex Changed: A History of Transsexuality in the United States*. Cambridge: Harvard University Press.

Noble, Bobby. 2006. "Our Bodies Are Not Ourselves; Tranny Guys and the Racialized Class Politics of Embodiment." In *Trans/Forming Feminisms: Trans-Feminist Voices Speak Out*, edited by Krista Scott-Dixon. Toronto: Sumach Press, pp. 95–104.

Overall, Christine. 2000. "Return to Gender, Address Unknown: Reflections on the Past, Present and Future of the Concept of Gender in Feminist Theory and Practice." In *Marginal Groups and Mainstream American Culture*, edited by Yolanda Estes, Arnold Lorenzo Farr, Patricia Smith, and Clelia Smyth. Lawrence: University Press of Kansas, pp. 24–50.

———. 2003. *Aging, Death, and Human Longevity: A Philosophical Inquiry*. Berkeley: University of California Press.

Penner, Mike (Christine Daniels). 2007. "Old Mike, New Christine." At http://www.latimes.com/sports/la-sp-oldmike26apr26,0,2084659,print.story (accessed April 27, 2007).

Pozner, Jennifer L. 2004. "Gender Immigrant: A Conversation with Jennifer Finney Boylan." *Women's Review of Books* 21(7): 5–7.

Raymond, Janice. 1979. *The Transsexual Empire*. London: Women's Press.

Rubin, Henry. 2003. *Self-Made Men: Identity and Embodiment among Transsexual Men*. Nashville, Tenn.: Vanderbilt University Press.

Scanlon, Kyle. 2006. "Where's the Beef? Masculinity as Performed by Feminists." In *Trans/Forming Feminisms: Trans-Feminist Voices Speak Out*, edited by Krista Scott-Dixon. Toronto: Sumach Press, pp. 87–94.

Scheman, Naomi. 1997. "Queering the Center by Centering the Queer." In *Feminists Rethink the Self*, edited by Diana Tietjens Meyers. Boulder, Colo.: Westview, pp. 124–62.

Spelman, Elizabeth V. 1988. *Inessential Woman: Problems of Exclusion in Feminist Thought*. Boston: Beacon.

Wilkerson, William. 2007a. *Ambiguity and Sexuality: A Theory of Sexual Identity*. New York: Palgrave Macmillan.

———. 2007b. "Choosing Desire, Choosing Identity: Freedom, Determinism, and Sexual Orientations." Paper presented at the annual meeting of the American Philosophical Association, Pacific Division, San Francisco, April 7.

2

Transsexuality and Contextual Identities

Georgia Warnke

Jan Morris begins her 1974 memoir with the words, "I was three or perhaps four when I realized that I had been born into the wrong body and should really be a girl."[1] Raymond Thompson writes, "My body didn't exist in the way it was born; for me it only existed in my inner identity as a male."[2] And in her 2003 memoir, Jennifer Boylan writes, "The awareness that I was in the wrong body, living the wrong life was never out of my conscious mind—*never*."[3] In this essay, I want to explore these claims. What does it mean to possess or inhabit the wrong body? Why does wrongness manifest itself as an issue of genitalia? What does it mean to think one should "really be a girl" or to possess the "inner identity" of a male? Here I am interested in the relation between one's body and particularly one's genitalia and one's felt identity. Because this relation is often viewed as one between physical sex and psychic gender, I begin with this relation.

Sex

Since Simone de Beauvoir wrote in *The Second Sex* "One is not born, but rather becomes a woman,"[4] it has been common, although not uncontroversial, for feminists and those in the field of women's studies to distinguish unchanging aspects of male and female biology—sex—from culturally and historically based differences in the roles, attitudes and behaviors of men and women: gender.[5] Beauvoir does not use this precise distinction in her book, and some theorists caution against applying it retroactively to it. Nonetheless, her sentence at least suggests a contrast between a female sex with which one is born and a feminine gender one acquires. Beauvoir also implies the contrast in the conundrum she raises at the beginning of her introduction:

"All agree in recognizing the fact that females exist in the human species....And yet we are told that femininity is in danger; we are exhorted to be women, remain women, become women."[6] Femininity can be in danger only if it is not naturally given with being female, only, in other words, if the feminine gender differs from the female sex. Female human beings can be exhorted to be, remain, and become women only if there are other options, only if they need not be, remain, or become women and, hence, again, only if there is a difference between being a female and being a woman.

The Second Sex serves as an extended inquiry into the myriad of historical, social, and cultural factors that combine to mold those sexed as females into those gendered as women. Yet, what is the sex being so molded? Judith Butler famously agues that sex is a fiction imposed on bodies by "various scientific discourses in the service of...political and social interests" and that, consequently, "the distinction between sex and gender turns out to be no distinction at all."[7] There are also more mundane reasons to question the category of sex. The first person to be advertised as the recipient of so-called sex reassignment surgery was Christine Jorgensen, who grew up as a "frail, tow-headed, introverted little boy who ran from fistfights and rough-and-tumble games." Yet, with her doctors, she insisted that she was only "seemingly male." Although her body made testosterone, she and her doctors claimed it made insufficient amounts of it to endow her with a male sex. Thus, in her view, her genital surgery was not actually a sex-change operation. Instead, she and her doctors called it the correction of a glandular problem.[8] Jorgensen's body was not really male and just needed help manifesting its real properties.[9]

Jorgensen's view of herself raises the question of which bodily factors are meant to comprise one's sex. Presumably, Jorgensen possessed a penis that had to be "corrected," and she may have had XY chromosomes. Do these factors not indicate which sex she really was? Was her insistence that she simply had a medical condition not simply a ruse to convince a hospital ethics board or the equivalent to give her the operation she wanted? If such questions are meant to tie sex to physical characteristics or chromosomes, it is worth pointing out that neither penises nor XY chromosomes are always sufficient to make one male. At least until recently, pediatricians recommended castrating infants with micropenises (penises less than about 2.5 centimeters long) and bringing them up as girls.[10] In its 2006 revision of its guidelines, the American Academy of Pediatrics did finally recommend that micropenises be left alone but insisted that outcomes were equally good if they were not. As for chromosomes, Androgen Insensitivity Syndrome (AIS) is a condition affecting XY individuals who inherit a nonworking androgen receptor gene and hence are not responsive to the androgens needed to develop immature genital buds in utero into penises. Such individuals are thus born with female genitalia, labia, clitorises, and short tunnels that stand in for vaginas. As adults, they can have generously sized breasts because their insensitivity to androgen renders them immune to the factors that restrict breast growth. This insensitivity also renders them immune to the factors that limit height and cause acne and thinning hair. In short, AIS individuals have the physiques usually only found in *Playboy* or the movies: "Good skin, great head hair, full breasts, tall stature," as Natalie Angier writes.[11] We typically assume AIS individuals are female—indeed, the paragon of femaleness. But then the question becomes how we ought to define sex: Does it lie in hormones or chromosomes? If the latter, then perhaps Jorgensen was born male; if the former, however, and her body could not produce or process large amounts of testosterone, perhaps she was born female.

Yet, the idea that Jorgensen was always female fails to comply with a number of legal decisions in the United States in which courts have insisted that sex *is* a matter of chromosomes. Take just one. The 1999 Texas case of *Littleton v. Prange* concerned the question of whether Christie Littleton could sue her late husband's physician for Jonathan Littleton's wrongful death. Before her marriage, Christie Littleton received genital reconstructive surgery, stopped living as a man, and began living as a woman. Although her husband was aware of her surgery, the Fourth Circuit Court of Appeals in Texas ruled that she had no standing to bring a suit as his wife. Christie Littleton's chromosomes proved she was male; hence her putative marriage to her so-called husband violated the Texas Family Code prohibiting marriages between members of the same sex. To be sure, the Texas court conceded, "a transsexual male can be made to look like a woman." Yet, because "the male chromosomes do not change with either hormonal treatment or sex reassignment surgery...biologically a post-operative female transsexual is still a male."[12] Of course, the same would seem to hold of Texan AIS supermodels but the court did not address this consequence.

A 2005 Illinois case, *In Re Marriage of Sterling Simmons and Jennifer Simmons*, confuses the question of sex yet further. Simmons had been born as Bessie Lewis but began taking testosterone at the age of twenty-one. Later, he had a hysterectomy and a bilateral salpingo oophorectomy removing his uterus, fallopian tubes, and ovaries. When he and his wife had a child through artificial insemination, he was listed as the father on the birth certificate. Nevertheless, when the couple tried to divorce, the court declared that the marriage had never existed because Simmons was a woman and his apparent marriage had therefore violated the restriction of marriage to opposite-sex partners. While the conclusion in this case is the same as the conclusions in the *Littleton* case, the reasoning is importantly different. According to the Illinois court, Simmons was female, not because he possessed an XX chromosomal pair but because he had not undergone all the operations necessary to make him male. In particular, he still possessed the external genitalia of a female. The appellate court wrote: "Based upon the testimony of all of the expert witnesses who testified at trial that petitioner still possesses all of his female genitalia, we find that the judgment of the trial court that he is a female and not legally a male was not against the manifest weight of the evidence."[13] Here, as in the case of surgically removed micropenises but not in the case of Christie Littleton, what sex you are depends upon what appendage you do or do not have.

In Jorgensen's case, the evidence of her sex, at least in her mind, lay in her hormones; in the *Littleton* legal case, the evidence of sex rested on chromosomes; in the *Simmons* case, as well as in most previous cases of surgically eliminated micropenises, the evidence of sex rested on external genitalia. Other cases and other courts offer other features as proof of sex. In a Spanish case, the court looked to the structure of the plaintiff's shoulders.[14] The upshot of these inconsistencies is to raise questions about the nature of the sexed bodies that transsexuals think they wrongly possess. As it turns out, medical and legal systems are in some disagreement among themselves as to what sex is.

Gender

If sex is mysterious, so is gender. What, we might ask, is the "inner identity as a male" that Thompson attributes to himself? What does Jan Morris mean by maintaining that she "should really be a girl"? What is the content of a given gender? One of the more concerted efforts to describe the content remains Nancy Chodorow's attempt to discover the consequences for psychosexual development that follow from the circumstance that infants' and children's primary caregivers are usually women. Despite increasing equality in domestic responsibilities between men and women, women continue to spend more time with infants and children than men and to be more involved in their daily lives. What follows? First, infants and children come to "expect and assume women's unique capacities for sacrifice, caring, and mothering." In contrast, children assume that men have separate lives from their own and, Chodorow says, identify them "with idealized virtues and growth." Second, because it is women who typically mother, daughters grow up identifying with their primary caregiver. They do so longer than boys do and exclude the father longer. In fact, according to Chodorow, their attachment to their mothers lasts even after they become attached to their fathers. As the little girl grows older and tries to achieve some distance from her mother, she does not completely reject her mother in favor of her father but, instead, adds her father to what becomes a triadic relation.[15]

The same attachment holds for the other side of the equation. While infants experience their mothers and fathers differently because of their respective primary and distanced relationships to them, the third consequence of women's mothering is that primary caregivers experience little boys and little girls differently as well. Chodorow claims that, because mothers were once little girls, they typically experience their infant and growing daughters as identical to themselves and care for them in ways that express this identity. In contrast, they experience their sons as different from themselves and care for them in ways that emphasize differences. Boys therefore acquire a gender identity that relies on differentiation from their primary caregiver and, indeed, on aligning themselves with a largely absent father. The opposite holds for girls: they grow into their gender identity in continuity with their primary caregiver insofar as that caregiver understands them to be like herself. The result is that girls and boys have different experiences of themselves and their relations to others. As Chodorow writes:

> Growing girls come to define and experience themselves as continuous with others; their experience of self contains more flexible or permeable ego boundaries. Boys come to define themselves as more separate and distinct, with a greater sense of rigid ego boundaries and differentiation. The basic feminine sense of self is connected to the world, the basic masculine sense of self is separate.[16]

Yet, ever since Chodorow first formulated this description of women's gender as a connected self, critics have worried that it describes race and class as much as it describes gender. Chodorow does not entirely ignore race and class differences in the way particular mothers mother. Nevertheless, she takes herself to be describing general core characteristics that hold independently of race and class. Because they are mothered the way they are and by whom they are, women are caring and other-related. Still, critics have insisted that gender cannot be simply stripped off of race and class and examined as a feature independently of them.

Patricia Hill Collins thus emphasizes the different form the relationship between a mother and daughter takes when the daughter's survival in a hostile social environment is at stake: "Mothers routinely encourage Black daughters to develop skills to confront oppressive conditions. Learning that they will work and that education is a vehicle for advancement can...be seen as ways of enhancing positive self-definitions and self-valuations in Black girls. Emotional strength is essential, but not at the cost of physical survival."[17] Likewise, Denise Segura and Jennifer Pierce stress the different form the mother-daughter relationship takes in a Chicana/o family with "multiple mothering figures,"[18] while Carol Stack's investigation of the neighborhood she calls "The Flats" "shows how misleading it is to regard child-keeping apart from residence patterns, alliances, and the interpersonal relationships of adults, and from the daily exchanges between kinsmen in the domestic network of the child."[19]

The example to which critics repeatedly return is the speech that Sojourner Truth's first biographer attributed to her. Although it is not clear that Truth ever gave the speech, it has become a touchstone for many theorists who focus on intersections between gender, race, and class:

> That man over there says that women need to be helped into carriages, and lifted over ditches, and to have the best place everywhere. Nobody ever helps me into carriages, or over mud-puddles, or gives me any best place! And ain't I a woman? Look at me! Look at my arm! I have ploughed and planted and gathered into barns, and no man could head me! And ain't I a woman? I could work as much and eat as much as a man—when I could get it—and bear the lash as well! And ain't I a woman? I have borne thirteen children, and seen them most all sold off to slavery, and when I cried out with my mother's grief, none but Jesus heard me! And ain't I a woman?[20]

The context of Truth's alleged remarks at the women's rights convention in Akron, Ohio, in 1851 suggests that they were meant to rebut the idea that women's gender identity rendered them too loving, care-oriented, and sentimental for any form of political participation. Yet, Truth counters, while some women may be brought up to be loving, care-oriented, and sentimental, others—field slaves, for instance—are brought up to be strong and assumed to be callous.[21]

The upshot of these examples is, at the very least, a disaggregating of gender. The gender of middle-class women and working-class women, white women and black women may be quite different, and, when we think we are describing gender, we may well be describing something else instead, not only race or class but nationality, age, and a host of different attributes. As Elizabeth Spelman notes, "It is only because whiteness is taken as a given that there is even the appearance of being able to distinguish simply between a person's being a woman and a person's being a man."[22] At the same time, more is at stake here than the simple disaggregating of gender into black and white gender identities, young and middle-aged gender identities, or middle-class and working-class gender identities. For the effect of examining our gender identities in these terms is that that the contours of their genderness tend to disappear. Being a woman is not necessarily to possess a sense of self that is connected to the world, nor is a feminine gender identity always bound up with nurturing or mothering. Indeed, women may have no features in common, and when we try to isolate gender from other attributes, we may discover that it is nothing at all.

Identity

Given the difficulties both sex and gender present, how are we to understand their relation to identity? And what exactly is identity? The statements that Morris, Thompson, and Boylan make implicitly rely on a distinction between sex and gender and use it to maintain that, while they feel themselves to be a certain gender, it is not the gender usually correlated with their sex. But if we have incompatible ideas of what sex is, and if gender seems to disappear into other variables such as race and class, what does it mean to possess a sex and gender that are not usually correlated? The question here is not why we should suppose that a certain sex typically links up with a certain gender. Beauvoir already traces this linkage to culture, society, and history. The question is, rather, what fails to go with what?

In the rest of this chapter, I argue that this question arises from a misunderstanding of what identities are. Identities, I claim, are interpretations of who we are, and as such they are intelligible only as parts of particular contexts. It follows that when they overflow these contexts, they create confusion. It also follows that, as interpretations, all identities have the same status. For this reason, I argue that transsexuality is no different from other changes of identity such as changes in nationality or sports team affiliation. Transsexuality is no more radical because sex and gender are no less context-bound.

Start with our understanding of the identity of the characters in a text. This understanding is contextual insofar as it is conditioned by our understanding of the meaning of the text as a whole. Who we understand Hamlet, the character, to be depends on how we understand *Hamlet*, the play. Seen as a play about disillusionment, we can understand Hamlet as a very young man trying to sort through competing feelings about his mother and the meaning of his past. If we understand the play as a play about interpreting signs, evidence, and the like, we can understand Hamlet differently, as an experimental scientist. How we understand Hamlet thus depends on how we understand the play. Conversely, how we understand the play depends, in part, on how we understand the character. Our understanding of texts and performances is a process of understanding the whole in terms of the part and the part in terms of the whole. If we can plausibly understand the play, *Hamlet* as a play about disillusionment, we can do so because this theme allows us to tie the different parts of the text together in a coherent way. Similarly, to the extent that it is possible to understand the play as a play about the interpretation of signs and evidence, it is possible because we can bring its parts together under this rubric. How we understand Hamlet depends on how we understand the play, and how we understand the play depends on how we understand characters such as Hamlet and their role in the play. Nevertheless, except in relation to the play, there is no way of understanding Hamlet at all. Indeed, except in relation to the play, he does not exist.

To be sure, in light of recent developments in literary theory such as deconstruction and neohistoricism, the idea that the integration of part and whole should serve as a criterion of interpretive adequacy may appear somewhat dated. Deconstruction emphasizes the degree to which what is not said undermines what is said. Nevertheless, to the extent that we understand what is being undermined, we necessaily do so in terms of the integration of whole and part. As for neohistoricism, the whole in which we may want to understand a particular text might also include the history of which it is a part. So, for example, the recent film version of Jane Austen's *Mansfield Park* emphasizes Sir Thomas Bertram's involvement with slavery in Antigua to illuminate possible reasons for his eldest son's descent into debauchery. This emphasis is legitimate as long as it allows us to understand the novel as an integrated unity of meaning and to understand who Tom Bertram is within it. The point remains, however, that outside of the novel, no matter how broadly we understand it, Tom Bertram exists no more than Hamlet does.

The same holds of males and females, as well as of men and women. To understand individuals in either sex or gender terms requires that we situate them within a text or context that gives them this meaning. It is not simply given with bodies that they can always be construed as male or female. Rather, to understand someone as a certain sex is to take certain aspects of the body—perhaps chromosomes or appendages or certain hormones—to be indicative of who the person is and to exclude other physical and biological features of bodies, such as knobby knees and muscle types. Determining what to include and what to exclude requires a frame of reference, a set of concerns or activities that justifies the inclusions and exclusions. Otherwise, why not include knobby knees? The context or frame of reference here is reproductive biology or what Butler more provocatively calls "compulsory heterosexuality."[23] Within a frame of reference centered on sexual reproduction, human beings may separate into different sexes. Moreover, by looking to the context of sexual reproduction, we may be able to determine which parts of the body are relevant parts of one's sex and which are not. It does not follow, however, that human beings separate into sexes outside of the framework of reproduction. Just as Hamlet is Hamlet only within *Hamlet,* males and females are males and females only within the context of reproduction. To interpret individuals in these terms outside of that context is equivalent to thinking one can deposit Hamlet into *Mansfield Park.*

If males and females are not males and females outside of the context of reproduction, the inconsistencies in the ways different legal and medical authorities define sex disappear. One is a male only when impregnating or trying to impregnate someone who is capable of being impregnated. And one is female only when one is being impregnated, trying to be impregnated, or giving birth. AIS individuals are therefore never one or the other. Indeed, no one is very often one or the other. Unless we are giving birth or engaged in potentially fertile sexual intercourse at all points of our lives, our reproductive capacities are absent from many if not most of the contexts in which we act and cannot provide coherent definitions of who we are within those contexts.

Linda Alcoff thinks that this sort of minimalism about sex underplays the influence of our bodies on our lived experience. Male and female human beings differ insofar as females have larger breasts, menstruate, lactate and are often capable of becoming pregnant. To be sure, not all female humans do give birth. Nevertheless, Alcoff insists that the perspective a girl has on her world, her life and herself is necessarily different than the perspective a boy possesses because of her awareness that she might become pregnant and might both bear and nurse a child. "The possibility of pregnancy, childbirth, nursing and, in many societies, rape are parts of females' horizons and they exist there because of the ways we are embodied."[24] Alcoff's analysis makes sense of the desire transsexuals possess to change their bodies. The suggestion we can infer from her account is that they want the embodied experience of the world that females have. At the same time, it is surely worth considering whether embodied experience divides along the lines of sex. Our lived experiences differ; different people have different lived experiences and they relate differently to the experience of possessing breasts, menstruating, and the like. Moreover, if the lived experience of having breasts differs from the lived experience of not having them, does the same not hold for the lived experience of having large breasts as opposed to the lived experience of having small ones or the experience of anticipating painful periods as opposed to anticipating unproblematic ones? Some people are also more adept than others at bringing their sexed identities into different contexts: Mae West comes to mind here. Yet, such identities are often incongruous and those who are part of the relevant context often find them to be incongruous with it. If someone remarks on the sex of a lab assistant, for example, the tension or even friction that arises is more than an objection to the relevance of the remark. It is, instead, a recognition that the lab assistant has been misidentified within the context, a misinterpretation of who he or she is that undermines the integration of part and whole or identity and context. Sexed persons are as misplaced in laboratories as Elinor Dashwood is in *Wuthering Heights*.

What about men and women? From what frame of reference, if any, can human beings be intelligibly understood as men and women? If we take the claims of Chodorow's critics seriously, it appears that there is no context within which individuals are women. The context of mothering breaks down into multiple mothering contexts for black women and white women and even further into black, middle-class women and white working-class women or divorced, white working-class women or middle-aged, divorced, white working-class women. In the end, it becomes unclear what the gender part of the complex is meant to describe.

In trying to combat such disaggregations of gender, Iris Marion Young appeals to Jean Paul Sartre's distinction between a series and a group. She thinks we can admit to the intersections of race, class, and gender and concede that white women and African American women, Asian American women, and Latinas or middle-class and working-class women may have no gender in common. Nevertheless, according to Young, we can conceive of genders just as we conceive of bus riders. Like women, bus riders may fail to possess a common feature that links them to one another. They are not on the bus for collective reasons, nor do they hold collective aspirations for the bus ride. Instead, they each have separate and individual relations to what Sartre calls a practico-inert reality: namely, the bus. Women, Young argues, are also a series. In this case, the relevant practico-inert realities to which she claims they are separately and individually related include pronouns, verbal and visual representations, clothes, cosmetics, social spaces such as sex-segregated bathrooms, and spaces associated with the sexual division of labor.[25]

As a guide to the context in which women are women, this list is somewhat problematic, however. Neither pronouns nor verbal and visual representations can serve as a context for interpreting individuals as women because they presuppose that the individuals at issue have already been interpreted as women. What is at issue here is what context or contexts makes that interpretation a plausible or coherent one. Sex-segregated bathrooms and the sexual division of labor are also problematic as contexts for understanding individuals as women. To see them as contexts in which individuals are women is to decide that in these cases part and whole, women and work or women and using a restroom cohere. But just as the phrase "driving while black" indicates a dissonance between context (driving) and identity (black), so too does understanding individuals as women while working or using a restroom. Those driving cars are drivers; those working are workers; those using restrooms are people who need to use a restroom. Of Young's practico-inert realities, then, we are left with clothes and cosmetics. Just as Hamlet is constituted as Hamlet only within *Hamlet*, women are constituted as women only within the context of clothes and cosmetics or, more generally, only when they present themselves as women.

Once we accept self-presentation as the context in which individuals are women, however, we are forced to restrict their gender identity in some ways and open it up in others. If women are intelligible only in the context of their own self-presentations, then they are not women unless they are part of this context. Just as we are not bus riders unless we are or are anticipating riding a bus, we are not women unless we are or are anticipating wearing dresses and cosmetics, sitting demurely, perhaps, and swinging our hips. Moreover, when we are engaged in these activities or anticipating doing so, we are. To wear Hamlet's costume, speak his lines, and perform his actions on a stage is to be Hamlet, whatever distinguishing characteristics we possess as individuals outside of the play. Likewise, to wear make up and to walk and talk in certain ways is just to be a woman, whatever body type we possess. Thus, we might say that we are women *only* when we are related to the relevant practico-inert realities and, additionally, that we are women *whenever* we are related to the relevant practico-inert realities.

In the literary domain, we acknowledge that texts can be understood in more than one way. Although our understanding of *Mansfield Park* as a whole provides the context within which we understand Tom Bertram and vice versa, we can understand both in more than one way. Take two different accounts of the novel appearing in the same 2004 issue of *Studies in English Literature, 1500–1900*. In one, "Ordination and Revolution in *Mansfield Park*," Michael Karounos argues that the heroine, Fanny

Price, and her cousin, Tom's brother, Edmund Bertram, are representatives, respectively, of gentility and religion. They are meant to serve Austen as Burkean figures who can help put a disordered society right. In the other article, "Austen's Later Subjects," Emily Rohrbach focuses on the spatial character of Austen's investigation of her heroine's subjectivity.[26] While the first interpretation focuses on the twin ordination of Fanny and Edmund as a way of illustrating Austen's conservative sensibilities, the second stresses Fanny's atemporality as a way of illuminating Austen's experimental attempts to depict a character's subjectivity. Neither interpretation necessarily precludes the other. Rather, in assessing the merit of any particular interpretation of a text, we ask how successful it is in revealing the text as a unity of meaning. We ask how our interpretation as a whole illuminates its various parts—not only its characters but also its plot development and the like—and how those parts reflect the meaning of the whole.

Ought not the same conditions apply to our understanding of women? Can individuals not possess different understandings of a particular context? If some of us understand women as those who relate serially to some of Young's practico-inert realities, cannot others understand them in different ways? To recognize the possiblilty of different, legitimate interpretations of a novel is not to claim that all interpretations are legitimate. Take Claudia L. Johnson's attempt to understand *Mansfield Park* as a parody, on the order of *Northanger Abbey*, although this time the parody is of what Johnson calls "conservative fiction" rather than gothic novels."[27] It is not clear that this interpretation allows us to make sense out of the unhappy fate Austen bestows on the Crawfords, in contrast to the one she bestows on the heroine of *Northanger Abbey*. Hence, we may have to conclude that Johnson's interpretation fails. Similarly, the question of who we are depends on the ways in which the interpretation of our identities can be successfully integrated with the contexts of which we are a part. Whether we can be successfully understood as men or women or as male or female will depend on whether understanding us this way illuminates the contexts of which we are a part and, conversely, whether a plausible understanding of the contexts we are in allows for an understanding of us as men and women or male and female.

This contextual way of looking at sexed and gendered identities, as context-limited interpretations of who we and others are, comports better with our understanding of identity in general. For, in most cases, the question of whether or not we possess a certain identity is a question of context. On a fashion runway, I may be a thin person, whereas in a hospital, I am an anorexic. In a legal context, I may be a juror, whereas in an educational context, I am a professor. In the context of sexual reproduction, I may be a female, but while at work, I am a writer. Certainly we can imaginatively set people in other contexts than the ones in which we find them acting. Thus, if we are watching a chess game and someone informs us that one of the players is the mother of two children, we can imagine the context within which this interpretation of who she is can be integrated, just as we can imagine contexts within which she is plausibly a woman or female. Moreover, while conceiving of contexts other than the one in which we find her acting allows us to register possible other meanings the chess player has in other contexts, conceiving of other contexts does not undermine the contextual character of identity, any more than imagining the meaning a word may have in another context undermines the meaning it has the present one.

It is also important to distinguish two differing questions: the hermeneutic question of what identities are and the moral psychological question of which of the identities we possess are the most important to us. Identities are contextual: who we are depends on the context of the question. We may be at different times and from different frames of reference, mothers, philosophers, Democrats, and rich people. At the same time, clearly some of these identities can be more important to us than others. I am not only and always a mother any more than I am only and always a pedestrian or a concert goer. Nevertheless, I may take my identity as a mother to be the core of who I am and that identity to which I give priority in conflicts of contexts. Nor need we all share the same senses of the identities that are and are not important to us. To some people, their contextual identities as males or females or as men or women may be far less important than their contextual identities as philosophers or Mormons. For others, sex and gender identities may be the most important contextual identity they possess, the one about which they spend the most time thinking and the one at which they want to do best.

Although it seems difficult to see, therefore, how we can demand standardization in which identities are to mean most to which people, it is important to note that K. Anthony Appiah comes to the opposite conclusion, at least in comparing race and gender and at least with regard to thinking about transsexuals. For those of "us in the modern West," he says, race, is less "conceptually central to who one is" than sex. His argument is a thought experiment. Suppose one undergoes a series of operations to alter all morphological markers of African descent. One lightens one's skin, straightens one's hair and "has...all the services of Michael Jackson's cosmetic surgeon." If one then asks oneself if one is still the same person, the answer, Appiah claims, for "almost everyone...must be yes." Perform the same thought experiment on morphological markers of being male or female, however, and Appiah thinks it is open to one to say no. Whereas the transracial cannot "disclaim the new person," the transsexual can.[28]

Appiah's test here for the virtually universal conceptual centrality of a given identity rests on whether a change in external markers triggers a change in one's sense of who one is. If that sense is open to transformation with changes in morphological markers, then the corresponding identity is conceptually central. If one's sense of who one is remains closed to transformation with changes in morphological features, then the identity is not conceptually central. Yet the question remains how we can make general assertions about the senses people, or even people in the modern West, have of who they are. The change in external markers that age brings may have profound significance for some people's sense of who they are and none at all for others. Moreover, what is conceptually central to different people can change over their lifetimes. At some point, it may be conceptually central to one that one is a mother. When one's children are grown, however, this identity may be far less central. Nor is it only external markers that can change people's sense of themselves. Surely if we ask a devoted mother if she would still be who she is if she killed her child, the answer would be no. Other people may think that they have become new people when they leave home, divorce their spouses, or learn French. For Morris, Thompson, and Boylan, sex and gender are surely central identities. Yet, it is not clear that they take themselves to be new selves after their genital surgeries. Instead, they appear to think they have finally become who they always thought themselves most importantly to be.

Conclusion

Once we distinguish moral psychological and hermeneutic conceptions of identity, the idea that Morris, Thompson, and Boylan became through genital surgery who they always thought they most importantly were is consistent with the claim that sex and gender are contextual identities. Being a woman is a core identity for Boylan and Morris; being a man is a core identity for Thompson. Neither is what they always are, however. There is thus nothing odd about the emphasis that Morris, Thompson, and Boylan put on the wrongness of their original bodies or original lives, even though that wrongness pertains to only small slices of their existence. For those slices are central to them. Furthermore, if we can distinguish between psychological and hermeneutic identity then we need not understand the sense of living the wrong life or of possessing the wrong body as a sense that marks out transsexuality from a number of other changes individuals go through in the course of their lives. For some people, the issue of their sex or gender identity (or both) is the overriding issue of their lives. It is conceptually central to who they take themselves to be and constitutes the core around which their lives revolve. Nevertheless, different identities are conceptually central to different people. For some people, their religious identity may be conceptually central to who they are; for others, it may be their status as a member of Red Sox nation. Moreover, even where a person's sex or gender identity is deeply important to that person, and even where that person also feels that his or her life as he or she presently lives it fails to express who he or she really is, we need not understand that person's felt need to change differently than we understand other changes in other identities. An Episcopalian may feel a real need to become a Jew and to feel that only as a Jew will he or she live the life he should be living. Similarly, an Australian may feel a real need to become an American, a lawyer to become a priest, or, perhaps less plausibly, a Red Sox fan to become a Yankees fan. At the same time, no matter how conceptually central an identity may be to us, there are contexts in which the identity is simply unintelligible. Running for cover in a tornado or brushing my teeth, I am neither a Democrat nor a woman.

These conclusions suggest that we ought to make much less, medically speaking, of the condition of transsexuality than we currently do. The 2000 revision of the *Diagnostic and Statistical Manual of Mental Disorders* maintains that a diagnosis of what it calls "gender dysphoria" or "gender identity disorder" must include three components. First, the patient must exhibit "a strong and persistent cross-gender identification, which is the desire to be, or the insistence that one is, of the other sex." This identification is found, for example, in a preference for the stereotypical toys of the other gender. Second, the patient's identification cannot be rooted simply in some idea of the cultural advantages that the other gender enjoys. Instead, one must possess a "persistent discomfort about one's assigned sex or a sense of inappropriateness in the gender role of that sex." Finally, "there must be evidence of clinically significant distress or impairment in social, occupational, or other important areas of functioning."[29] If we take an interpretive view of what sex and gender identities are, then the dismay of at least some members of the transsexual community at this definition is justified. For suppose we were to substitute religion for gender or sex. We would then define religious dysphoria or religious identity disorder in terms of an analogous three components. There would have to be a strong and persistent cross-religious identification, which would express itself as the desire to be, or the insistence that one is, of another religion. Presumably the corollary of enjoying the other gender's toys here would be an interest in the other religion's rites and rituals. One would also have to possess a "persistent discomfort about one's assigned religion or a sense of inappropriateness in the religious roles of that religion." Finally, there would have to be "evidence of clinically significant distress or impairment in social occupational, or other important areas of functioning." Clearly, we do not call a feeling that one belongs to the wrong religion a disorder. Nor do we require that those seeking to change their religious identities be persistently uncomfortable, distressed, or "impaired" under their previous religious identities. To be sure, some are, but some are not and, in any case, whether they are or not is not the business of the medical community.

Understanding identities as context-bound interpretations also has consequences for the legal system. For doing so suggests that we should disestablish sex and gender just as we have disestablished religion.[30] The legal cases we looked at concerned the dissolution or invalidation of a civil marriage due to a court's determination that each involved two men or two women. Yet why should we suppose that, in the United States, civil marriage is a context or "whole" for which men and women are intelligible parts? From an interpretive point of view, the question is not whether and how much genital surgery is sufficient to change one's status from male to female or female to male for the purposes of civil marriage. Rather, the question is why determining whether or how much genital surgery is sufficient should be any more relevant than determining whether and how many religious rituals are sufficient to change one's status from Catholic to Mormon or Mormon to Catholic for the purposes of civil marriage. We determined from the beginning in the United States that the right to civil marriage was not a right of a Catholic to marry anyone but a Mormon. We determined much later that it was not a right of a white person to marry anyone but a nonwhite person. It may be possible to understand it today as the right of a man to marry anyone but a man or a woman to marry anyone but a woman. Nevertheless, it is certainly not clear why sex and gender identities should have any more purchase on marriage than a series of other identities the courts have excluded, including not only racial identities but also identities as prison inmates and identities as indigent noncustodial parents.[31]

The upshot of this analysis is that we must try to be clearer than we have thus far been about the contexts within which different identities have their home. This necessity is all the more crucial for such identities as sex and gender, as well as race.

For by allowing them to overflow the frameworks in which they retain their intelligibility, we cause psychological pain and social injustice.

NOTES

1. Jan Morris, *Conundrum* (New York: Harcourt Brace Jovanovich, 1974), p. 3.

2. Cited in Jay Prosser, *Second Skins: The Body Narratives of Transsexuality* (New York: Columbia University Press, 1998), p. 77.

3. Jennifer Finney Boylan, *She's Not There: A Life in Two Genders* (New York: Broadway, 2003), p. 21.

4. Simone de Beauvoir, *The Second Sex* (1949), trans. and ed. H. M. Parshley (New York: Knopf, 1993), p. 281.

5. Toril Moi, *What Is a Woman and Other Essays* (Oxford: Oxford University Press, 1999), p. 3.

6. Beauvoir, *Second Sex*, p. xlv.

7. Judith Butler, *Gender Trouble: Feminism and the Subversion of Identity* (New York: Routledge, 1990), p. 7.

8. Christine Jorgensen, *Christine Jorgensen: A Personal Autobiography* (New York: Paul S. Eriksson, 1967), p. 111.

9. See Jorgensen's letter to her parents in ibid., pp. 123–26.

10. Anne Fausto-Sterling, *Sexing the Body: Gender Politics and the Construction of Sexuality* (New York: Basic, 2000), p. 59

11. Natalie Angier, *Woman: An Intimate Geography* (New York: Anchor, 2000), p. 37.

12. *Littleton v. Prange*, 9 S.W. 3d 223, at 230–31.

13. *In Re Marriage of Sterling Simmons and Jennifer Simmons*, 355 Ill. App. 3d 942, at 948.

14. Fausto-Sterling, *Sexing the Body*, pp. 1–2.

15. Nancy Chodorow, *The Reproduction of Mothering: Psychoanalysis and the Sociology of Gender* (Berkeley: University of California Press, 1978), pp. 83, 129.

16. Ibid., p. 169.

17. Patricia Hill Collins, *Black Feminist Thought: Knowledge, Consciousness and the Politics of Empowerment* (New York: Routledge, 2000), p. 184.

18. Denise A. Segura and Jennifer L. Pierce, "Chicana/o Family Structure and Gender Personality: Chodorow, Familism, and Psychoanalytic Sociology Revisited," *Signs* 19, no. 1 (Autumn 1993), p. 62.

19. Carol Stack, *All Our Kin* (New York: Basic, 1974), pp. 64–65.

20. Quoted in Aida Hurtado, "Relating to Privilege: Seduction and Rejection in the Subordination of White Women and Women of Color," *Signs* 14, no. 4 (Summer 1989), p. 842.

21. See also Kimberle Crenshaw, "Mapping the Margins: Intersectionality, Identity Politics and Violence against Women of Color," *Stanford Law Review* 42 (July 1991), p. 1252.

22. Elizabeth Spelman, *Inessential Woman: Problems of Exclusion in Feminist Thought* (Boston: Beacon, 1988), p. 134.

23. Butler, *Gender Trouble*, p. 18.

24. Linda Martín Alcoff, *Visible Identities: Race, Gender, and the Self* (Oxford: Oxford University Press, 2006), p. 176

25. Iris Marion Young, "Gender as Seriality: Thinking about Women as a Social Collective," *Signs* 19, no. 3 (Spring 1994), pp. 713–38.

26. Michael Karouno, "Ordination and Revolution in *Mansfield Park*," and Emily Rohrbach, "Austen's Later Subjects," *Studies in English Literature, 1500–1900* 44, no. 4 (Autumn 2004), pp. 715–36 and 737–52.

27. Quoted in Rohrbach, "Austen's Later Subjects," p. 751.

28. K. Anthony Appiah, "'But Would That Still Be Me?': Notes on Gender, 'Race,' Ethnicity as Sources of 'Identity,'" in *Race/Sex: Their Sameness, Difference, and Interplay*, ed. Naomi Zack (New York: Routledge, 1997), pp. 78–79.

29. American Psychiatric Association, *Diagnostic and Statistical Manual of Mental Disorders*, 4th ed., Text Revision (Arlington, Va.: American Psychiatric Publishing Inc., 2000), p. 576.

30. David B. Cruz, "Disestablishing Sex and Gender," *California Law Review* 90, no. 4 (July 2002), pp. 997–1086.

31. For example, *Loving v. Virginia*, 388 U.S. 1; *Zablocki v. Redhail*, 434 U.S. 374; and *Turner v. Safely*, 482 U.S. 78. See also Georgia Warnke, *After Identity: Rethinking Race, Sex and Gender* (Cambridge: Cambridge University Press, 2007), chap. 6.

3

Tracing a Ghostly Memory in My Throat

Reflections on Ftm Feminist Voice and Agency

C. Jacob Hale

It is from all those who have abandoned the traditional conception of sexual morality that the transsexuals differ. Unlike militant homophiles, enlightened therapists and liberated women, transsexuals endorse such traditional values as heterosexuality, domestic roles for women, the double standard of sexual morality, the traditional division of tasks and responsibilities, and the discreditation of deviant sexuality. Unlike various liberated groups, transsexuals are reactionary, moving back toward the core-culture rather than away from it. They are the Uncle Toms of the sexual revolution.

—Thomas Kando, *Sex Change*

Female-to-constructed-male transsexuals are the "final solution" of women perpetrated by the transsexual empire. ...Female-to-constructed-male transsexuals neutralize themselves as biological women and also their potentially deviant power. This is merely the most extreme form of neutralization that is taking place also with unnecessary hysterectomies and with the movement toward androgyny. The biological woman is not only neutralized but neuterized.

—Janice G. Raymond, *The Transsexual Empire*

There are also female transsexuals. They have been studied less, since they appear to be less common. They are also less spectacular. Theirs is not the Star System; rather, they ground their beings in the dullness of male attire. As one

surgeon has remarked, they want to be like everyone else,
that is, men. Women are never like everyone, for they do
not make the world. To be a man, in short, is to be part of
the common lot. This, it appears, is what female transsexuals aspire to: they want to be fellows, fellows of their
fellows.

—Catherine Millot, *Horsexe*

Demanding sex change is...part of what constructs the
subject as a transsexual: it is the mechanism through which
transsexuals come to identify themselves under the sign
of transsexualism and construct themselves as its subjects.
Because of this, we can trace transsexuals' agency through
their doctors' discourses, as the demand for sex change
was instantiated as the primary symptom (and sign) of the
transsexual.

—Bernice Hausman, *Changing Sex*

and I doubt I should answer
that unspoken question with a scream
for fear of discovering I no longer exist
for perhaps my voice too is no longer alive
except as a memory in my throat—

—Xavier Villaurrutia, *Nostalgia for Death*

The meeting of the Society for Women in Philosophy (SWIP), Pacific Division, on
May 20, 1995, was the first time I presented an academic paper on an overtly transgender topic from an openly ftm subject position.[1] This was the day after I received
my first injection of exogenous testosterone. Despite being beside myself from the
profound shifts in consciousness engendered by that first shot of boy-juice, trepida-
tion about the reactions I would meet slipped through the haze of my excitement.
I was fearful that some of the feminist philosophers active in Pacific SWIP would
ostracize me. Later that evening, I asked those who had stayed to share dinner,
drinks, and conversation if they thought I should continue teaching "Philosophy and
Feminism." I was temporarily reassured to hear the verdict they reached after a long
discussion: having seen the world as a woman and as a man, I would have a unique
perspective from which to approach the subject.[2]

During the fall of 1995, I asked the same question on the message board,
SWIP-L. Although there was much that was useful in the ensuing discussions, I met
three distinct types of erasure:

1. Responses in which I was classified as still a woman; this was usually accomplished by use of feminine pronouns or my former name.
2. Responses that invoked oppressive, totalizing, distorting constructions of transsexuality, abundant in medical, psychotherapeutic, social science, and some feminist and critical studies discourses. For example, my transition was equated with "sex change surgery," and it was expected that I should welcome discussions of Janice Raymond, whose 1979 *The Transsexual Empire* is widely regarded in trans community circles as the paradigm example of transphobic hate literature; among ftms, Raymond's notoriety is surpassed only by Leslie Lothstein's 1983 *Female-to-Male Transsexualism.*
3. Responses in which my question was figured—reconfigured, that is—as tantamount to asking "Can men be feminists?"

It may seem strange that I took (3) as an erasure, especially since I took being classified as a woman as an erasure. Leaving aside for a moment the varieties and complexities of ftm embodiments and subjectivities, one reason I took this as erasing the specificities of my subject position was that the paradigmatic men whose participation in feminist politics and theorizing has been the site of contestation are not transsexual. The dialogue proceeding from this paradigm elided differences between ftms' and nontranssexual men's relationships to feminist theory and practice, as well as erasing differences between our relationships to other cultural structures of power, oppression, and regulation. This set of erasures results from a familiar coupling: the binary assumption that one who is not a woman must therefore be a man, conjoined with the normatively paradigmatic status of nontransgendered people, in—and on—whose terms most feminist, queer, antiracist, postcolonialist, and other resistant discourses are conducted.

Evidently, the obvious points of difference between ftms and nontranssexual men were not obvious, or not obviously relevant, to those who participated in this discussion. Unlike nontranssexual men, ftms have lived parts of our lives as girls and as women with fairly unambiguous female embodiments and all that means in this cultural and historical moment. Thus, we have had years of experiencing the oppressions to which women and girls are subjected: differently, depending on our racial, ethnic, class, geographical, and other locations, and differently, depending on how we resisted the attempts at female socialization to which we were, still differently, subjected. Some ftms have long histories of participation in women's communities in ways that, usually, men are not allowed to participate, although these experiences may have been fraught with anxiety for us. Some ftms have had years of experience living as lesbians, some as heterosexual women, some as bisexual women, and some occupying all of these subject positions.

Unlike most nontranssexual men, most ftms have had months or years of experience moving about the world—or attempting to—as highly gender ambiguous. Sometimes this occurs before medical transition; sometimes it occurs only after medical transition begins. Here, one sees different kinds of oppressions than those seen by people for whom other's gender attributions are fairly univocal and confident.

During periods of gender ambiguity, we tend to develop finely grained observations about how gender attribution works and about our degrees of agency in manipulating the cultural meanings of gendered bodies, and we are subjected to firsthand experiences of the abjection—falling out of realm of social existence, entering a field of deformation and abjection—which Judith Butler writes accrue to people who fall outside the established gender boundaries (Butler 1987, 132; Butler 1993, 16). Insofar as gender-ambiguous people and people who claim transsexual subject positions are sometimes taken to be male-to-female transsexuals, some ftms learn from personal experience about how mtfs are treated in this culture. In my personal experience, being taken to be mtf has led to being verbally abused at top voice in public and to attempted rape.

Self-identification provides another nexus of differences between ftms and nontranssexual men. While many ftms self-identify as men simpliciter, not all ftms self-identify as men in any simple, stable, or nonproblematic way. Some nontransgendered people with fairly unambiguous male embodiments do not identify as men either, but the range of identificatory alternatives available to ftms is different. Some ftms, such as David Harrison, self-identify as transsexual men and view that as "a different gender from what people commonly think of as 'man'" (Due 1995, 18; Harrison 1996, 36).[3] Michael Hernandez (n.d.) writes, "My sexual orientation is queer. I consider myself to be a hybrid of woman and man, thus lesbian as well as gay." Just as some mtfs, such as Kate Bornstein (1994), self-identify as neither man nor woman, some ftms discursively position themselves as neither, or both, or "all of both and neither of either," or as members of a third gender, or look "forward eagerly to the day when there [will] be more genders from which to choose" (Devor 1995). Some ftms, such as myself, are profoundly uncomfortable with all of the already given sex and gender categories. However, in some situations we are forced to locate ourselves within these categories; for example, my U.S. passport must bear one of two designations, "F" or "M," and which of these two it bears matters for my mobility and my safety. In some situations, we may choose tactically to locate ourselves within already given sex and gender categories to achieve particular ends; for example, in this essay, I claim a right to speak as one, assuredly not representative, ftm transsexual, although in some other situations, I resist location of myself within the category *transsexual* as a means of disrupting certain aspects of hegemonic gender taxonomy. Further, we may be located in already given sex and gender categories against our wills in some situations; for example, sometimes other transsexuals insist on referring to me as a transman, transmale, or MTM despite my objections to being so positioned.

In this essay, I try to speak from my subject position as it is constituted by those multiple, apparently indiscriminate, erasures to which I am subjected. From this subject position, I chart the contours of an epistemological subject position from which some ftms can engage productively in feminist theorizing and practice. It is important to stress that this is not the only possible nor the only legitimate ftm feminist subject position: differences within the category *ftm* are exemplified in different ftm projects of self-construction, which lead to different types of political projects. My project aims to unsettle the category *man*, to trouble totalizing constructions of the category *ftm*, to suggest some particular contributions ftms might have to make to feminist theorizing, and to articulate some particular problems we face in undertaking feminist projects. Thus, my project in this essay is simultaneously political, ontological, and epistemological.

Flesh and Blood, Memory, Narrative, and Consciousness: A Whirlwind Tour of a Contested Gender Colony

Colonization of transsexuals crucially shapes our discursive and political situations in ways that directly influence ftm feminist voice and agency. In this section, I articulate those aspects of this colonization salient to ftm feminist voice and agency. In the next section, I directly address ftm feminist voice and agency.

In her landmark essay "The *Empire* Strikes Back: A Posttranssexual Manifesto" (Stone 1991, Stone 1992), Allucquère Rosanne (Sandy) Stone began the project of articulating transsexual academic resistance to our production and containment within binary, phallocentric, misogynistic, medicalized, and pathologizing gender purity genres: "The people who have no voice in this theorizing are the transsexuals themselves" (Stone 1992, 163). Stone's title responds directly to Raymond's *The Transsexual Empire*—aptly, since Raymond singled Stone out to vilify for her participation in the Olivia women's music collective as a recording engineer (Raymond 1979, 101–3; cf. Gabriel 1995 and Stone 1992, 154). Stone charts some of the similarities between discourses about transsexuality and other minority discourses that may be more familiar to nontranssexuals. She reads the historical movement from the first autobiographical accounts of mtf "sex change" to establishment within psychiatric nosology (in 1980) as exhibiting the following broad structure: "The initial fascination with the exotic, extending to professional investigators, denial of subjectivity and lack of access to the dominant discourse; followed by a species of rehabilitation" (Stone 1992, 163).

This "species of rehabilitation" is deeply pathologized: it is part of a system which requires that we get ourselves diagnosed with *DSM*-IV 302.85 (Gender Identity Disorder in Adolescents and Adults) before obtaining medically regulated embodiment technologies, many of which nontranssexuals obtain without inserting themselves into psychiatric nosology.[4] For transsexuals, inserting ourselves into this nosology is often necessary for exercising agency over our own bodies. It is also an act of complicity with our own erasure, for no one need listen when we claim a place for our voices in theorizing about us. As Susan Stryker writes: "I live daily with the consequences of medicine's definition of my identity as a mental disorder. Through the filter of this official pathologization, the sounds that come out of my mouth can be summarily dismissed as the confused ranting of a diseased mind" (Stryker 1994, 144).[5]

By accepting this "species of rehabilitation," transsexuals are forced to submit to an intricate, tightly woven set of regulatory regimes. If we desire medically regulated technologies, we must either insert ourselves into these regimes or forego adequate medical care and access to juridical mechanisms for changing sex and gender status on legal documents that require certification from physicians. As Stryker points out, "the current medical system imposes some tough choices on transsexuals about how we exercise power over our own bodies" (Stryker and High 1995, 228). That we confront these "tough choices," that we often experience ourselves—to borrow Marilyn Frye's words out of context—as "caged in: all avenues in every direction, are blocked or booby trapped" (Frye 1993, 4), can best be explained by noticing that the presence of such "double-bind" situations is constitutive of oppression. As Frye argues:

> One of the most characteristic and ubiquitous features of the world as experienced by oppressed people is the double bind situations in which options are reduced to a very few and all of them expose one to penalty, censure, or deprivation.
> One can only choose to risk one's preferred form and rate of annihilation. (2–3)

It is only by ignoring that this is an effect of oppression that Raymond can attempt to impale mtf lesbian-feminists on the horns of the following dilemma:

> The question of deception must also be raised in the context of how transsexuals who claim to be lesbian-feminists obtained surgery in the first place. Since all transsexuals have to "pass" as feminine in order to qualify for surgery, so-called lesbian-feminist transsexuals either had to lie to the therapists and doctors, or they had a conversion experience after surgery. I am highly dubious of such conversions, and the other alternative, deception, raises serious problems. (Raymond 1979, 104)[6]

Ignoring Frye's insight and its applicability to transsexuals also enables more recent discussions about whether transsexuals are duped or duplicitous, or both (Hausman; Shapiro 1991, 251; cf. Halberstam 1996).

Stone argues that "the [gender] clinic is a technology of inscription" of a dissolving ontology of gender as essential, natural truth (Stone 1992, 164). In the wake of the demise of most U.S. gender clinics and programs, technologies of inscription, domination, containment, and colonization of transsexuals' gendered embodiments, identifications, and performativities have become more diffuse. Currently, these technologies circulate through a number of structures, in addition to the remaining gender clinics and privately practicing psychiatrists, psychotherapists, endocrinologists, plastic and reconstructive surgeons, gynecologists, urologists, internists, and general practitioners.

The American Psychiatric Association is another such structure, which regulates gender through its *Diagnostic and Statistical Manual* codifications of Gender Identity Disorder (GID) in Children, GID in Adolescents and Adults, GID Not Otherwise Specified, and Transvestic Fetishism. Another regulating structure is the Harry Benjamin International Gender Dysphoria Association, Inc. (HBIGDA), an organization of predominantly nontranssexual medical and psychotherapeutic "professionals" which has appointed itself to set and promulgate "standards of care" for transsexuals. HBIDGA's standards of care are misleadingly named: although the phrase "standards of care" usually refers to standards of medical quality within particular medical communities, HBIGDA's standards of care are almost exclusively standards for access to medical technologies. Those involved in enacting and applying regulations governing change of name and sex or gender designations on legal documents—legislators, judges, and a wide variety of federal, state, county, and municipal employees—constitute another regulatory nexus.

Gender colonization resituates from imperialization of blood, soil, natural resources, national treasures, memory, narrative, and consciousness to territorialization of flesh, blood, memory, narrative, and consciousness. This is effected not by guns and tanks but by the conditions under which scalpels, syringes, pills, and sex and gender markers on legal documents are accessed, withdrawn, or denied. These conditions not only regulate culturally meaningful gendered embodiment, they constitute it by establishing, marking, and policing boundaries between those embodiments that have cultural meaning and those that are abjected from social ontology.

Heterosexism, phallocentricity, and illusions of a natural order of sex and gender are written on our very bodies. Here's a quiz for nontranssexual readers: What's wrong with these pictures?

1. Before performing penile inversion vaginoplasty (in which penile skin forms the inner lining of the neovagina), Eugene Schrang (Neenah, Wisconsin) measures the penises of his mtf patients to ensure that they are long enough to provide "adequate vaginal depth." If not, Schrang grafts skin from other bodily zones to achieve "adequate vaginal depth." Basing their judgments on the appearance and functionality of Schrang's results, many mtfs consider him to be the most skilled surgeon currently performing vaginoplasty in the United States.

2. At the First Annual FTM Conference of the Americas in 1995, Michael Brownstein (San Francisco, California) asserts that, although a number of his ftm patients seeking breast reduction or chest reconstruction tell him that they do not wish to have their nipples or aureole reduced, almost all ftm patients need such reduction. He also told his mostly ftm audience that, prior to surgically reconstructing ftm chests, he measures his own chest to ensure proper proportions. Many ftms believe that Brownstein's "top surgery" results are the best currently available in the United States for ftms who require mastectomy rather than other surgical techniques.

3. Also speaking at the First Annual FTM Conference of the Americas, Donald Laub's (Palo Alto, California) presentation on phalloplasty includes a slide bearing nothing but black serif uppercase type on a white background: "THE PROBLEM: NO PENIS" (Rubin 1996, 174–75).[7] Laub, along with David Gilbert (Norfolk, Virginia), is currently considered to be one of the two best phalloplastic surgeons in North America.[8]

4. At the 1991 Southern Comfort convention, Gilbert tells his audience that he will not construct a scrotum from labia when performing genital surgery on an ftm patient, since labial tissue is "girlie tissue." At the 1993 HBIGDA conference, Gilbert states that he will not allow his ftm phalloplasty patients to retain their vaginas because to do so would be to make "a chick with a dick—and no one would want that!"[9]

These examples foreground medical refusals to grant transsexuals agency over our own embodiments; however, they also point toward ways in which medical power focuses on our tongues: simply by writing this, I risk foregoing any further surgical alterations of my body. That Brownstein, Laub, and Gilbert clearly have the upper hand in systematic power relations is shown by the fact that they made their remarks from conference podiums to audiences composed primarily of transsexuals. Further,

I intend these examples to make unavoidably clear to theorists who would critique medical alterations of transsexual bodies that those of us who are directly subjected to this medical regime are in privileged epistemological positions from which to launch such critiques.

As is the case with other colonized peoples, transsexual problems with voice and agency are deeper than that those of us in privileged epistemological positions are coerced into silence or are dismissed as mad when we do speak. Silencing techniques exerted on us often reinscribe our words within nontranssexual discourses when we speak in ways that do not fit their monolithic constructions of us. Sometimes this is performed by nontranssexuals' self-imposition of a kind of selective deafness. For example, at the First Annual FTM Conference of the Americas, endocrinologist Richard Cherlin declared that ftms do not have pap smears as often as we should because we hate our vaginas. Cherlin's remark came in answer to a question from an ftm who had asked the medical panel whether he might face any possible medical complications were he to retain his vagina after metaoidioplasty. Clearly, this ftm's relationship to his vagina was not the hatred that Cherlin attributed to ftms.

Sometimes such silencing is performed by nontranssexuals' unwillingness to transfer principles from other contexts to considerations of transsexuality. For instance, at the SWIP table at the American Philosophical Association Eastern Division reception in 1994, I found myself arguing with a feminist philosopher about her contention that transsexuals cannot exist because feminist philosophers have shown that Cartesian dualism fails and transsexuals say they are women trapped in men's bodies. Would she similarly have used a recent Weight Watcher's commercial in which a woman said that she had known all along she that was a thin woman trapped in a fat woman's body to argue that fat women cannot exist? In another context, Carole S. Vance writes: "When we come to sex, our minds grind to a halt: normal distinctions become incomprehensible, and ordinary logic flies out the window" (Vance 1989, 17). This seems especially true of much nontranssexual thinking about transsexuality. When we think about a desire to lose weight, we realize that there are nondualistic ways to express this desire, that limits of contemporary discourse on a topic are not limits to all possible discourse on that topic, and that difficulties with expressing a desire in extant discourse do not necessarily delegitimate that desire but may, instead, point to problems with the discourse. When we think in contexts of nontranssexual feminist, lesbian/gay/bisexual, or queer theorizing and activism, we are familiar with using tactics of inversion to disrupt hegemonic assumptions of male, heterosexual, or normally sexualized centrality. Why, then, should nontranssexual feminist or queer theorists profess to be confounded by the phenomenology of transsexual desires, as if their own nontranssexual desires were utterly transparent standards of reference for transsexual desires? (cf. Scheman 1996)

Marjorie Garber's *Vested Interests* is a prime example of nontranssexual unwillingness to transfer epistemological and political tenets from other contexts to theorizing about transsexuality. Garber recognizes problems with medicalized discourses when speaking about nontranssexual subjects and succinctly states that "reading *through*...puts the interpreter in the position of the subject who knows—knows somehow 'better' than the person whose life is under scrutiny" (Garber 1992, 171);

however, she forgets this in her chapter about transsexuality. Garber adopts psycho-analytic psychiatrist Robert Stoller's conception of the demarcation between "male" transvestites and "male" transsexuals, which locates categorical differences in differ-ences between their allegedly obsessive relationships to their penises as insignia of maleness. She achieves this by conjoining three rhetorical techniques: uncritically quoting Stoller, citing his authority as "one of the most widely respected interpreters of gender identity today," and lauding his narrative style as "both sympathetic and empathetic, adopting the affective subject position of the transvestite" (95).

On this construction, Stoller knows at least as much about mtfs as they know about themselves and empathetically occupies a subject position that can serve as a stand-in for mtfs themselves, so there is no need to examine what mtfs might have to say about themselves. In fairness, I must note that Garber also cites several mtf auto-biographies and transvestite erotica in support of her claims. However, she overlooks the cultural and historical forces that produce these genres and their relationships to community discourses. Thus, Garber has cleared the path for her conclusion that, while transvestism and transsexuality threaten to radically undermine gender identity essentialism (Garber 1992, 102), "male transvestites and transsexuals radically and dramatically essentialize their genitalia" (98); in so doing, Garber's use of "*male* transvestites and transsexuals" (italics mine) reasserts the propriety of birth-assigned sex or gender for people assigned male at birth, reinscribing the very phallic essen-tialism for which she is faulting "male" transsexuals and transvestites.[10]

What, then, does Garber see when she reads through those of us whom she, asymmetrically, terms "female-to-male transsexuals"? She uncritically quotes Leslie Lothstein, totalizing his transphobic claims even more than he does. For example, after recounting Lothstein's remarks about *two* ftms who "developed massive cas-tration anxiety" after serious post-phalloplasty difficulties, Garber comments: "*The* female-to-male transsexual . . . gets more than he (or she) bargained for: together with the penis, he/she . . . gets not only castration anxiety but something that sounds very much like castration: his (or her) penis falls off, and has to be replaced (again)" (Garber 1992, 103; italics mine). At Garber's hand, ftms become penis-obsessed, deluded (both because we conflate the penis with the absolute insignia of maleness and because, according to Lothstein, some ftms go bare-chested in public despite poor mastectomy results), and uncritical victims of the misogynist notion that "a 'real one' can't be made, but only born" (104–5).[11]

Garber proposes a new project for gender studies, one predicated on denying transsexual agency in the critical gender discourse which is to built on a discourse about us: "It is to transsexuals and transvestites that we need to look if we want to understand what gender categories mean. For transsexuals and transvestites are *more* concerned with maleness and femaleness than persons who are neither transsexual nor transvestite" (Garber 1992, 110). Who speaks, in Garber's text, for those whose lives are under scrutiny? Nontranssexuals, including two of the most transphobic psychotherapists who have been actively engaged in pathologizing and regulating gender embodiment, identification, and expression—and a feminist literary critic. Are we to presume these theorizing subjects know more or better about our lives than do we, the objects of their scrutiny?

Another silencing technique is deployed when transsexuals are folded into non-transsexual paradigms, and our words, subjectivities and subject positions are understood in nontranssexual terms. This is the type of silencing to which I was subjected when my question on SWIP-L was treated as reducible to a question about the politics of nontranssexual men teaching feminism. Another example of this occurred at the first American Philosophical Association Pacific Division meeting I attended after beginning medical transition. During the discussion period, I spoke about how all three papers presented on gay and lesbian issues differently elided transgendered phenomena directly relevant to the topics of those papers. Since each of these three papers accomplished these elisions differently, it took a few minutes to make them visible to a nontransgendered panel and audience. Afterward, a feminist philosopher told me that now that I was a man I seemed all too ready to take up too much verbal space. With no more than a modification in tense—"Because you used to be a man"—the same rhetorical device could have been used equally well to erase the words of an mtf transsexual speaking from her mtf transsexual subject position. In both cases, our transsexual subject positions are reduced to nontranssexual manhood in an explanatory and dismissive scheme in which the complex specificities of our transsexual subject positions are folded into nontranssexual paradigms. It is not that ftms and mtfs bear no relationships to masculinity, manliness, or manhood; of course we do. Rather, my point is that these relationships are complicatedly different from those had by nontranssexual men, so simple assimilations of our words to paradigms of nontranssexual manhood function to erase the specificities of our subject positions.

Transsexuals are convenient sites for colonization predicated on our discursive erasure and for struggles between gender colonizers of all kinds and political locations. Insofar as there is such a monolithic entity as *the transsexual*, this peculiar object is—to borrow Frantz Fanon's psychoanalytic concept from a different context—"a phobogenic object, a stimulus to anxiety" (Fanon 1967, 151). This phobogenic object is a monolithic fiction constructed stunningly well not only to stimulate anxiety but also to function as a depository for nontranssexuals' gender anxieties. Because of our multiply ambiguous relationships to paradigmatic constructions of manhood and womanhood, totalized mtf and ftm transsexuals serve equally well as sites for anyone's anxieties about their own or another's masculinity or femininity, maleness or femaleness, manhood or womanhood.

Not only does this preposterous construct stimulate and absorb others' displaced anxieties, it is a device of containment; indeed, it must be to serve its function as a phobogenic object. This totalization is a stabilizing structure: compared with transsexual lives as lived, the transsexual is ontologically stable, for this stability is necessary to the maintenance of the illusion of a relatively sharp boundary between transsexuals and nontranssexuals. Containment and inscription of radical difference between subjects and others who are constructed as markers of their radical difference, encoded in categories of differential diagnosis as well as in wider cultural totalizations, are twin boundary-marking effects that enable domination, colonization, and oppression: individual transsexuals are figured as mere instantiations of the construct *the transsexual*, our specificities and complexities are policed and erased, our embodiments heavily regulated, our voices silenced, our subjectivities restricted and elided, and our radical threats contained and plundered in service of gender hegemonies.

Insofar as our practices of self dislodge familiar, comfortable notions about the naturalness of bodies and the natural foundations of the relationships between bodies, selves, others, and the rest of the world, we are cultural placeholders for anxieties about nature versus culture, artifice, perversity, human dominion over nature, natural limitations on human manipulation and control, science versus culture, normal versus pathological, inside versus outside, relationships of alterity, spectacle versus propriety, display versus taboo, agency versus domination, self versus body, self versus culture, and self versus other. Because different regimes of power compete to control cultural discourses of the sexed or gendered subject in relation to these distinctions, we become contested battlezones: psychiatry and other medical specialties, different psychological and psychiatric schools of thought, psychology, sociology, anthropology, feminist theory, and queer theory compete for hegemony over the terrain of transsexual representation and production. Since the structure of the sexed and gendered world rests on foundations belied by our practices of self, we are a system of interlocking fault lines threatening to undermine that world's structure, to shake it off its foundations and bring it crashing to the ground. With so much at stake, is it any wonder that so much meaning, so much tension between so many competing meanings, circulates through transsexual bodies (cf. Halberstam 1996 and Stone 1992, 164), that so many people have so much invested in controlling our unruly pluralities by figuring that placeholder for their anxieties, that phobogenic object: *the transsexual?* With so much invested in and contested on our bodies, on our tongues, how can we speak in and on our own terms?

Moreover, our ability to speak with our own voices is limited by, as Stryker puts it, "the inability of language to represent the transgendered subject's movement over time between stably gendered positions in a linguistic structure" (Stryker 1994, 241). For example, once when my father started telling a story about a memory of me as a child, he said: "When Jake was a little boy—I mean a little girl—I mean a little child—he—I mean she—I mean—I don't know what I mean!" There he broke off. My father was right to be frustrated, for there are no available grammatical structures with which he could compose one sentence that referred to me both as a girl child and as an adult man. Additional complications come to the fore when we consider references to a transitioning transsexual. The linguistic problem is deeper than temporality: representations of me as a *stably* gendered girl child (or boy child) or as a stably gendered adult man (or adult woman) would all be false. Structurally, insertion into language—therefore, into social ontology—requires gendered stability both over time and at any given time that some of us lack.

For those of us on whom the limits of already available discourse press the most closely, it would seem that refusing colonizing discourses leaves us in a position of near speechlessness: reverse discourse (Stryker 1994, 240). Yet we know that sounding trumpets of resistance will not, by itself, fall flat on the arid earth of those walls of oppression that shut us out of the city of language, out of social ontology, out of intelligibility. If some queer feminist ftm can speak only reverse discourse, how can he speak with a feminist voice?

Displaced Persons: Discursive Dislocatedness and Ftm Feminist Agency

> And we do have something else to say, if you will but listen to the monsters: the possibility of meaningful agency and action exists, even within fields of domination that bring about the universal cultural rape of all flesh.
>
> —Susan Stryker, "My Words to Victor Frankenstein" (250)

> May we have to be monstrous enough to greet our predicament?
>
> —Nicholas Mosley, *Hopeful Monsters* (3)

> I suggest we think carefully, butches and FTM's alike, about the kinds of men or masculine beings that we become and lay claim to: queer masculinities, ultimately, will fail to be queer to the extent to which they fail to be feminist.
>
> —Judith Halberstam, "Female-to-Butch" (173)

> The core of one's being must love justice more than manhood.
>
> —John Stoltenberg, *Refusing to Be a Man* (185)

On January 17, 1994, the Northridge earthquake left me a "displaced person." This media construction meant that I was not homeless, although I did not have a place to live: I did not have to sleep in a park, at a Red Cross shelter, or on the street. Since I had financial resources and documentation verifying the legality of my residence in the United States, I was able to find another home after four months. About a year later, I entered a more enduring displacement, constituted by my permanently transsexing embodiment and by my discursive dislocatedness.

In this section, I map the contours of one possible ftm subject position from which to engage in feminist theorizing and practice. There are many viable ftm subject positions quite different from mine, which will lead to different ftm feminist projects. The subject position that I claim here is one of displacement, dislocation, and erasure, yet it is also a space of creative reconstruction.

My discussion of discursive dislocatedness builds on the view of definitions of gender category terms that I developed elsewhere with regard to the category *woman* (Hale 1996). I advanced a descriptive reconstruction of the contemporary U.S.-dominant cultural definition of "woman," which has thirteen defining characteristics, clustered into several different groups, and weighted differently. None of these thirteen characteristics is necessary or sufficient for membership in the category *woman*; instead, together they are Wittgensteinian family resemblance criteria. On this view, some members of one category may be more paradigmatically or centrally located with that category than other members of the same category in virtue of possessing more or more heavily weighted defining characteristics, and category boundaries are fuzzy. Borders between gender categories, then, are zones of overlap, not sharp lines.

Those of us who are dislocated from already given gender categories, both normative and nonnormative ones, are dislocated in that we cannot fully inhabit any of them. We place ourselves and are placed by others in the margins of any number of gender categories, never close to the paradigmatic core of any but also never falling fully outside all. I am, for example, not fully man nor woman nor male nor female nor hermaphrodite nor drag queen nor butch leatherman nor lesbian man nor faggot butch dyke nor transsexual nor ftm nor transgendered nor third gender nor anything else, since I do not fit the paradigms of any already given gender categories. I flit about the margins of each of these categories. Since some of these categories share unions with one another, I flit through overlapping border zones constituted by the margins of several gender categories.

Flitting about the margins is not a refusal to own my location, nor is it valorization of gender play or gender fluidity. Flitting is a type of movement proper to ghosts: creatures abjected from full social existence who, instead, have only partial, limited social existence. For reasons as personal, various, and idiosyncratic as the personal, various, and idiosyncratic connections border zone inhabitants draw between our embodiments, self-identifications, and subjectivities, already given discourses offer us little else than indefinite sequences of indiscriminate erasure. Already given discourses may elide the specificities of those with firm locations within already given categories, but not to the same degree that they elide the specificities of the dislocated. Those of us who live in border zones constituted by the overlapping margins of categories do so because our embodiments and our subjectivities are abjected from social ontology: we cannot fit ourselves into extant categories without denying, erasing, or otherwise abjecting personally significant aspects of ourselves. The price of committing such violence against ourselves is too great, though our only other option is also very costly for the dislocated have fallen through the cracks in the structure of the gendered world. Having slipped off all the handholds we have ever tried to grasp, we have fallen between the cracks of language and life. Unintelligible to ourselves and to others, we are driven to search for new category terms, since category terms are the signal-flags of social ontology, and we desperately long to reenter the world. Having been thrown tumultuously out of the world of social existence already, ghosts never again expect a social world, structured by discourse, to provide homely comforts; we have already learned that home was an illusion, so we forego nostalgia for origins lost because never properly had. While we try to carve out zones of safety in which to create new discourses—structures and category terms—with which to call ourselves and others into fuller social being, we recognize that such social existence will always be precarious and partial. So we are always cautious, drawing tentatively on the various discourses of those locations we only partially inhabit, always ready to shift in resistance to the tactical shifts of hegemonic, normalizing, totalizing, and colonizing forces. Here is queer gender, here is genderqueer: a range of abjected subject positions, dislocated locations, from which the displaced can speak. Here is where I stake my place between places.

"Dislocated locations" may sound paradoxical, but it is not, for dislocatedness is not utter absence of location. Rather, our dislocatedness is constituted by our locations in the overlapping margins of multiple gender categories. Different genderqueer border zone denizens are, of course, differently located: not only do we exist in the areas of overlap of different gender categories, but also our placements in those areas of overlap are different. Only by speaking quite specifically about those located elements of our dislocatedness can those who dwell in border zones speak at all. Such lengthy, detailed specifications do not provide the material for full occupancy of social ontology, which presently requires more central, less multiple instantiation of social categories.

The concept of world traveling that María Lugones develops in "Playfulness, 'World'-Travelling, and Loving Perception" (1990) provides conceptual tools for understanding the epistemological subject positions of genderqueer border zone denizens. On Lugones's conception, a "world" is always presently inhabited by some flesh and blood people; it need not be a construction of an entire society, and it may be incomplete in that things in it may not be altogether constructed or some things in it may be negatively constructed. Thus, a world may be an incomplete, visionary, nonutopian construction, or it may be a traditional construction of life; some of the inhabitants of a world may not understand or accept their constructions within it (Lugones 1990, 395). From this base, Lugones argues that some of us, especially "those of us who are outside the mainstream U.S. construction or organization of life," travel between worlds and that some of us are in more than one world at once (396). When we travel between worlds, we "have the distinct experience of being different in different worlds and ourselves in them," and we are more at ease in some worlds than in others (396). We may be at ease in a world in any of four ways: (1) by understanding the norms and discourses in that world; (2) by being normatively happy because in agreement with the world's norms; (3) by being humanly bonded with others within that world; and, (4) by sharing a history with others in that world. A person is maximally at ease in a world in which that person is at ease in all four senses (397).

Dislocated genderqueers cannot be at ease in Lugones's second sense: since we are only marginally within any gender category, we will not be normatively happy because we will not be in agreement with the norms that constitute that gender category's core. Yet we may be at ease in many worlds in each of Lugones's other three senses. We may understand the norms within worlds of the normatively gendered, within transsexual worlds, within ftm-specific worlds, and within other queer worlds; we may have close, loving, human bonds in each of the worlds about whose margins we flit; and we may share histories with others in many worlds. Thus, we may have more plural self-images than those double images of ourselves that Lugones locates in our memories of ourselves in different worlds (Lugones 1990, 398); we may travel to indefinitely many worlds, and, thus, see indefinitely many images of ourselves, and we may also see ourselves as constructed differently than we construct ourselves in indefinitely many worlds. Some of these constructions of ourselves may be such that we cannot recognize even shreds of ourselves; for example, I cannot recognize myself in Kando's Uncle Tom of the sexual revolution, Raymond's "final solution," or Millot's fellow who aspires to be a fellow of his fellows, or Hausman's transsexual whose agency is fully contained by a demand for sex change and thus can be read off from medical discourse. Such hostile worlds may be ones that we need rapidly and with finality to exit, or they may be worlds in which we must try to exercise agency to bring about change. Choosing between these alternatives is always a decision about which resistant tactics will produce the most gender-liberatory results for all peoples subjected to gender oppression.

World-traveling genderqueers' subject positions lead to particular kinds of gender theory, politics, and practice, forged from the particular zones of overlap that we occupy and through which we travel. In the rest of this essay, I explore two clusters of such projects of particular ftm feminist concern: (1) our relationships to manhood, manliness, and masculinity, and (2) creating wider conditions of possibility for genderqueer discursive agency and bodily autonomy.

Problems of manhood, manliness, and masculinity are especially poignant to dislocated genderqueers assigned female at birth who have traveled and still travel in feminist worlds. Our lived histories as girls and women have given us many of the same experiences of oppression as normatively gendered women, for our bodies have carried cultural meanings similarly embedded in misogyny and male dominance, yet we are deeply implicated in masculinities.

Compared with nontranssexual men, we have both advantages and disadvantages with regard to feminist theory, politics, and practice. Our lived experiences tend to give us epistemological advantages of the sort I have already noted. Beyond this, though, we tend to experience much more directly that how we embody masculinity, manliness, and manhood is a matter of existential choice—that "masculinity is what we make of it," as Halberstam writes (Halberstam 1996, 1998)—to which we bring feminist and other genderqueer political standards. Indeed, for some ftms, one of the more disconcerting aspects of transition is the extent to which we become privy to displays of nontranssexual men's sexism as our gender presentations and embodiments come to elicit attributions as fellows of our fellows. Thus, we are in strong positions from which to be reticent to fit ourselves into already given models of masculinity, most of which, it must be said, have been given by dominant men (Harrison 1996, 34). We must be willing to examine our implications in masculinities and to hold masculinities that attract us—and ourselves—to feminist and genderqueer political standards of nonoppressiveness. To do this, we must hold onto those human bonds and histories we share with nontranssexual and transsexual feminist women: that is, to continue to move in our feminist worlds.

Continuing to participate in feminist worlds can be especially difficult for genderqueers assigned female at birth. Nontranssexual men have never been told by feminists that they simply delude themselves into thinking that they exist or that they are the final solution to women. Never having been women, nontranssexual men are not told they are gender traitors grasping at male privilege by leaving the category *woman*. Nor are nontranssexual men's masculinities subjected to the tightly coercive structures that control access to medically regulated technologies for reembodiment.

Although we face difficulties, we bear moral and political responsibility for that which we make from already given masculinities. Remaining in our feminist worlds, even if only marginally, may require that we exercise great patience with ourselves and with others, and that others exercise similar patience with themselves and with us. The easiest course would be simply to walk away from our feminist worlds when faced with the silencing techniques I have outlined earlier in this essay. Effort and pain are involved in self-examination, and attempts to work through erasure to a vista from both men's domination of normatively gendered women and normatively gendered colonization of nonnormatively gendered peoples can be held simultaneously within the same visual field. Only when genderqueers and feminist women can hold both simultaneously within our visual fields are we in positions from which to engage problems of manhood, manliness, and masculinity, for these constructs have been produced in opposition to normatively gendered womanhood, womanliness, and femininity and in opposition to abjected gender subjectivities and embodiments.

To engage these problems productively, we must be cautious of the identifications we make. Self-identity is always doubly relational (at a minimum). We form and maintain our identities by making continually reiterated identifications *as* members of some category U(s). This is accomplished both positively and negatively by repeated identifications *with* some (not necessarily all) members of U, and by reiterated identifications *as not*-members of some other category T(hem). Identifying *as* and identifying *with*, while closely related, are not identical. Identifying *as* U always involves identifying *with* some members of U, but the converse does not hold; for example, I identify *with* leatherdykes, as a result of historical ties, continuing friendship circles, and some affinities of sensibilities and values, but I no longer identify *as* a leatherdyke. Some members of U serve as positive identificatory referents, whereas some members of T serve as negative identificatory referents.[12]

The multiple alterities of border zone–dwelling ftms provide many possibilities from which to select primary positive and negative identificatory referents. There are many pressures on us to select dominant men as our primary positive identificatory referents and lesbians, particularly butches, as our primary negative identificatory referents, yet in making our identificatory choices we can exercise moral and political agency rather than succumb to imperialist coercion. In making our identificatory choices wisely, we will gain much from conversations with others who face similar yet different choices, particularly feminist butches and feminist (or antisexist or pro-feminist) nontranssexual men. We must be particularly cautious when forming identifications with nontranssexual men and in locating nontranssexual men as our primary positive identificatory referents. Holding those whom we locate as primary positive identificatory referents, as well as those with whom we identify more loosely, to feminist and other gender liberatory principles is, fundamentally, holding ourselves to our own moral and political principles in our acts of self-construction.

We may find that self-definitions in which we take our gender identifications as core aspects of our beings will obstruct our abilities to construct selves with which we can live morally or politically. As John Stoltenberg writes: "We must be transformers of selfhood—our own and others'. If we are not, we will have betrayed women's lives utterly, and we will have lost a part of ourselves that is precious and rare on this earth" (Stoltenberg 1989, 198). My claim is not that we must jettison our gendered subjectivities, embodiments, and self-identifications to live in a fictional space of gender transcendence but, rather, that we may need to make our gendered self-identifications subsidiary to other aspects of those selves we construct: we must care more about our moral and political values than we do about our gendered self-identifications. At the level of self-identification, this would mean that we self-identify primarily as particular kinds of moral and political beings and that our primary positive identificatory referents would be other people with similar moral and political self-identifications. If those moral and political self-identifications that we select to constitute central aspects of ourselves are based on feminist and other gender-liberatory principles, our primary positive identificatory referent class will likely include more nontranssexual women than nontranssexual men; it might include more mtfs than ftms, and it will be heavily populated by other genderqueers.

For some dislocated genderqueer ftms, locating our moral and political values at the cores of our beings may lead to refusing to be men, as Stoltenberg urges for nontranssexual men.[13] While it is difficult to make such refusals legible to others, we can write creatively on context-sensitive paper. Our refusals may be verbal or textual, or they may be more visual public displays. Writing about drag queens, Richard Smith remarks that "homosexual effeminacy is less about wanting to be a woman, and more about wanting to be a man" (Smith 1994, 237). In some contexts, such as an ftm gathering, doing drag or even just over-the-top nellie camping is often read as a powerful refusal of manhood.

Whether manhood is a morally and politically viable subject position is an issue that needs further investigation, and this investigation will be most productive if engaged across boundaries of gender identity categories with people who share feminist and other gender-liberatory political commitments and if engaged performatively, as well as in more traditional prose forms. I have argued elsewhere for a multiple-strategies approach to struggling against the oppression of women, an approach that both remakes the category *woman* from the inside, redefining and revaluing womanhood out from under heterosexism and male domination, and encourages gender proliferation (Hale 1996). A similar approach is necessary with regard to the category *man*. This is not because *woman* and *man* are parallel categories but because the category *man* must be remade lest it continue to be oppressive to all of us who are not within that category or who are not centrally or solidly within that category. This consideration holds independently of whether manhood is a morally and politically viable subject position. Further, some genderqueer feminist ftms may be in better positions than nontranssexual men, for reasons I have suggested earlier, to re-create manhood from the inside.

Whichever strategy an ftm chooses, he will necessarily be locating himself marginally, as a flittingly disruptive border zone presence. We must be monstrous enough to meet our moral and political predicament, to exercise our ghostly agency in accordance with feminist and other gender-liberatory principles. We must also be monstrous enough to restructure the world, to create spaces for new cultural formations and new forms of discursive agency that recognize those fractures that already exist between the aspects of embodiment, subjectivity, performativity, and self-identification taken to constitute unitary sex/gender/sexuality status, and which broaden the conditions of possibility for new fault lines to appear. In so doing, we may be creating conditions that will preclude our own obsolescence.

The politics of bodily autonomy provides fairly smooth links between feminist political efforts regarding reproductive technologies and transsexual political work on access to medically regulated technologies. Moreover, political goals of ending sexist and heterosexist gender role and performativity restrictions provides links between feminist, lesbigay, and transgender political concerns about regulation of gender embodiment, subjectivity, performativity, and self-identification. Insofar as medicine, psychotherapy, and the law constitute formidable regulatory structures, they are institutions on which our political work must focus.

There are powerful alliances to be forged between lesbigay efforts to end the psychiatric abuse of gender-variant lesbigay children under GID diagnoses (Burke 1996); feminist attempts to ensure women's autonomous access to reproductive technologies and to end coercive abuse of such technologies through sterilization abuse and female genital mutilation; intersex activists' work to stop genital mutilation of intersexed infants and children (Chase 1988); sex radical activist goals of removing adult, consensual sex from the *DSM*; and transsexual political objectives of breaking the medico-therapeutic-juridical power that enables our colonization and puts psychotherapists, physicians, lawmakers, judges, and government bureaucrats in positions to regulate theoretical and political beliefs about gender, as well as specific gender performativities, in antifeminist and heterosexist ways. Psychiatric nosology draws and polices taxonomic divisions that make these fruitful areas of alliance opaque. Yet if we were to eliminate the strategies of colonization and containment that focus specifically on transsexual bodies, we would thereby create a world in which the technological and performative means for embodiment of sex, gender, and sexuality would be available on the basis of desire alone. Such a world is one in which there would be greater freedom to think and enact gender as existential choice, made in accordance with moral and political principles.

The structures of such a world are not predictable from our vantage point in this heavily regulated world, but we can be sure that it would be one in which unforeseen categorical, discursive, and cultural formations would appear and in which many of our present formations would become archaic. If we are serious about eradicating those structures that comprise the architecture of contemporary gender oppressions, we must form stronger alliances based on shared feminist, lesbigay, queer, intersex, transgender, transsexual, and genderqueer moral and political values. Even though some of our short-term goals may be antithetical, if those of us who are working to end the cultural rape of all flesh do not strengthen such alliances, we will leave some structures of gender oppression in force on our bodies, our tongues, and our hearts.[14]

NOTES

A longer version of this essay was originally published in T. Digby, ed., *Men Doing Feminism* (New York: Routledge, 1998).

1. Throughout this essay, I use "ftm" as a primitive, not necessarily abbreviatory, term of self-identification; I attempt to signal its primitiveness by disrupting the customary capitalization of "FTM." "Female-to-male" is the most common specification of FTM, though FTM is sometimes used as an abbreviation for nonstandard self-identifications such as "female-toward-male," which I sometimes apply to myself to disrupt the assumption that I am striving for "complete" male embodiment. Adjectivally, ftm can modify "transgendered" or "transsexual," or both, if *transsexual* is viewed as a subcategory of *transgendered*. Some people prefer "MTM" (male-to-male) as a self-identificatory term indicating that they are acquiring male embodiments in line with their already male self-identifications. Others prefer the terms "metamorph" (Morton 1994), "transmale," "transman," or "MBF" (man born female). At this and other points in this essay, I cannot supply adequate citations, since much newly forming, contested ftm community discourse circulates through informal conversations that carry the presumption of confidentiality.

2. At the time, I was so afraid of being called a gender traitor yet again, of facing yet again the presumption that my transition is a grasp for male privilege (as in Cromwell 1994), that I felt comforted by their verdict about my epistemological privilege. Later, I became troubled by the suggestion that ftms have better epistemological positions than nontranssexual women from which to make claims about nontranssexual women's oppression, because it too easily warrants dismissing nontranssexual women's claims about their own oppressions.

3. Many ftms and MTMs who self-identify as transsexual men do not take this to be a gender category distinct from *man*; "transsexual man" is often used to indicate a different route to manhood or a different location within the category *man*.

4. The most controversial political issue among contemporary U.S. transsexuals is whether we should work to remove Gender Identity Disorder (GID) from the *DSM*. Some transsexuals fear that our abilities to access medically regulated technologies for reembodiment would be compromised were there no such diagnosis (e.g., Stryker 1996).

5. "These are my words to Victor Frankenstein, above the village of Chamounix. Like the monster, I could speak of my earlier memories, and how I became aware of my difference from everyone around me. I can describe how I acquired a monstrous identity by taking on the label 'transsexual' to name parts of myself that I could not otherwise explain. I, too, have discovered the journals of the men who made my body, and who have made the bodies of creatures like me since the 1930s. I know in intimate detail the history of this recent medical intervention into the enactment of transgendered subjectivity: science seeks to contain and colonize the radical threat posed by a particular transgender strategy of resistance to the coerciveness of gender: physical alteration of the genitals" (Susan Stryker, "My Words to Victor Frankenstein," 244). Stryker's formulation reflects a confluence of dominant cultural, medical, legal, and mtf transgender community discourses that tend to situate the penis as transsexuality's placeholder. By contrast, I claim that coerced complicity with medico-juridical power structures functions to contain and colonize the numerous radical threats posed by transsexuals' use of a wide variety of medically regulated technologies to alter surgically and hormonally a wide range of

culturally marked bodily zones, including breasts and chests, internal and external reproductive organs, genitals, voice, hair growth and distribution, musculature, and skin texture, many of which nontranssexuals alter by means of the same technologies without similar regulation. This is not to contest the claims that the penis bears more cultural meaning than any other piece of flesh and that nontranssexual regulation of transsexual bodies fastens more compulsively onto the penis than onto any other bodily zone.

6. Most psychiatrists, psychotherapists, and surgeons who control access to reembodiment technologies no longer enforce a heterosexuality requirement, although they still often impose heterosexist gender norms on transsexuals.

7. My notes from this conference disagree with Rubin with regard to Luab's punctuation.

8. Phalloplasty and metaoidioplasty are the two procedures available for surgical construction of ftm neophalluses. Phalloplastic techniques, available to nontranssexual men and ftms, use skin grafts to construct a neophallus within the size range typical for nontranssexual males. Ftms disagree about the adequacy of phalloplasty with regard to eliminatory and sexual function, sensation, and appearance. Metaoidioplasty is an ftm-specific procedure by which a small but sensate neophallus with erectile capabilities is constructed from erectile tissue already enlarged by testosterone. Urethroplasty and vaginectomy are separate procedures. (On these procedures, see Green 1995 and Leonard 1996.)

9. Jason Cromwell told me about Gilbert's Southern Comfort remark and Susan Stryker related Gilbert's 1993 HBIGDA assertion to me; both were in the audiences. The latter remark implies that mtfs who have not had penectomy—as well as ftms who have not had vaginectomy—are undesirable, as well as erasing ftm subjectivity with regard to gender identifications by positioning some of us as "chicks."

10. On the paramount role of the penis in sex and gender assignment of infants, see Chase 1988 and Kessler 1994, 223–24, 227–28.

11. Since the primary use for which phalloplastic techniques have been developed is reconstruction of nontranssexual men's penises after damage in combat or in accidents, Garber's feminist analysis of the reasons for the inadequacies of these techniques is misguided. If patriarchy wanted anyone to have a fully functioning penis, would it not want to bestow that honor on war heroes along with their Purple Heart decorations?

12. Identifications *with*, *as*, and *as-not* may be partial, incomplete, mediated, or crossed, as becomes clear in José Esteban Muñoz's exposition of his different though related concept of disidentification (Muñoz 1996, 145).

13. At first, this seems much easier for Stoltenberg to say than for an ftm since nontranssexuals assigned male at birth who opt out of manhood on moral or political grounds face quite different consequences. It is less likely that they will be told that they are women. Even if they are, their histories and embodiments give this very different meanings from those for ftms. Further, nontranssexual men will not face the same types of violence used to police gender boundaries and performativities, especially vaginal rape. However, if I am to take seriously my claim that moral and political values provide a better core for my sense of self than gendered subjectivity, then I must also take seriously its implication that it should be less damaging to be discursively located by others as having a gender category membership at odds with my self-identifications than it would be to lose a more central aspect of my subjectivity.

14. In Hale 1998 I also explore themes of resisting definition of "transsexual" as a political tactic, ftm construction of butches as primary negative identificatory referents, disclocatedness,

and border zone defense. For productive conversations on topics of this essay or for help with sources, I thank Talia Bettcher, Kate Bornstein, Cheryl Chase, Jason Cromwell, Dexter Day, Ann Garry, Judith Halberstam, Sandra Harding, Michael M. Hernandez, Jordy Jones, C. Julian Leonard, Jay Prosser, Rebecca Rugg, Naomi Scheman, Ben Singer, and Susan Stryker.

WORKS CITED

American Psychiatric Association, *Diagnostic and Statistical Manual of Mental Disorders*, 4th ed., Text Revision (Arlington, Va.: American Psychiatric Publishing Inc., 2000).

Bornstein, Kate. 1994. *Gender Outlaw: On Men, Women, and the Rest of Us*. New York: Vintage.

Burke, Phyllis. 1996. *Gender Shock: Exploding the Myths of Male and Female*. New York: Anchor.

Butler, Judith. 1987. "Variations on Sex and Gender: Beauvoir, Wittig and Foucault." In *Feminism as Critique: On the Politics of Gender*, ed. Seyla Benhabib and Drucilla Cornell, 128–42. Minneapolis: University of Minnesota Press.

———. 1993. *Bodies That Matter: On the Limits or Discursive "Sex."* New York: Routledge.

Chase, Cheryl. 1998. "Hermaphrodites with Attitude: Mapping the Emergence of Intersex Political Activism." *GLQ: Journal of Lesbian and Gay Studies* 4, no. 2.

Cromwell, Jason. 1994. "Default Assumptions, or the Billy Tipton Phenomenon." *FTM Newsletter* 28 (July): 4–5.

Devor, Holly. 1995. "The Fallacy of Duality in Conceptualizations of Sex, Gender and Sexuality." Plenary speech presented at the 38th annual meetings of the Society for the Scientific Study of Sexuality, San Francisco.

Due, Linnea. 1995. "Genderation X." *SF Weekly* 14, no. 37 (October 25–31): 12–14, 16–17, 18–19.

Fanon, Frantz. 1967. *Black Skins, White Masks*. Trans. Charles Lam Markmann. New York: Grove.

Frye, Marilyn. 1983. *The Politics of Reality: Essays in Feminist Theory*. Freedom, California: Crossing Press.

Gabriel, Davina Anne. 1995. "Interview with the Transsexual Vampire: Sandy Stone's Dark Gift." *TransSisters: Journal of Transsexual Feminism* 8 (Spring): 14–27.

Garber, Marjorie. 1992. *Vested Interests: Cross-Dressing and Cultural Anxiety*. New York: HarperPerennial.

Green, James. 1995. "Getting Real about FTM Surgery." *Chrysalis: Journal of Transgressive Gender Identities* 2, no. 2: 27–32.

Halberstam, Judith. 1996. "Right Bodies, Wrong Bodies, Border Bodies: Transsexualism and the Rhetoric of Migration." Paper presented at the American Studies Association conference, Kansas City, Mo.

———. 1998. "Butch/FTM Border Wars and the Masculine Continuum." *GLQ: Journal of Lesbian and Gay Studies* 4, no. 2.

Hale, C. Jacob. 1996. "Are Lesbians Women?" *Hypatia* 11, no. 2 (Spring): 94–121.

———. 1998. "Consuming the Living, Dis(re)membering the Dead in the Butch/FTM Borderlands." *GLQ: Journal of Lesbian and Gay Studies* 4, no. 2.

Harrison, David. 1996. "Becoming a Man: The Transition from Female to Male." In *Assaults on Convention: Essays on Lesbian Transgressors*, ed. Niocola Godwin, Belinda Hollows, and Sheridan Nye, 24–37. New York: Cassell.

Hausman, Bernice L. 1995. *Changing Sex: Transsexualism, Technology, and the Idea of Gender*. Durham, N.C.: Duke University Press.

Hernandez, Michael, 1998. "Holding My Breath under Water." In *Looking Queer*, ed. Dawn Atkins, 199–204. Boston: Hayworth Press.

Kando, Thomas. 1973. *Sex Change: The Achievement of Gender Identity among Feminized Transsexuals*. Springfield, Ill.: Charles C. Thomas.

Kessler, Suzanne J. 1994. "The Medical Construction of Gender: Case Management of Intersexed Infants." In *Theorizing Feminism: Parallel Trends in the Humanities and Social Sciences*, ed. Anne C. Herrmann and Abigail J. Stewart, 218–37. Boulder, Colo.: Westview.

Leonard, C. Julian. 1996. "Phallusies: Exploding the Myth of 'Penis Formation.'" *TransFagRag* 1 (Fall): 8–9.

Lothstein, Leslie. 1983. *Female-to-Male Transsexualism: Historical, Clinical and Theoretical Issues*. Boston: Routledge and Kegan Paul.

Lugones, María. 1990. "Playfulness, 'World'-Travelling, and Loving Perception." In *Making Face, Making Soul / Haciendo Caras: Creative and Critical Perspectives by Feminists of Color*, ed. Gloria Anzaldúa, 390–402. San Francisco: Aunt Lute Books.

Millot, Catherine. 1990. *Horsexe: Essay on Transsexuality*. Trans. Kenneth Hylton. New York: Autonomedia.

Morton, Shadow. 1994. "A Man by Any Other Name." *FTM Newsletter* 27 (April): 11.

Mosley, Nicholas. 1990. *Hopeful Monsters*. New York: Vintage.

Muñoz, José Esteban. 1996. "Famous and Dandy Like B. 'n' Andy: Race, Pop, and Basquiat." In *Pop Out: Queer Warhol*, ed. Jennifer Doyle, Jonathan Flatley, and José Esteban Muñoz, 144–79. Durham, N.C.: Duke University Press.

Raymond, Janice G. 1979. *The Transsexual Empire*. London: Women's Press.

Rubin, Henry S. 1996. "Report on the First FTM Conference of the Americas: A Vision of Community." *Journal of Gay, Lesbian, and Bisexual Identity* 1, no. 2 (April): 171–77.

Scheman, Naomi. 1996. "Queering the Center by Centering the Queer: Reflections on Transsexuals and Secular Jews." In *Feminists Rethink the Self*, ed. Diane Tietjens Meyers. Boulder, Colo.: Westview.

Shapiro, Judith. 1991. "Transsexualism: Reflections on the Persistence of Gender and the Mutability of Sex." In *Body Guards: The Cultural Politics of Gender Ambiguity*, ed. Julia Epstein and Kristina Straub, 248–79. New York: Routledge.

Smith, Richard. 1994. "Frock Tactics." In *Drag: A History of Female Impersonation in the Performing Arts*, by Roger Baker with contributions by Peter Burton and Richard Smith, 236–62. New York: New York University Press.

Stoltenberg, John. 1989. *Refusing to Be a Man: Essays on Sex and Justice*. New York: Meridian.

Stone, Sandy. 1991. "The *Empire* Strikes Back: A Posttranssexual Manifesto." In *Body Guards: The Cultural Politics of Gender Ambiguity*, ed. Julia Epstein and Kristina Straub, 280–304. New York: Routledge.

———. 1992. "The *Empire* Strikes Back: A Posttranssexual Manifesto." *Camera Obscura* 29 (May): 151–76.

Stryker, Susan. 1994. "My Words to Victor Frankenstein above the Village of Chamounix: Performing Transgender Rage." *GLQ: Journal of Lesbian and Gay Studies* 1, no. 3: 237–54.

———. 1996. "Delusions of Gender." *Out*, no. 37 (October): 34.

Stryker, Susan, and Kathy High. 1995. "Across the Border: A Discussion between Susan Stryker and Kathy High on the Anarchorporeality Project." *Felix: Journal of Media Arts and Communication* 2, no. 1: 228–36.

Vance, Carole S. 1989. "Social Construction Theory: Problems in the History of Sexuality." In *Homosexuality, Which Homosexuality?*, by Dennis Altman, Carole Vance, Martha Vicinus, Jeffrey Weeks, and others, 13–34. London: GMP Publishers.

Villaurrutia, Xavier. 1993. *Nostalgia for Death*. Trans. Eliot Weinberger. Port Townsend, Wash.: Copper Canyon.

4

Transsexuality and
Daseia Y. Cavers-Huff

Naomi Zack

I'll start with my qualifications. I am *not* a transsexual. I know very little about transsexuals. About eight or nine years ago, a graduate student where I was teaching produced an elaborate example, intended to make an epistemological point, which began, "What if Naomi (Zack) is really a man?" I wondered why he had chosen that question and whether others in my department might think that I was a transsexual. In that context, had I been a transsexual, my self-presentation as a woman would have counted as a form of "passing," because it is commonly assumed in our society that those who are "women" have been female since birth. That is, my impression was that it would not have been "acceptable" for me to have been born male and present myself and identify as, a woman, which is what my "really" being a man implied.

In thinking about whether other graduate students and colleagues thought that I "really" was a man, I noted that such a belief or perception would be factually absurd because I had given birth to two children. But I did wonder why they might believe I was a transsexual. I produced two hypotheses: I am a woman who looks like she "really" is a woman, but who often operates like a man in philosophical argument; I am mixed race and being difficult to categorize in that regard opens up the possibility of other categorical slippage. That I found it necessary to come up with some explanation for the student's example suggests that I felt my gender identity to be unstable. I believe this reveals something about gender identity in general and not just mine in particular.

Gender identity is plastic and malleable. While I was a girl and young woman, in the 1950s, 1960s, and 1970s, even stereotypical heterosexual women pondered whether they were sufficiently "feminine." Girls and women today have more options for gender expression than their mothers and grandmothers did, including a degree of choice in sexual orientation. They give considerable thought to their gender possibilities. Any of these gender possibilities can still work as an ideal that women may fail to attain. Failing to fulfill a gender ideal can degrade feelings of self-worth. If we do fail in this way, we react as though we were responsible for our gender, not only because it is ours but also because we assume that we are able to do something about it. Gender thereby imposes a kind of moral responsibility.

In recent liberatory scholarship, to write credibly about a subject, one should be knowledgeable about the literature and have an identity that lines up with the subject. Homosexuals write about gay and lesbian issues; Hispanics write about Latin American issues; African Americans write about slavery, affirmative action, and racism; most feminists are women. Over the past ten years, I have met and conversed with three transsexuals, one male-to-female and two female-to-male, all at philosophy conferences. I have seen some documentaries, read a few books and articles, and watched several movies about transsexuality. I am less than "hardly an expert" on this subject.

Nevertheless, last year I was asked by a publisher to write an endorsement for Mattilda's *Nobody Passes*,[1] an anthology composed of essays written by transsexuals. Many of the contributors were also multiracial, and they expressed discomfort with both the racial and sexual labels that others had insisted on assigning to them. My understanding was that I had been asked to review that manuscript because I have written extensively about multiracial identity, some of it from the perspective of my own experience. Mixed-race people often pass. Indeed, the ability to pass, and decisions about when and where to pass, come with the first-person identity and third-person identification of mixed race. Thus, the qualification I was presumed to have for writing the endorsement might have been life experience and ongoing interest in "passing," a choice or imposed circumstance that transsexuals experience in terms of gender identification. As in my experience with the student using my hypothetical transsexuality as an epistemological example, there might have been a perceived similarity between mixed race and transsexuality as identities. It also occurred to me that I was perhaps invited to contribute to this volume for the same reason. I do not mean to suggest by this that the editors of either book think that multiracial and transsexual identities are, in reality, similar.[2] Rather, they may be aware, as I am, that in the amorphous nowhere of the public imaginary, there is a category of the not-normal, which in encompassing both race and sex pertains to both transsexuality and mixed race.

Returning more narrowly to the question of my qualifications in this context, a small amount of direct experience is sometimes sufficient to initiate a critique that addresses both a subject at hand and other subjects in which one has more experience. I would like to suggest that gender identities are relational identities rather than substances in human beings. I have claimed in *Inclusive Feminism* that being a woman means that one identifies as a member of, or has been assigned to, a disjunctive historical category of female birth designees, biological mothers, or men's primary sexual choices (category FMP, standing for "birth females, or mothers, or men's primary sexual choices").[3] One does not have to be any of the disjuncts to be a woman: a man can be a woman if he identifies with the group of women. On the basis of such a unifying definition, the differences among women can be explained in terms of their varied circumstances. Women's different circumstances of race, class, sexual preference, or sex at birth are contingent.

One can put oneself in the place of a very different other, as a free subject—not just via one's own freedom but in imagining the freedom of that very different other. For all their attention to human dignity and autonomy, philosophers in their daily professional lives often fail to do this because they believe that some others are just too "different." I return to this problem in the profession at the end of this chapter. Until then, in the work of the chapter, I engage in an inclusive exercise of imagining the autonomy of transsexuals through a discussion of transgression, normality, and freedom. It should be evident in this exercise that the matter of inclusion includes my own presence in this volume. At the end, I return to the importance of relational definitions, broadly understood as a way of being humanly inclusive. The shame of a particular recent case of exclusion by academic philosophers then becomes the issue.

Transgression

Sexual identity in a dimorphic male-female system is not much like racial identity in the present U.S. system of four or five races, mixed-race, and Hispanic or non-Hispanic ethnic identity. Accepted and recognized racial categories in even one time and place are far more varied than accepted and recognized sexual categories. The racial system is known to be different from country to country, region to region, century to century, and even decade to decade, whereas the sexual system is relatively stable. There is more extended history and biological reality underlying sexual differences than racial ones. All of this is quite obvious.

However, the way that the difference in underlying reality plays out in human psychic reactions is quite interesting, on account of differences in the degree of *social transgression* expressed by strong deviations from and repudiations of the received categories of race and sex. Mixed race is increasingly evident; interracial marriage is no longer as taboo as it used to be; and racial passing is not only ordinary, but many people "play" with it in personal style: for example, bleached blonde hair with dark skin or Jeri-curls and dreadlocks on Anglo-Saxons scalps. The idea of racial passing is now a "classic" with many derivatives; "passing" can now be applied to almost any nonracial situation in which individuals are (in some "deeper" and more abiding sense) different from how they represent themselves or permit themselves to be perceived.

It is thus no longer as *transgressive* as it used to be for individuals to change their racial identities. But it remains transgressive to the point of being life-threatening for individuals to change their sexual identities. This ugly fact is true "on the ground," while at the same time, the topic and representation of transsexuality is no longer particularly shocking or transgressive. The topic and representation of transsexuality is now part of acceptable mass entertainment. For example, one of the lead characters in the hit television show *Ugly Betty* is a male-to-female transsexual.

Transsexuality is not merely a matter of action or doing but of identity or being. It is one thing to do something transgressive and quite another to be transgressive as a part or whole of one's identity. Transgressive actions can be corrected, punished, regretted, and separated from those who do them. Smoking cigarettes, for example, has become a socially transgressive activity (in many quarters), but if one quits, one can become socially separate from the group of smokers (in those same quarters). And if one obeys the signs and wishes of others, one can even continue to smoke, without harm to assessments of one's other actions or character. Transgressive being or identity, however, is not in the same way distinguishable or separable from other aspects of its bearer or, indeed, the bearer as a whole.

It is a profoundly alienating experience that probably approaches what Kristeva scholars mean by the term *abject*, to experience one's being as transgressive. Such experience is of course the result of social interactions. Few create feelings of being transgressive beings on their own or in isolation (although prolonged isolation in itself can be very transgressive). Physically changing one's sex is undoubtedly a transgressive act in our society, and not identifying in society as the sex one was designated at birth makes one a transgressive being. Transsexuals are thereby doubly transgressive.

If the double transgression of transsexuals were simply a matter of their being exceptions, then they would be no different from others who are odd because they were uncommon or rare. In principle, transsexuals would be no different from biological intersexuals, for example. There are more intersexed than transsexed people, but beyond the fact that comparatively very few people become the sex they are by deliberating changing the physical sex they were assigned at birth or by socially identifying as a sex different from the one assigned at birth, the oddity of transsexuality lies in its deliberate qualities.

Freedom

The transsexual transgresses by being too mobile. Transsexuality is an exercise of too much freedom. To have that much freedom requires an ability to detach oneself from the received *fundamental—immanent* in the culture. By "fundamental," I mean foundational, that on which other things are based and from which they derive; by "immanent," I mean thing-like, determined, that which can be objectified and may be appropriate to objectify (i.e., treat as an object or a thing). The more fundamental and immanent the division crossed, the greater the freedom exercised and displayed in crossing it. The fascinating questions that arise here involve the nature of what it is that detaches itself from a physically sexed body and whether this detached "something" already has a sex.

Let's say that it is the mind which is capable of rejecting its body as the right sex for it. Clearly, this mind insists that for its body to be the right sexed body for it, it must be the same sex as itself. Does this mean that the mind has a sex? Obviously, the mind doesn't have a physical sex because it isn't a physical body, but the mind does carry a sense of the whole person as being male or female and, in doing so, the mind is capable of assessing whether all of the major aspects, if not the literal components, of the person, are coherent. The extent to which this mind itself is male or female will depend on which gendered roles the mind identifies as appropriate for the whole person and what kind of gendered physical appearance and structure best express its own sense of itself. The capacity to reject the physicality we find ourselves with, because we prefer a different one, suggests that there is something in the view of the self and one's own relationship with oneself that can assert a degree of mastery over found physicality, on the grounds of a desired self-identity or gender ideal.

The capacity of our minds to reject something about our bodies, in the interests of a desired identity, is not limited to transsexuality. In fact, this is a very general capacity, evident in desires for health and beauty. But transsexuality does appear to be the most extreme example of this capacity. When I taught at the University at Albany, Eric Sprague was a graduate student there. Sprague is now world famous for his project of changing his skin and skeletal structure toward that of a reptile.[4] He is a *transspecieist*.[5] During the 1990s, when Sprague was first developing his project, he occasioned some surprise and aversion from both faculty and students. But as far as I know, no human specieists or herpetophobes threatened him while he was at our institution.

Individuals who change religions and nationalities are also tolerated or "accepted" in our culture. Transsexuality, by contrast, is a dangerous transgression when practiced by ordinary people. This suggests that male or female sex is a more fundamental marker of identity than race, religion, nationality, and even species. We are expected to accept immanence in male or female gender. We are not only expected to accept our gender immanence, but the vast majority of individuals are fully comfortable in doing so. They not only easily identify with the sex assigned to them at birth but also, on a daily basis, continue to view their entire persons as holistically coherent with their bodies as they were "sexed" at birth. The transsexual reminds us that there is a mind (or a spirit, psyche, consciousness, or self) that is not completely captured by its objectified or objectifiable, physical, sexual embodiment.

However, the language of transsexuality often obscures the freedom I am inferring. We hear that a person felt or feels like "a woman trapped in a man's body" and also the obverse, although less often. (Why is that?) This language is Platonic in holding that the soul (or mind) can be imprisoned by the body. It also obscures the fact that transsexual transformation is deliberate, so that gender is thereby chosen. The opacity is accomplished via the "normal" language of gender. People are believed to be "natural women" or "real men." If how they feel and what they want to be is at odds with one of these disjuncts, it must be the result of some force over which they have no control. The discourse about people trapped in bodies of the wrong gender obscures not only choices to change gendered physicality but the ways in which those of us who accept our birth sex assignment have chosen to do that. The transsexual-trapped discourse attempts to make transsex natural and real in the same way that nontrans male or female sex is believed to natural and real.

Instead of this false Platonism, a Foucaudian discourse would be better, whereby the body is the prisoner of the mind. And better yet would be a more Sartrean construction, whereby the connection between my body and my self is avowedly a purely contingent one, which I have to choose and construct. We hear in the popular discourse about transsexuality that people who want to change from male to female feel as though they are already women in some way so essential that for it not to be expressed is a grievous, lying, form of living death. But we also hear another theme, that of not wanting to either disclose whether one has "had the surgery yet" or not wanting to be specifically identified as either the sex being left or the one that is the destination.[6] Perhaps such resistance to disclosure expresses the anguish in realizing that in having chosen to change their sex, those transsexuals have experienced their freedom from their physical sex, and that newly experienced freedom is threatened by an insistence on their supposed new immanence. Perhaps there is a fear that others will entrap and objectify them by their precise knowledge of which genitalia they have, an entrapment all too familiar given the transsexual's experience of having a psychic gender attached to a physical body that does not express that psychic gender. Perhaps in not wanting to fully disclose which genitalia they have at any given time, some transsexuals want to retain their freedom from whatever genitalia they may have, that is from an identification of personhood with specific genitalia, in general.

The freedom of the successful transsexual, or even mere transsexual imaginings, must be one of those ultimate freedoms of consciousness, precisely because it is *possible* for a human being to undergo such a complex transformation. Without a hero's acclaim, and with much abuse, the choice to trans-sex probably must be made for its own sake because it is something that the transsexual *wants* to do, for and with the self. Thus, transsexuality appears to be first and foremost an issue of the person's own sexual identity, for that very person. (Homosexuality, by contrast, can leave the sexual identity a person is born with more or less intact insofar as it is a matter of the sex of those who are desired.)[7]

Just thinking about transexuality in these terms is vertiginous. Most of us, no matter how well adjusted we are in our lives, and to our bodies, would rather not be reminded that we have a choice and certain powers to effect change in the fundamental immanent domain of our sexual identity. The transsexual transgresses not only our sex identity categories but also our ideas about our own freedom. Most of us do not want to know that we are free to be either male or female—or neither, or both.

Ruth Applewood and Christine Jorgenson

As I have suggested before, Americans have a double standard about who may be permitted to transgress via transsexuality. Generally speaking, those who may transgress in other areas with impunity—that is, the rich, famous, and beautiful—can be glamorized after they change their sex. But ordinary people who change their sex have considerably more difficulty and are thereby more transgressive and abject than their celebrated counterparts. It is instructive to specifically consider just such a comparison, between the character Roy "Ruth" Applewood in the 2003 HBO movie, *Normal*, and the persona of Christine Jorgensen, who achieved world fame as the result of sex reassignment surgery in 1953. Because transsexuality seems to have become more acceptable over time, one would expect Christine to have had a more difficult time than Ruth. That this is not the case highlights the gap between celebrity and ordinariness.

Christine Jorgensen was born George William Jorgensen Jr. in New York, 1926. Jorgensen described herself as frail, introverted, and fearful as a young boy. George was drafted into the Army in 1945 and on returning home heard about sex reassignment surgery. He received both hormone therapy and surgeries in Denmark, returning as "Christine Jorgensen." (The name "Christine" was chosen in honor of Dr. Christian Hamburger, who had pioneered the addition of hormone therapy to earlier surgical procedures for sex reassignment.) On December 1, 1952, after Christine returned home, a headline in the *New York Daily News* read, "Ex-GI Becomes Blonde Beauty." Jorgensen remained famous and went on to become a talk show celebrity, an actress, and a nightclub performer. Before she died in 1989, she was proud of having given the sexual revolution, "a good swift kick in the pants."[8]

In the HBO movie, *Normal*, Roy and Irma Applewood are depicted as a middle-aged, middle-class, midwestern, church-going couple, married for twenty-five years after having been high school sweethearts. The characters, as played by Jessica Lange and Tom Wilkinson, are wholesome-looking and unglamorous. They still love each other, and the viewer is invited to witness a depiction of how their idealized love is tested when Roy realizes that he has always been a woman and decides to embark on gender reassignment. Indeed, the way in which so much of the film is about the effect of Roy's transformation on Irma shifts the story from a dramatization of transsexuality to a glorification of true love in marriage. In her interview remarks, Lange refers to transsexuality as a "natural upheaval." This is precisely the abrogation of responsibility alluded to earlier, whereby the free choice is reconfigured as something just as compelled, and thereby natural, as the birth sex. Because *Normal* depicts that place where marriage is between a man and a woman, if Roy is seen to freely choose to become a woman, then how could he still be a good husband?

We have a "real life" view of Roy/Ruth in interview remarks made by Wilkinson and Lange. Lange describes Wilkinson as "very manly." When asked about her reaction on seeing him in women's clothing, she says, "Well, it's pretty scary. It's pretty fucking scary," and she and the interviewer laugh.[9] Lange's take on Roy and Irma seems to be that because they love each other so much and because Irma is so compassionate and giving, their marriage and family survive the transformation. It's clear that, as herself, Lange is repelled by the idea of being married to a male-to-female transsexual. She can only make sense of it for her character by viewing a transsexual husband as a freak who a loyal wife will stand by, not because she wants to or enjoys his new persona, but because she is so good that she cannot stop loving the man who she has loved all her life—even if he becomes a woman.

In his interview, Wilkinson echoes the way in which the film is an endorsement of family values. He sympathetically describes how difficult Roy's transformation is for Irma and praises Roy for wanting to keep his family together. However, Wilkinson is somewhat skeptical that Roy could succeed in this family unity after his surgery. He also admires Roy's courage, several times, and closes his interview with this comment: "It's remarkable, I would recommend it to everybody, every now and again you just put a dress on, see what it feels like, because it's, it's interesting. A whole complex series of thoughts and feelings assail you as you look at yourself."[10] This comment is interesting because it is the first time in either the film or the actors' interviews when anyone suggests that there might be intrinsic value in transsexuality. The rest of the treatment in and about *Normal* has the connotation of dealing with an unfortunate accident that victimizes, and thereby tests, all concerned.

From the perspective of a member of the audience in both cases, neither Jorgensen nor Applewood is fully transgressive. Jorgensen lived in an imagined celebrity sphere to which the rest of the American public had no direct access. Of course, there were people who knew her personally and interacted with her on that basis, but insofar as she was a celebrity, her transformation and performance of it could remain in the sphere of entertainment. It might have helped the general increase of freedom in sexual matters (for which she takes credit), but it did not specifically affect anyone except herself.

The difference between celebrities and ordinary people who transgress by becoming transsexuals amounts to a difference in social embeddedness and relation. The transsexual celebrity appears as a portrait image or an individual figure on a stage. Only the transsexual identity is displayed in such portrayals, and in this sense the display is purely formal. The ordinary-person transsexual is part of—that is, a functioning member of—a family, intimate relationships, and a community. For ordinary people, transsexuality cannot be a purely formal matter of displaying a new identity because their transsexuality has consequences in their relationships with others. Because these others are affected by the transgression of sex categories which they themselves still view as unchangeable parts of their own identities, the concrete fact of transsexuality has more content and is thereby more transgressive than the transsexuality of images or public figures.

On first consideration, the film *Normal* is not seriously transgressive because of all the accompanying lip service paid to family values and the implication of abnormal, albeit natural, forces. The message is that such forces can and will be tamed and contained by middle-class goodness. But in another sense, the film is strongly transgressive because it does depict the disruptive effects of transsexual transformation for ordinary people. It also dislodges comfortable assumptions about the ongoing immanence of gender because Roy Applewood is not a likely character for any kind of behavior, or even aspiration, that would go against the identity of average and approved American masculinity. It is assumed within the film and in the actors' interviews, that the fact of transsexuality is far more difficult for "normal" people in "normal" places to accommodate than it would be for (imagined) cosmopolitan denizens of world-class cities. As a result, the mere depiction of that kind of gratuitous difficulty is in itself transgressive of the sense of life-style security enjoyed by all the folks who live in "*Normal*."

Moreover, *Normal* transgresses in its implication that the more tightly the normal folks grasp their respectable sexual goodness and propriety, the more these comforting personal and social assets slide out of their control. Irma teeters on a dangerous edge in staying with Ruth, against the advice of others, including her minister. Although she clings to him as a good heterosexual woman standing by her man, because he is her "heart," as she puts it, staring her in the face is the inevitable consequence that if the Applewoods do succeed in holding their marriage together after Roy has become Ruth, then they will both become lesbians.[11]

Freaks

Regarding my scant qualifications for writing this, I first emphasized them so as to signal my intention not to give offense. I now want to return to those qualifications by way of examining whether or not I am offended if I speculate that editors assume I am qualified to write about transsexuality by virtue of being multiracial. I am going to cut to the chase by considering the concept of a "freak."

When John Locke addressed how "monsters," infants born with what we would consider birth defects, ought to be classified, he illustrated his more general nominalism. According to Locke, what counts as a human being has an arbitrary foundation and to some extent an arbitrary application. We decide what the criteria for membership in the human group are, and we decide whether those criteria have been fulfilled in any given case. Our concepts, according to Locke, are creations of the mind, imposed on reality by the mind. So when Locke considered an offspring of a woman that looked like an animal (a sheep was his example), it was a genuine question for him whether such a "monster" would be considered a human being.[12] Locke's willingness to have an open mind on the issue is very strange to us because we now have the benefit of the science of biology, with its taxonomic and evolutionary subfields, which is something that Locke lacked. We know that apart from the kind of medico-technical intervention that did not exist in Locke's day (e.g., embryonic transplants and possibly also genetic engineering), any animal automatically has the same species membership that its parents have. A human female simply cannot give birth to any nonhuman animal (e.g., a lamb). Anything she gives birth to will be human. In this sense, we are not as nominalistic about biological natural kinds as Locke was.

How, then, do we classify those members of the human family that Locke identified as monsters? Without the cognitive option of relegating them to another species, we have classified them as "human oddities" or "natural-born freaks." The circus sideshow spectacle of such individuals, natural or embellished, is an institution of the past, for obvious reasons. (I am old enough to remember it, however.) What made the sideshows fascinating to their audiences was precisely the fact of *natural* oddity. If the "bearded lady" did not have a natural beard but a fake one, she was a "fake." However, over the past thirty or forty years, given general theoretical and moral progress in social justice, the concept of the "freak" has changed. It is no longer appropriate to designate someone a "freak" because of birth oddities. The people who are most likely to be considered freaks today are not those who are born with abnormalities or atypicalities but those who construct or invent them. But, and here is the new cruelty, viewing someone as a freak in the constructed or invented sense also bestows on that person the past human degradation of being a "natural-born freak." It is a degradation because it destabilizes a "natural" normality.

So here is how this process works, with specific examples. Barack Obama is a mixed-race black and white man who identifies as black. As a black man, he is highly respected and revered, even though part of his political viability derives from the fact that he has white ancestry as well as black. People relate positively to Obama in this regard. He is not considered a freak. Tiger Woods is a mixed-race, black, white, and Asian man who has insisted that he is mixed race. His reward for that has been public vilification for having tried to come up with a racial name that would encompass all of his racial ancestry (Calabalasian). People relate to Tiger Woods negatively in this regard. Naomi Zack is a black, white, and Native American woman who has publicly identified as mixed race, albeit in polite (academic) company. Nobody blames me for having had parents with different racial identifications, but the fact that I insist on being considered mixed race in a system that is still largely either/or when it comes to black and white race may make me appear to be more qualified than I am to comment on transsexuality.

However, I now, finally, do understand this, and having understood it, I am perfectly comfortable with it. I was not born "multiracial" insofar as that is a social designation. My mother, who was Jewish (which is now considered white), raised me to pass as Jewish, doing the best she could do to conceal my father's identity from me.[13] It took painful work to get her to admit who my father was, and it took more painful work to acknowledge that my nonwhite appearance was something for which I had to take responsibility. Once I did that, it required the research and thought that went into several philosophical books for me to decide that I was not black because my father was black (or, more precisely, black, white, and Native American) but, rather, mixed race—if "race" as a term for ancestry and human biology has any meaning, which it does not.[14]

Permit me to emphasize the seriousness of the term "work" in this regard. Neither nonwhite racial self-discovery nor the creation of academic philosophy books on the subject of race is a recreational activity. And I would assume, neither is it a recreational activity to tell your nearest and dearest that you want to change your sex, not to mention submitting to surgeons' scalpels or biochemistry to effect that change. To the extent that the public expects that transsexuals, mixed-race people, and other self-identified freaks come to tragic ends, to that extent do we collectively fail to recognize individual freedom. Why? Because some rely on what received opinion is known or intuited to be as a source of rationalization and excuse for not making certain choices, when they might otherwise *want* to make them for good reasons. And others tend to go along with the majority view in not recognizing the autonomy and freedom of those who have made such unpopular choices.

So, yes, to the extent that there is a deliberate action or project involved in insisting on a mixed-race identity if one has black ancestry, to that extent do I recognize a commonality with people who have, for whatever reasons, undertaken the project of becoming designated men if they were born designated women, or designated women if they were born designated men. All I can say, as I've suggested before, is that transsexuality is a *heroic* undertaking and an exercise of the freedom that we all have, with all of our fundamental identities, but which so few dare to acknowledge. If that makes those of us avowedly belonging to either category—that is, mixed race or transsexual—*freaks*, well, that's just another term for "known to be free." A freak is anyone who deliberately transgresses an important category of social identity.

Daseia Y. Cavers-Huff

Daseia Y. Cavers-Huff was a junior colleague of mine, with whom I was friends for a while during the late 1990s. Cavers-Huff received her Ph.D. in philosophy from the University of California, Riverside, in 1997. The title of her dissertation was *Cognitive Science and Metaphysics Revisited: Toward a Theory of Properties.* I published an article she wrote, "Cognitive Science and the Quest for a Theory of Properties," which was based on a chapter in her dissertation, in my edited anthology, *Women of Color and Philosophy.*[15]

Daseia had a very difficult childhood and adolescence that included sexual abuse, drugs, violence, and periods of homelessness while growing up in Cleveland, Ohio. She had a number of medical problems, not the least of which was a permanent internal shunt for the drainage of excess spinal fluid from her brain into her stomach. She identified as African American, but she had green eyes, blonde hair, and a skin tone that many associate with mixed-race genealogy. She had a highly developed sense of style and dressed very fashionably. She was about five foot, two inches tall and weighed over three hundred pounds, although during the time I knew her, she insisted that she was perfectly healthy and would proclaim that she was a "sexual ideal" for many macho men, both black and white. Her hair and makeup were always flawless, and the countertops surrounding her bathroom sink were full of trays containing scores of bottles of nail polish and lipstick tubes, along with arrays of perfume, eyeliner, powders, and so forth. She wore a diamond ring on every finger and boasted that she liked to acquire her jewelry in pawn shops in white neighborhoods; she said the quality was better there and that she enjoyed exploiting the bad luck of white people. (I told her that was mean.) She was an outrageous personality, intellectually and psychologically brilliant in conversation, but self-absorbed in every detail of herself, to an extent that listening to her for three or four hours at a stretch felt like an exhausting day's labor. When she told me the story of her doctoral defense, she began with a description of what she wore that day. Her outfit included a leopard skin pillbox hat that she had found in a thrift shop—and not fake fur, either! Need I say that Daseia Cavers-Huff was *transgressive?*

Daseia *chose* to successfully pursue a doctorate in philosophy while she was also a tenured professor at Riverside Community College. She also *chose* to pursue a law degree. And, at some point, after the time we'd been in regular contact, she *chose* to undergo stomach reduction surgery for weight loss. (She didn't tell me this directly at first but said that her surgery had been performed to remove scar tissue from previous surgeries. In time, however, it became assumed and known that it had been an elective procedure for weight loss.) There were complications, mainly centered on the fact that her body began to lose its ability to absorb nourishment. The last time I saw her, she had lost over one hundred pounds. She told me that when she took the California bar exam, she had worn a backpack containing fluids that entered her system intravenously. She took the bar exam on an IV! Need I say that she was *a freak?*

In May 2007, after several years of illness and inability to work, due to her worsening inability to absorb nourishment, Daseia was found dead in her apartment in Southern California. The coroner determined cause of death to be a heart attack related to her other medical problems. She was forty-five.[16]

After I heard of Daseia's death, I sent emails to her dissertation co-chairs and the last chair of the department at which she had been employed. I asked if they would join me in writing her memorial for publication in the American Philosophical Association's annual bulletin that honors our colleagues who have died over the past year. Both dissertation co-chairs declined on the grounds that they had been out of touch with her in recent years; I did not receive a reply from Daseia's last department chair.

Daseia claimed that she had been the first African American to receive a Ph.D. in philosophy at UC Riverside. She was proud of this accomplishment. As far as I could determine, Daseia had been well established and was highly regarded at Riverside Community College. In 2002, she was voted by colleagues to deliver the Distinguished Faculty Lecture of the Year; she had also served as a member of the academic senate.[17] Daseia was aware that people gossiped about her and that some of her academic colleagues expressed aversion to her. Certain transgressions could not fail to attract notice: representing and performing a black ghetto background in academic society, asserting and performing exaggerated female heterosexuality against prevailing ideals of respectable feminist androgyny, resorting to the violence of surgery for the sake of appearance, and publicly displaying the required therapy (i.e., the IV backpack) that resulted from the cosmetic surgery. How many African American women with doctorates in philosophy take bar exams wearing IV backpacks as the result of cosmetic surgery? That stunt in itself is a fascinating transgression of the boundaries between public and private because it brings the intensely personal into a hyperstructured, formal, public place. How could people not gossip about Daseia?

But, as far as I know, Daseia's very public personal behavior did not diminish the quality of her work or her ability to fulfill professional obligations, before she became ill. I think that some of the negative personal reactions to her support a view that part of what was obnoxious may have been the freedom that she evidently exercised. We academics, as a group, tend to be restricted and somewhat drab in how we dress and groom ourselves. We do not as a rule publicly perform identities that depart from a staid, middle-class repertoire. We are not known for using surgery to change our appearance toward increased sexual desirability, according to the norms of contemporary culture. We tend to forget that our restraint in such matters is chosen.

It is possible that if academics exercised more freedom with their personal identities, the result would be the recognition and exercise of more intellectual freedom. That could lead to different kinds of responsibilities and connections with the world outside of academia. None of this is to claim that Daseia Cavers-Huff did not suffer. Freedom is not necessarily enjoyable; it is not a feeling but the ability to make choices. Freedom does not always result in a "happy ending" in the stories of real lives. We are responsible because we are free—*"ought* implies *can"*—but the consequences of our choices need not make us happy or better off. These consequences can very well make us miserable and kill us. Just as freedom is not a pleasant feeling, responsibility is not an emotion of satisfaction or gratification. The consequences of particular choices may not be what we hoped for or wanted, and we may not recognize the self we wanted or hoped to be after making the real life choice to become it.

It could be objected that the foregoing is an overly grim and technical view of freedom. Isn't freedom at least sometimes enjoyable, as in instances of "playing" with the categories of race and gender in personal styles of passing and drag? Earlier on in this essay, weren't those very examples used to show that stylistic racial passing is no longer a big deal? I think that's precisely the point. Freedom is a form of play, when the transgression is not fundamental. Thus, before a sympathetic audience, cross dressing is a form of entertainment, and in social contexts that acknowledge more than a black and white racial grid, the same can be said of obvious passing. Nevertheless, we need to remember that play in one context may be deadly serious work in another. We need to respect that a transformation of play to work can constitute the core of the commitment made to transformative identities by those who earn the label "freaks."

The Humanity of Philosophy

Philosophy is an ancient discipline and many of its practitioners believe that they are working in the humanities. We are (so far, until genetic technology changes that) all homo sapien sapiens. Nothing human should be alien to us. As Cornell West once said,[18] this is not solely a shared practice of walking upright or the presence of certain cognitive capacities, but it importantly includes the tradition of burying our dead. Those philosophers who do not in life practice the simplest rituals of humanity, such as putting someone to rest in the virtual reality that is our intellectual community, have in a basic way overlooked a shared humanity. The category of human freaks is quite diverse and interesting for the experiments in living that it proffers up for everyone else.[19] To the extent that an enclave as cloistered as academic philosophy has had and continues to have some freaks in its ranks, this is not cause for shame but for celebration.

I said at the outset that an inclusive feminism can begin with a relational definition that women are those who belong to a historical group. Humanity is a simple biological matter, so far. The groups within humankind are social divisions based on culturally selected differences. An inclusive humanity would include all "races" and genders of human beings. An inclusive philosophy would include all philosophers, defined as those who have identified and been duly designated as philosophers (e.g., by having been granted a Ph.D. in the field). It doesn't matter how personally jarring or different philosophers may have been or continue to be as particular individuals. They are philosophers nonetheless, one of the human groups, which as such, buries its dead, in deed and word.

I am sorry that Daseia Y. Cavers-Huff did not have a longer life. I am happy to have had her as a friend and colleague. May she rest in peace.

NOTES

My thanks to Laurie Shrage and an anonymous reviewer for Oxford University Press for suggestions that much improved this piece.

1. Mattilda, A.K.A. Matt Bernstein Sycamore, ed., *Nobody Passes: Rejecting the Rules of Gender and Conformity* (Berkeley: Seal, 2006).

2. Laurie Shrage is a highly respected and respectful professional colleague of mine who is extremely knowledgeable about my work on race, gender, and feminism. She is also one of the most highly principled people I have ever known. I know that she would never objectify me or any other colleague on the basis of demographic information.

3. Naomi Zack, *Inclusive Feminism: A Third Wave Theory of Women's Commonality* (Lanham, Md.: Rowman and Littlefield, 2005), chaps 1, 2, 3, et passim.

4. At www.thelizardman.com (accessed May 2007).

5. In this way, Sprague's project is the reverse of Dr. Moreau's in H. G. Wells's novel, *The Island of Dr. Moreau.* See Naomi Zack, "*The Island of Dr. Moreau:* Interpretation of Images of Race and Species," in *SciFi in the Mind's Eye: Reading Science through Science Fiction*, ed. Margret Grebowicz (New York: Open Court, 2008).

6. The sensitivity to "Have you had the surgery yet?" was explored by Talia Mae Bettcher in "Hallucinating in the Borderlands: Reflections on Transphobic Violence and the Politics of Illusion," a paper presented at the Pacific Division Meeting of the American Philosophical Association in Portland, Oregon, on March 25, 2007. The resistance against male or female identity is a frequent theme in the articles in Mattilda's *Nobody Passes.*

7. There are numerous examples of male to female transsexuals who continue to prefer women as sexual partners, after they themselves become women. (One of the most famous twentieth-century examples is Myra Breckinridge in Gore Vidal's novel by the same name (Gore Vidal, *Myra Breckinridge/Myron* [New York: Little Brown, 1968]).

8. At http://en.wikipedia.org/wiki/Christine_Jorgensen (accessed May 2007); see also *Christian Jorensen: A Personal Autobiography* (New York: Bantam, 1967).

9. At http://www.hbo.com/films/normal/interviews/ (accessed May 2007).

10. Ibid.

11. I think this is a killing irony. It dimly occurred to me while I was watching the movie, but I thank Laurie Shrage for making the point in the context of suggestions for revising this essay.

12. For Locke's treatment of "monsters" in the context of his nominalism, see John Locke, *An Essay Concerning Human Understanding*, ed. Peter H. Niddich (Oxford: Oxford University Press, 1975), pp. 338–40, 414–15, 454.

13. When my mother first made this decision in 1944, Jews were not as securely white as they are now. Please see the introduction to Naomi Zack, *Race and Mixed Race* (Philadelphia: Temple University Press, 1993).

14. Naomi Zack, *Philosophy of Science and Race* (New York: Routledge, 2002).

15. Naomi Zack, *Women of Color and Philosophy* (Boston: Blackwell, 2001).

16. I am grateful to Travis Gibbs, who was a colleague and friend of Daseia's for many years, for having informed me about her death and the circumstances surrounding it.

17. Gibbs, personal communication.

18. West said this at a talk he gave to a student group at the University of Albany, State University of New York, in, I believe, fall 1998. I do not remember if he meant to claim that human groups are the only animals who bury their dead, but I find it unlikely, insofar as it has been well known for a while that elephants also bury their dead. (I am grateful to Chaone Mallory for having pointed out this about elephants to me. If the reader is skeptical, please see Rosella Lorenzi, "Elephants Mourn Their Dead," *Science*, November 4, 2005, at www.abc.net .au/science/news/stories/s1497634.htm.)

19. This was exactly John Stuart Mill's famous utilitarian point in *On Liberty*: namely, that society is inclined to be censorious and judgmental regarding those who do not conform, but if we respect the full liberty of others in areas where their actions mostly concern them, in the long run, everyone benefits.

5

The Sexual Schema

Transposition and Transgender in Phenomenology of Perception

Gayle Salamon

> The body...is always something other than what it is,
> always sexuality and at the same time freedom.
>
> —Merleau-Ponty, *Phenomenology of Perception*

> What I am, all told, overflows what I am for myself.
>
> —Merleau-Ponty, *The Visible and the Invisible*

Phenomenology and Ambiguity

In *Phenomenology of Perception* Maurice Merleau-Ponty makes but a single reference to what might be called mixed-gender embodiment: "A patient feels a second person implanted in his body. He is a man in half his body, a woman in the other half" (88). This remark would not seem to promise much for thinking about nonnormative gender configurations. We are introduced to this person of indeterminate gender as a "patient," already marked by some indistinct but defining sign of emotional or mental distress. That patient is doubly confined within a binary system of gender. Even though this patient is, phenomenologically speaking, both a man and a woman, this gender configuration is not thought as some new third term that might exceed the binary of man and woman but is conceived by Merleau-Ponty as a man, intact and entire, somehow fused with an also properly gendered woman, with the body divided down the middle neatly between them.[1] Despite this, I want to argue that, even given the dearth of attention to nonnormative genders in this text, the phenomenological approach to the body that Merleau-Ponty offers in *Phenomenology of Perception* can be uniquely useful for understanding trans embodiment.[2]

Perhaps the most vital aspect of phenomenology is its insistence that the body is crucial for understanding subjectivity rather than incidental to it or a distraction from it. And one of the most important aspects of the body is its manifestation and apprehension of sexuality. Though Merleau-Ponty has been criticized for his masculinist approach, his insistence that sexuality is vital for understanding both the human body and subjectivity offers at least the promise of new ways of conceptualizing each that would seem to be aligned with feminism and trans studies.[3] That his work has not been much utilized in this way speaks perhaps to the strangely liminal position that sexuality holds within his work: embodied yet not entirely physical, inescapable yet inchoate, both persistently present and impossible to locate.[4] In Merleau-Ponty's work there is something essentially *ambiguous* in sexuality. I suggest that this ambiguity need not be read, as it most often has been, as a phobic or hostile "avoidance" of sexual difference but, rather, as a more purposeful confounding of that category.[5] There is something enabling in this philosophy of ambiguity; it is precisely the ambiguity attending sexuality that can become the means for understanding bodies, lives, and especially *relationality* outside the domains of male or female.

Merleau-Ponty describes that ambiguity through his explication of the sexual schema. Like the body schema, the sexual schema is a temporal affair and, like the body schema, the presentness of the sexual schema is inescapable and spans different temporalities, always pointing both to the past and to the future. This temporality of the sexual schema extends forward insofar as that which animates my body through desire depends on those sensations, either compelling or painful, that I have previously experienced—my history shapes my desire. It also extends backward, in that those things that I have previously experienced coalesce into a recognizable whole for me, to which I then give a narrative. My sexual desire, located always in this futural mode, thus marries with my sexual history, located in my past, and creates a sexual self. The sexual schema both depends on my history and makes a history out of my past.

There is a danger of overstating the confluence of sexuality and identity, and this danger is particularly acute in relation to transpeople. Second-wave feminist receptions of transsexuality,[6] some recent biological theories about transsexuality,[7] and popular misconceptions of trans all share this conflation of gender expression with sexual expression.[8] Historically, transsexuality has often been fantasized to be—and thus described as—a kind of hypersexualization; some trans writers' effort to *disengage* transgenderism from the realm of sexuality stems from this historical conflation of transgenderism with sexuality. For example, Christine Jorgensen's autobiography, in which she claims to have no sexual feelings at all, can be read as a counterargument to the assertion that transsexuality is really "about" sexual desire rather than gender expression and that transformation of gender at the level of the body is only undertaken for the purposes of a closed circuit of sexual gratification.[9] The trans body thus becomes something akin to a fetish, and those aspects of bodily transition in particular or transgender experience in general that are motivated by a desire for a specific kind of gender presentation, rather than a specific kind of sexual expression, drop out of the model entirely.

But deemphasizing sexuality to avoid the perils of fetishization would seem to be accompanied by a different set of perils, for it is certainly an impoverished account of subjectivity that cannot make room for desire, and we might ask what sorts of contortions result when trans subjects are required to suppress or deny their sexuality. Might there be a way of avoiding the groundless conflation of transsexuality with sexual fetishism without denying trans subjects a sexuality altogether? Is there room in this picture for desire?

The Sexual Schema

Merleau-Ponty opens his inquiry into the nature and experience of sexuality and its importance to embodiment in a curious way by offering sexuality as a causal impetus for beloved objects in the world. "Let us try to see how a thing or a being begins to exist for us through desire or love" (154). This is not only an acknowledgement of the difficulty that we have, as embodied subjects, in recognizing other embodied subjects as subjects, the sometimes surprising efforts required, both rational and affective, for us to recognize that *this other who stands before me is like-me but not-me.* I only become bound to this other through "desire or love," and through that relation of desire or love the other comes to exist for me as a thing or being. But through a revisitation of Descartes and a tour through empiricism's correspondence problem, Merleau-Ponty comes to ask after the being of the self, the ontological solidity of *my* body, and not just the body of the other. What he eventually concludes is that I, too, am brought into being through desire or love. The beloved other comes to exist in my phenomenological field as such to the extent that she comes to exist *for me*. But I, too, come to exist *for myself* in this scenario, and only to the extent that either the other exists *for me* or I exist *for the other*, or perhaps both. Sexuality may be ambiguous, but it has an immensely generative power, a power that refuses to be distributed along familiar lines of heteronormative procreation. Indeed, this power to bring about the self is realized insofar as it refuses lines of procreation that would be either heteronormative on the one hand or autogenetic on the other. The former would require that the other and I are in some sense *for* a third, and the latter would have me only *for myself.*

What might it mean to suggest that the body itself comes to be though desire? This claim underscores the degree to which our embodiment is intersubjective, a project that can only be undertaken in the presence and with the recognition of other embodied beings.[10] Merleau-Ponty's project must then be read as a radical unsettling of the Cartesian tradition that understands me to be a subject only to the extent that I am distinct and separate from others, where physical confirmation of that separateness can be found in the perfect boundedness of my body. These boundaries, Merleau-Ponty will suggest, are dissolved by sexuality. In this way, sexuality is more than just an affective response to a bodily event; there is, he claims "nothing to be said" about affectivity in this regard (154). This can be read as a reaction against aspects of the psychoanalytic model of sexuality, which he understands to be both determinative (bodily morphology determining psychic structures, anatomy is or as destiny) and programmatic (any somatic symptom lends itself to only one interpretation, that of sexual repression). Merleau-Ponty is writing specifically against Freud here, and this section of the *Phenomenology* is offering the least interesting reading possible of Freud's theories of sexuality. For all his quarrel with psychoanalysis,

Merleau-Ponty is in fact not rejecting understandings of either the mind *or* the body that psychoanalysis offers, but merely moving the capacities of the unconscious from the domain of the mind to the domain of the body and thus reconfiguring the imaginary topography of the subject rather than diminishing its capacity by doing away with the unconscious altogether. Unincorporated traumatic events from a "past that was never a present" (164–65) thus find both their retention and expression through a bodily, rather than a psychic, unconscious.[11]

Nevertheless, just as proprioception offers us a way of reading and understanding the body beyond the visible surface of its exterior, so too does sexuality make of the body a thing that is internality and externality folded one around the another. Indeed, internality and externality are themselves not perfectly bounded, and sexuality is described in terms that precisely match a psychoanalytic, proprioceptive model of embodiment. The description of sexuality that Merleau-Ponty offers, its suffusion of the body entire and its transformation of the body into something whose erotogenic zones are almost entirely labile, maps almost perfectly onto the topography of sexuality that Freud lays out in *Three Essays on the Theory of Sexuality*.[12]

Sexuality is a matter not of seeing but of *sensing*, which takes place below and beyond the threshold of the visible: "The visible body is subtended by a sexual schema, which is strictly individual, emphasizing the erogenous areas, outlining a sexual physiognomy, and eliciting the gestures of the masculine body which is itself integrated into this emotional totality" (156). In this description, sex is not simply compared with or analogized to proprioception: sexuality *is* proprioceptive (and so, too, is sex—but more on that below). There is the visible body, the for-itself as viewed by others, the material stuff of flesh that is animated and inhabited by a sexual schema. That sexual schema delivers to the subject a sexual physiognomy, just like the body schema delivers to her a bodily morphology. We might even say that the sexual schema in this moment exists prior to the bodily schema: Merleau-Ponty begins with a body, visible but vaguely defined, and then moves to a consideration of the sexual schema beneath it, only after which the physiognomy of the sexual regions of the body become delineated. It is only after that delineation wrought by desire that gender appears, first as a bodily fact ("the masculine body") and finally as an emotional one.

Merleau-Ponty's description of the visible body subtended by its sexual schema offers us two different kinds of gender. The presumptive masculinity of the ostensibly universal subject is unremarkably present, as it is throughout Merleau-Ponty's work. But there is a more nuanced and productive account of gender here as well, subtending Merleau-Ponty's more orthodox account of male bodies. Masculinity is specifically described as *gestural* rather than anatomical—and the very purpose of the body's materiality is finally to transmit this inchoate but expressive gesture. There is also a double mimeticism at work here, whereby the gesture becomes the property of the body by virtue of being elicited *by the sexual schema itself*. This masculinity is also mimetic because it is citing, perhaps even soliciting, an other masculine body, a body located in some remote elsewhere, yet proximate enough to function as a structuring ideal. What is perhaps most surprising in this account is its insistence that the sexual schema is neither *one*, that which might describe the presumptively masculine, nor *two*, that which might encompass the excluded feminine and thus might be parsed between masculine and feminine or male and female. The sexual schema is instead, Merleau-Ponty writes, *strictly individual*. This theorization of bodily inhabitation is simultaneously dependent on the "individual," and thus grounded in particularity, but also insisting on relation, and as such cannot be attached to one singular region of physicality or even one singular mode of being. Merleau-Ponty suggests that a systematic and rigid notion of erotogenicity will not do, that it is not my morphology but rather my experiences and mental representations that fundamentally constitute which regions of my body will give me pleasure, and how.

We are offered here a view of sexuality that is fantastically ambiguous, so much so that it should come as little surprise that it has not been taken up as a model by more identitarian conceptions of sexual difference and sexual identity.[13] An insistence that phenomenological experiences of the body and the subject are individual rather than categorical situates the subject differently, temporally and socially. In terms of social organization, this insistence on particularity frustrates categorical summary; it means that neither sexual embodiment nor situatedness nor expression can be predicted by membership in any particular category of gender or sex. The implications of this disarticulation are more profound than the comparatively clearer decoupling of sexed identity (male or female), gendered identity (man or woman, femme, butch or trans), and sexuality (lesbian, gay, bisexual, or heterosexual). Nor is this an articulation of the now familiar enough notion that feminine desire is by its nature unlocatable, diffuse, ambiguous (we might think of Irigaray again here).

I am interested in arguing that an embodied response to desire is, through its radical particularity, unpredictable and impossible to map on the morphology of the body. A woman's experience of sexuality may be tightly and intensely focused on a particular region of the body, or it may be distributed throughout the body. So, too, might a man's. That is: we have zones of intensely erotic pleasure, but the relation between a body part and its erotogenic or sexual function is perhaps one of lightly tethered consonance rather than a rigidly shackled indexical mapping. And while a sexual physiognomy might be "outlined" by the erotogenic zones, the body's morphology is neither determinative of the location or behavior of those zones but, rather, is determined *by* them. Merleau-Ponty is insisting that sexuality is not located in the genitals, nor even in one specific erotogenic zone, but rather in one's intentionality toward the other and toward the world.

Desire and Transposition

Merleau-Ponty contends, in *Phenomenology of Perception*, that desire always puts me in relation with the world. Through desire, my body comes alive by being intentionally directed toward another, and I myself come into being through that desire. This does not mean that my desire is always gratified or that the existence of my desire alone is sufficient to secure a particular kind of relation to one beloved other or many, or, indeed, any reciprocated relation at all to an other. Desire may be frustrated or unsatisfied, or find—one could hardly call it a *choosing* since I am often unfree to choose either the inclination or expression of my desire—an object that is unattainable, structurally or otherwise. Desire in these moments may feel only like a constraint or an isolation. But withdrawing from desire, or attempting to stage its death, inevitably involves a truncation of one's own capacities to exist outside oneself. Desire involves, desire *is*, a being toward the other, and this necessarily conjoins me with, makes me part of, the world.

As we saw above, the organization of desire across different temporal modes and into a narrative coherence is sexuality. Sexuality, Merleau-Ponty writes, "is what causes man [*sic*] to have a history" (158). It is embodied and lived rather than excavated and analyzed. It is not only that which suffuses life; life is not possible without it.

> Sexuality is neither transcended in human life nor shown up at its centre by unconscious representations. It is at all times present there like an atmosphere.... From the part of the body which it especially occupies, sexuality spreads forth like an odour or like a sound. Here we encounter once more that general function of unspoken *transposition* which we have already recognized in the body during our investigation of the body image. When I move my hand towards a thing, I know implicitly that my arm unbends. When I move my eyes, I take account of their movement, without being expressly conscious of the fact, and am thereby aware that the upheaval caused in my field of vision is only apparent. Similarly, sexuality, without being the object of any intended act of consciousness, can underlie and guide specified forms of my experience. Taken in this way, as an ambiguous atmosphere, sexuality is coextensive with life. In other words, ambiguity is of the essence of human existence. (168; emphasis mine)

What we are asked to consider in this passage is sexuality, taken as a condition not of human *meaning*, as psychoanalysis would have it, or of *identity*, as some strains of lesbian and gay studies would have it, but of *life itself*. And desire in this most resolutely physical sense is embodied but—importantly—not located. When Merleau-Ponty writes, "From the part of the body which it especially occupies, sexuality spreads forth," this may be read as something other than a phallic reference veiled by some coyness that forbids his naming the part. There is an important ambiguity secured with Merleau-Ponty's refusal to name the penis as an encampment of sexuality, an ambiguity that performs an unyoking of bodily parts from bodily pleasures. The join between desire and the body is the location of sexuality, and that join may be a penis, or some other phallus, or some other body part, or a region of the body that is not individuated into a part, or a bodily auxiliary that is not organically attached to the body. This passage asserts that the most important aspect of sexuality is not any particular part, not even the behavior of that part, but the "general function" which causes that part to be animated, the means through which it is brought into my bodily sense of myself and is incorporated into my self-understanding through a reaching out toward the world. Merleau-Ponty designates that function as *transposition*.

The engine of sexuality is transposition; we are offered transposition as a model for understanding what sexuality is for, does with, and brings to me. But what precisely is it? Merleau-Ponty at first makes an analogy between transposition and the ordering and use of the body that is the corporeal schema, suggesting an equivalence, or at least a strong resemblance, between transposition and the function of proprioception. Both are general in the sense that they take place below the level of conscious thought. Both function as conduit between bodily materiality and intention. But there is a difference in that proprioception emphasizes the relation between one part of my body and another part, the assemblage that constitutes my felt sense of my body as a whole. This sense is, of course, gained as I make contact with the world around me, but it is at its core a consciousness that is of and in my body. Transposition describes a slightly different phenomenon, a sense of self that is not additive or cumulative but a function that emphasizes a shifting from one mode of being or bodily inhabitation to another, involving something like a substitution.

This is a substitution that relates to my material being, and is in some sense an intermediary for it, but cannot be reduced to a function of materiality as such. It is assuredly not a linguistic substitution, for Merleau-Ponty designates this transposition as "unspoken" and emphasizes, just as he does in his discussion of proprioception, the unthought and nearly reflexive nature of my relationship to the sexual schema. In the quoted passage, transposition describes a kind of chiasmic crossing that transforms both body and desire as each comes to stand in the other's place, and with that displacement becomes confused with its other. Transposition describes the process by which the desire that houses itself in my body *becomes* my body itself—not held proximately by thought, but felt and experienced (as opposed to only referred to) through and as the body. If I can be said to have desire, this is only so to the extent that I find it as my body. Simultaneously, my body, in its desire, *becomes* desire itself. The flesh of it is felt only as an animated leaning, intentional in the sense that the desire animating it has an object—it is desire to the extent that it is desire *of*—but also intentional in that my sense of it coalesces around a purposeful being toward this desired object. My body becomes a leaning or a yearning, a propulsive force that negates any sense of my body as solid or still, or indeed as *mine*, in that this sensation owns me more than I own it.

We are given an eye and a hand in this passage, offered a description of one kind but two expressions of desire, the desiring look and a desire that motivates the reach of a hand. In the desiring look, the eye that comes to rest on an object finds there a still point, an anchor that grounds vision itself and transforms it so that what is, factually speaking, a blurring upheaval in the visual field is sensed as an unremarkable shift of focus through this process of transposition.[14] My look has an object, and I trust that object to ground my look and thus know that the world itself is not turning, that the "upheaval" that occurs when I turn my head and look at something is both occasioned by that desired object and quieted by it. This experience, though entirely mundane and unremarkable, is a decentering of the self that happens because I turn toward another, and yet that other magically restores me to myself by persisting as the focused and sustained object of my look. The reach, too, is something that is simultaneously disorienting, dizzying, decentering, *and* consolidating, purposeful, incorporative. When I am thirsty, I move toward the glass on the table, unbend my arm, grasp the glass, move it up to my lips, and drink. This is not a matter of cognition but of changing my comportment, my embodiment, my bodily being so that it encompasses the object of my desire and interacts with it. My body comes into concert not only with those objects in the world toward which my desire is intended but also with itself in that moment—it becomes purposefulness. The transpositional paradox comes when my arm, that which allows me to take hold of the glass, fades from my experience even and only through the act of the reach. In reaching, the arm itself tends to recede from view or disappear as both an object of consciousness and a phenomenological presence. The object of desire supplants the self as center.

Is the scenario different if our body impels us toward another subject rather than an object? What is my experience of my own body if, rather than thirst making me reach for a glass of water, desire causes me to reach toward another person? Instead of reaching toward a *what* that is an object, I am reaching toward a *who,* another subject, and this renders the situation both similar and different. When I reach for the other, I do not feel *my arm* but an intensification of both the proximity and the absence of the one for whom I am reaching. My sensation can in some sense feel itself to be located in that other, and my arm, unbent and reaching out is no longer the location of my sensation but rather becomes the gesture through which I am toward the other. The arm is the conduit of desire but not the seat of its sensation. My body is the vehicle that puts me into compelling and sometimes heady proximity to the objects of my desire in this way, and, in the case of sexual desire, my body comes alive through being intentionally directed toward another.

This then is the substance of the transposition which, according to Merleau-Ponty, animates my body in desire: my sensation becomes more ambiguous and diffuse even as it intensifies because I am suddenly spread out as a sensing subject, located both in my body and that toward which my body bends. The locus of my sensation seems to shift, and my arm, if I reach out, is experienced phenomenologically less in its function as *my arm* and more in its function as *toward you.* This dispersal and transposition need not be read as diminishing either the sensation or the body part in question, but might instead be a way of understanding how in sexuality I am dispossessed of my body and delivered to it at once. A sexual transposition also involves a displacement of the body as a coherent amalgam of conscious thinking, which is surely obvious enough. But this transposition, even as it is the intensification of bodily pleasures, also involves a dissolution of the body as material ground, as phenomenological center of its own world. That center, suddenly, is shared. So self and other together comprise not only the joined unit of my affective life but also the phenomenological pivot of sensory apprehension of the world.

But if I am found in the other, so, too, am I lost there. The "me" that is conjoined with the world in this way is already displaced, disassembled. Phenomenology would suggest, and psychoanalysis would agree, that the object of desire is never a person whole and entire but a fixation on this particular part or that, or a number of parts in succession. There is already at the heart of sexuality something disassembled about the body as an object of desire, and also *as* the vehicle *of* my desire, to the extent that various areas of my body may be differentially called forth through my desire, that the intensity of my sexual feeling would manifest more intensely in some regions than in others. We unmake the other even as we create hir as an object of our desire.

What significance might this notion of transposition have for transpeople? This phenomenon of transposition is no less true for transpeople than it is for normatively gendered people. Transposition, in the case of transpeople, is also the process in which sensations become animated through the body and the body becomes animated by sensation. Desire is experienced bodily through a series of substitutions or reconfigurations that are also present, though perhaps less marked, in normatively gendered people.

What happens, in particular if I am a transperson reaching toward that other? Or if it is a transperson toward whom I reach?

Sex and Transcendence

> Existence is indeterminate in itself, by reason of its fundamental structure, and in so far as it is the very process whereby the hitherto meaningless takes on meaning, whereby what had merely a sexual significance assumes a more general one, chance is transformed into reason, in so far as it is the act of taking up a *de facto* situation. We shall give the name "transcendence" to this act in which existence takes up, to its own account, and transforms such a situation. Precisely because it is transcendence, existence never utterly outruns anything, for in that case the tension which is essential to it would disappear. (169)

When it is misconstrued as pathology, transsexuality has most often been characterized as a mental disturbance in which a person fantasizes hirself to have the genitals of the sex to which sie does not belong. It is on the basis of this fantasy, whereby a misrecognition of one's own body is understood to signal a break from reality, that transsexuality has been characterized as a psychosis rather than a neurosis. As this logic would have it, the materiality of the body is the arbiter of reality; the presence of, say, the transman's phallus is a hallucination if he has not had bottom surgery and merely "ersatz" if he has.

But phenomenology, as we have seen, is a realm in which one's own perceptions retain pride of place as a means of determining truth. My own phenomenological mode of embodiment—of bodily configuration or comportment—is itself understood as constituting a truth. This does not mean that I construct the truth, whole cloth, from the cloister of my own experience, neither does it provide hallucination with the stamp of legitimacy. What it means is that my experience of my body, my sense of its extension and efficacy, the ways that I endeavor to make a habitable thing of it, and the use I make of it—or in the throes of desire, perhaps the use that it makes of me—are my necessary relation to whatever materiality I am. The sexual schema is rather a way of becoming uncloistered in the body in that it delivers my own body to me through the movement of my body toward another. Thus through desire, my body is no longer a conglomeration of its various parts in their expressions as "inner phenomena" but is suddenly the vehicle through which I am compelled into relation with the world, where it is finally only that relation that gives me a body.

Merleau-Ponty suggests that sexuality is transformed into something of a more "general" significance and seems then to be suggesting that sexuality itself, or the baser realm that it may occupy, is transcended and we are delivered into some more rarified realm. The merely sexual is meaningless; it is only once the sexual achieves a more general significance that it achieves meaning. But it is also true that

Merleau-Ponty uses sexuality as the exemplar of transcendence; transcendence is the name he gives to the relation between self and world that is sexuality. He wants to claim both that sexuality only means something once it means something greater than itself and, at the same time, that sexuality need not point to some more momentous aspect of existence to be significant because sexuality is itself coextensive with existence: "There is interfusion between sexuality and existence, which means that existence permeates sexuality and *vice versa*, so that it is impossible to determine, in a given decision or action, the proportion of sexual to other motivations" (169). This confusion is not incidental. Merleau-Ponty's paradoxical conclusions regarding the status of sexuality—does it matter or does it not?—mirrors the status of sexuality itself, which is constantly "interfused" with existence.

Sexuality offers itself as one means by which a transformation from ideality to particularity becomes possible. We might even say that sexuality is the means by which Merleau-Ponty most thoroughly revises our inherited Cartesian presumptions about body and world. It is through sexuality that the body—and thus the *self*—is transformed from a thing that is concerned with itself to a thing that is concerned with others. Sexuality as a mutual project offers another person's body to me as an object of desire, as "not just a body, but a body brought to life by consciousness" (167), and my body, in turn, is visible and vulnerable to the other in this same way. Sexuality then becomes relation itself, not in the sense that all relations are at their heart sexual, or that sexual relations are about the masquerade of one thing for another (as bad readings of Freud would have it) but that sexuality is always offering my embodied existence as held in this inescapable and tensile paradox: I am for me, and I am for the other, and each of these modes of existence realizes itself in my body. Sexuality is perhaps the only way I can experience both these modes simultaneously, and can be the means by which the distinction between myself and another can dissolve, enacting the confusion that will become transcendence.

"In the Full Flesh"

The 1999 film *Boys Don't Cry* is based on the story of Brandon Teena, a young Nebraska man who is killed when he is discovered to be transgendered.[15] There is a scene in the film where Lana Tisdale, Brandon Teena's lover, is confronted by two of her friends, John Lotter and Tom Nissen. They have heard rumors that Brandon is not really a man but in fact a woman only pretending to be a man, and have come to Lana's house looking for Brandon, with plans to forcibly strip him and lay bare his "true" identity. This is undertaken to punish and humiliate Brandon, and the wrong that Brandon is being punished for is not just misrepresenting his gender but misrepresenting it *to Lana*. Thus forcibly stripping Brandon is only part of their aim—it is not enough that they see Brandon's nakedness, what they then want is for Lana to see it. They do not want merely to satisfy their own suspicion that Brandon has no penis and is therefore not male; they also want to force Lana to look at Brandon's naked body in their presence. The nature of the assault sets Lana up as the arbiter of Brandon's gender.

Thus humiliation is conceived by Lotter and Nissen as the way to "protect" Lana from being duped by Brandon and his duplicitous presentation of the "wrong" gender. Lana's response to this is to protect Brandon: she attempts to call Lotter and Nissen off by telling them, "I seen it."

"Mom, I seen him in the full flesh. I seen it. I know he's a man. Problem done. Now let's go to bed."

How ought we read that claim, "I seen it?" Is it just an untruth offered by Lana as a form of protection, to spare Brandon the violence that threatens him at this point in the film, a violence that will kill him by its end? I want to ask whether Lana's statement might be understood as something other than an instrumental lie. The "it" that she has seen is unspecified; Lotter and Nissen and perhaps the audience understand her to be referring to a penis, but she will not name the part as such. In declaring "I know he's a man," she is pointing not only to Brandon's own conviction but also to her understanding of him and his gender; her utterance serves to confirm Brandon's masculinity and his sense of himself as male by asserting that she shares that sense. That knowledge of his masculinity is emphatically bodily but also ambiguous. She knows him to be a man because she has "seen him in the full flesh," a statement of embodiment rather than the naming of a body part, an ambiguity that enables both Brandon's gender identification and Lana's recognition of that gender.

There is a dual ambiguity contained in Lana's statement, situated in the relationship between materiality and "flesh," and also surrounding perception itself. The "full flesh" does more work than simply act as a veil for the phallic reference, and "flesh" does a great deal of theoretical work. I suggest that the work done by that use of the word "flesh" in Lana's utterance can be explicated by considering its meaning in the phenomenological vernacular and that Lana's description of flesh has useful concordance with "flesh" in the Merleau-Pontian sense of that word, what he describes as a carnal relation with the world. It can name an aspect of embodiment that is not quite the body or a dimension of the world that is not quite quantifiable.

Merleau-Ponty considers perception to be a relational structure, where those relations do not map neatly onto the relation between subject and object. He attempts to frustrate this distinction between subject and object, between the seer and seen, between inside and outside, by according relation a primacy that had previously been reserved for the object itself. His final, unfinished work, *The Visible and the Invisible*, can be read as an attempt to show the ways in which familiar philosophical distinctions—and even familiar experiential ones—between subject and object, between the hand that touches and the hand that is touched, between our visible, bodily being and those aspects of ourselves that are not visible, are undermined by the importance of the relations between these categories. If the physical body can be thought as a discrete and bounded entity, capable of being distinctly set apart from the ground that is its world, this identification is less a matter of disconnection or differentiation and more a product of relation. A body becomes so by virtue of its interaction with what surrounds it, not because it is composed of a stuff that is radically foreign to its surroundings.

How are we to understand the relation between body and world and our perceptions of those relations? We are certain of our perceptions of the world, we are sure that they "belong" to us, and we are sure that they show us the world as it "truly" is.

And yet, a reliance on perception to confirm our certainly about what we know of the world can be misleading in that it cannot always account for those nameless structures that are true to experience but foreign to an objective assessment of that experience. If I stand in the middle of the road and survey it as it stretches before me, I see that it differs in width as it approaches the horizon, but "the road close up is not 'more true': the close, the far off, the horizon in their indescribable contrast form a system, and it is their relationship with the total field that is the perceptual truth" (22). In this way perception points toward a network of relations rather than confirming the material "truth" of any single element in that network or system. In considering perception in this way, "every distinction between the true and the false, between methodic knowledge and phantasms, science and the imagination, is ruined" (26).

This conclusion might seem at first to difficult to support, since it is one thing to claim that our perceptions of the world are inescapably perspectival and another to claim that this collapses distinctions between true and false, between methodic knowledge and phantasms. In the case of the body, the distinction that Merleau-Ponty wishes to challenge would seem to be the very distinction that allows the body to be thought as a bounded and legible entity. Ultimately, the act of perception "ruins" any clean division between the body and the world in which that body is situated, and if my body can still be understood as mine, it cannot be thought as more proximate to me than the world through which my body moves: "What I 'am' I am only at a distance, yonder, in this body, this personage, these thoughts, which I push before myself and which are only my least remote distances; and conversely I adhere to this world which is not me as closely as to myself, in a sense it is the only the prolongation of my body" (57).

How is it possible to understand the world as something capable of being as close to me as I am to myself, that the entire world is felt and functions as an extension of my body? This is an account of ontological "truth" that refuses to give primacy to either the perceiver who registers perceptions of the world or the world as a material fact over and against our perceptions of it. The "truth" of being exists somewhere in between these two registers, between what appears (the visible) and that which cannot be captured by flat and factual assertions about the appearances of the world (the invisible). The way in which Merleau-Ponty offers the category of the phantasmatic is significant in its restructuring of the relation between the visible, the invisible, and bodily being. We might expect the phantasmatic to be paired with "materiality," thus presenting an opposition (even if a collapsing one) between the phantasmatic and the invisible and that which is visible, material, and substantive. The phantasmatic is instead paired with "methodic knowledge," suggesting a relation of opposition between the phantasmatic and what we can know rather than the more familiar opposition between the phantasmatic and what we can see. If the phantasmatic can be described as something (or, more properly, some non-thing) which escapes our attempts to grasp or survey it, it would seem that the aspect of the phantasmatic that retreats from our perception is not the solidity of its materiality but the solidity of our own knowledge of it. Merleau-Ponty reconfigures the phantasmatic, transforming it from a register characterized by a lack of materiality into a register characterized by an ungraspability. The phantasmatic may or may not be material. It is not necessarily invisible, but it is indefinable, rendering the phantasmatic as that which cannot be encompassed by our knowledge of it rather than that which cannot be perceptually grasped. There exists a certain borderlessness to the phantasmatic; a methodical attempt to survey it as we would any commonplace object always fails to fully encompass it and can neither give a thorough account of its material dimensions nor translate that material into meaning.

This failure of perception to account for the totality of a thing is, of course, true of any object in the world toward which perception might be intended. Every object is shot through with an infinite number of possible appearances which no single act of perception can encompass and no series of perceptions can exhaust. Even a perception in which we have all faith, which seems to deliver a truth about the object, cannot encompass the reality of that object because " 'reality' does not belong definitely to any particular perception…In this sense it lies *always further on*" (41). Perceptual faith cannot help us locate the "reality" of the object—it is not even able to finally decide on its *own* location, seeming sometimes to emanate from the presence of the object and sometimes to be located in the body of the perceiver, and the incompossibility of these two positions (my perception cannot be both in the thing itself and in me) leaves the question of the location of perception undecidable. Yet perception is not impoverished by its inability to deliver the "whole" of any object; perception always gives us something less than this whole but also something more through the multitude of connections it makes between the perceiver and the thing perceived. For Merleau-Ponty, perception is not a passive activity whose aim is to capture a quantifiable measurement of the world through recording and measuring the qualia of any particular object within it. Perception produces our relations with other objects and subjects, and these relations are, finally, the location of the object's meaning. The perceptual truth of the object becomes the creation of its meaning, a meaning that is produced rather than found.

What consequences might this theory of perceptual truth have for thinking gender variance? First and most obviously, it suggests the possibility of a lack of accord between the object as it is delivered by our perception and the "reality" of the thing perceived, a reality that always lies "further on" than any objective perception. What one might "read" from the contours of the body is something less than the "truth" of that body's sex, which cannot be located in an external observation of the body, but exists instead in that relation between the material and the ideal, between the perceiver and the perceived, between the material particularity of any one body and the network of forces and contexts that shape the material and the meaning of that body. The perceptual truth of the body is not necessarily what we see, and the traditional binary of sexual difference might have less purchase on the body's "truth" than other ways of apprehending its lived reality. Or, to turn again to the film, Brandon's sex "close up" is not more true than Brandon's sex "far away," just as "the road close up is not more true than the road far away."

The category of the "flesh" also offers a way of thinking embodiment which takes seriously the productive capacities of its psychic investments and understands the phenomenological experience of the body to be as vital as an objective assessment of the body's corporeality. So what is "flesh"? Merleau-Ponty offers a theorization of "flesh" in which it is not reducible to the material and is a product of relations between myself, the other, and the world. Of course, the term is often employed as if its referent were clear and obvious: flesh is understood as bodily substance.[16] This has been true in discussions of the transgendered body in particular: Jay Prosser describes the body's "fleshy materiality," making no distinction between these two terms. It is simple, it is visible, it is material, and, in both of these instances, the term is deployed to dispel the cloud of linguistic abstraction that is thought to attend discussions of the body. More colloquially, the term "flesh" is used to describe a mode of being allied with visibility and presence and often indicates a certain relational component to that being. To say that one is present "in the flesh" connotes being present to or for someone else, an observing or other entity differentiated from the self and for whom the flesh becomes a display, a guarantor of the embodied presence of personhood. (The phrases "in the flesh" and "in person" are practically interchangeable—the former acts as a guarantor of the latter.)

Merleau-Ponty's definition of flesh shares with the colloquial, everyday deployment of the term the notion of relation but is both more restricted (my flesh and my person are not the same thing) and more expansive (my flesh need not be coterminous with my body but can extend into the world, which itself has a flesh). He asks: "Do we have a body—that is, not a permanent object of thought, but a flesh that suffers when it is wounded, hands that touch?" (137).

In working to differentiate body from flesh, Merleau-Ponty opposes them, attributing to one the characteristics of an object and to the other the characteristics of a subject. The first distinguishing property of flesh is *that it suffers*, it is only secondarily important that it has "hands that touch." This is not quite a distinction between passivity and activity—suffering may be as active an engagement with the other as touching. (Recall that the body is active when it "opens itself to others," including opening itself to the possibility of being wounded by the other.) It does, however, draw a distinction between the body as it is seen (as object) and the body as it is felt, as it is phenomenologically experienced. And herein lies the greatest difference between Merleau-Ponty's explication of flesh and flesh thought as merely the material stuff of the body. Flesh is that which, by virtue of psychic investment and worldly engagement, we form our bodies into rather than the stuff that forms them.

To become flesh is to enter the world and engage with it so fully that the distinction between one's body and the world ceases to have meaning. It is to inhabit one's body, "to exist within it, to emigrate into it, to be seduced, captivated, alienated by the phantom, so that the seer and the visible reciprocate one another and we no longer know which sees and which is seen" (139). Flesh is the world's seduction of the body and the body's incorporation of the world into itself.

Merleau-Ponty continues:

> It is this visibility, this generality of the Sensible in itself, this anonymity innate to Myself that we have previously called flesh, and one knows there is no name in traditional philosophy to designate it.... The flesh is not matter, is not mind, is not substance. To designate it, we should need the old term "element," in the sense it was used to speak of water, air, earth, and fire, that is, in the sense of a general thing, midway between the spatio-temporal individual and the idea, a sort of incarnate principle that brings a style of being wherever there is a fragment of being.... Flesh is an ultimate notion, that it is not the union or compound of two substances, but thinkable by itself. (139–140)

Merleau-Ponty insists that flesh is not a singular substance, but neither is it the "union or compound of two substances, but thinkable by itself." Flesh designates a certain unlocatablility of the body, neither the substance of the thing nor a pure ideality but that which is constructed somewhere between these two. When Merleau-Ponty asks, "Is my body a thing, is it an idea?" he answers that "it is neither, being the measurement of things. We will therefore have to recognize an ideality that is not alien to the flesh, that gives it its axes, its depth, its dimensions" (152). The body itself is, finally, a mixture or amalgam of substance and ideal, located somewhere between its objectively quantifiable materiality and its phantasmatic extensions into the world. Merleau-Ponty suggests a mode of bodily inhabitation through which we allow ourselves to be seduced by the phantasmatic aspects of the body, suggests that we give ourselves over to the world in affirming the flesh that is not-quite-the-body, and thereby find a more deeply rooted and expansive engagement with the other and the world.

Flesh then is a thing that is thinkable, but a thing that has not been thought. Flesh is neither matter nor mind but partakes of both these things, and yet cannot be described as a mixture of them. It is forged through our relations with others, in all their phenomenological particularity, yet is itself "a general thing." What, then, might we take from this theorization of the flesh to help us understand transgendered embodiment? Merleau-Ponty's description of flesh sounds, in many ways, like a description of transgenderism or transsexuality: a region of being in which the subject is not quite unitary and not quite the combination of two different things. An identity that is not secured by the specificity of the materiality of the body or by a particular mental quality but is something involving both. It can be thought by itself yet has been unnameable. Neither a singular substance nor a union of two substances. In both, too, the question of relation is primary. To feel one's own flesh, or to act as witness to another's, is to unsettle the question of subject and object, of material and phantasmatic, in the service of a more livable embodiment.

NOTES

1. Maurice Merleau-Ponty, *Phenomenology of Perception*, trans. Colin Smith (New York: Routledge, 1962). This fantasy of a magical fusion of sexes and its production of a body cleaved exactly in half might be understood as the dominant fantasy about nonnormative sexes, inclusive of both hermaphroditism and transsexuality, since the dually sexed creature of Ovid's *Metamorphosis*. For a history of gendered bodies beyond the binary in classical antiquity, see Luc Brisson, *Sexual Ambivalence: Androgyny and Hermaphroditism in Graeco-Roman Antiquity* (Berkeley: University of California Press, 2002). For a depiction of how such fantasies of bodily division in which sex cleaves the body into two halves persists in depictions of hermaphroditism, see Elizabeth Grosz, "Intolerable Ambiguity: Freaks as/at the Limit," in *Freakery: Spectacles of the Extraordinary Body*, ed. Rosemarie Garland Thompson (New York: NYU Press, 1996). Compare the critical account of transsexuality offered in the final pages of Elizabeth Grosz, *Volatile Bodies: Toward a Corporeal Feminism* (Bloomington: Indiana University Press, 1994).

2. Phenomenology has been utilized variously by authors doing trans work. For example, Henry S. Rubin, "Phenomenology as Method in Trans Studies," *GLQ: Journal of Lesbian and Gay Studies* 4, no. 2 (1998): 263–81. His most recent book is a sociological account of transmen that uses Merleau-Ponty's *Phenomenology of Perception*; he reads phenomenology's

insistence on the perspectival situatedness of subjects as shoring up and fortifying both the speaking "I" and the truth claims of that "I" (Rubin, *Self-Made Men: Identity and Embodiment among Transsexual Men* [Nashville: Vanderbilt University Press, 2002]).

3. Irigaray's is perhaps Merleau-Ponty's most trenchant critic here. See "The Invisible of the Flesh," her engagement with Merleau-Ponty's *The Visible and the Invisible*, in *An Ethics of Sexual Difference*, trans. Carolyn Burke and Gillian C. Gill (Ithaca: Cornell University Press, 1993). For a reading of Irigaray's engagement with Merleau-Ponty, see Tina Chanter, "Wild Meaning," in *Ethics of Eros* (New York: Routledge, 1995), and Penelope Deutscher, "Sexed Discourse and the Language of the Philosophers," in *A Politics of Impossible Difference: The Later Work of Luce Irigaray* (Ithaca: Cornell University Press, 2002). Judith Butler suggests that Irigaray's trope of two sets of lips speaking finds its inspiration in Merleau-Ponty's *deux lèvres* in "Merleau-Ponty and the Touch of Malebranche," in *The Cambridge Companion to Merleau-Ponty*, ed. Taylor Carman and Mark B. N. Hansen (Cambridge: Cambridge University Press, 2005). Butler offers a different reading of the intersection of phenomenology and feminism in "Sexual Ideology and Phenomenological Description: A Feminist Critique of Merleau-Ponty's *Phenomenology of Perception*," in *The Thinking Muse*, ed. Jeffner Allen and Iris Marion Young (Bloomington: Indiana University Press, 1989). See also Linda Martin Alcoff's essay, "Merleau-Ponty and Feminist Theory on Experience," in *Chiasms: Merleau-Ponty's Notion of "Flesh,"* ed. Fred Evans and Leonard Lawlor (Albany: SUNY Press, 2000), for a feminist critique of Merleau-Ponty's approach. For a more optimistic reading, see Roslyn Diprose's reading of Merleau-Pontian embodiment as a site for a transformed kind of ethics in *Corporeal Generosity: On Giving with Nietzsche, Merleau-Ponty and Levinas* (Albany: SUNY Press, 2002).

4. Iris Marion Young's essay "Throwing Like a Girl" (*The Thinking Muse*, ed. Jeffner Allen and Iris Marion Young [Bloomington: Indiana University Press, 1989]), her follow-up essay "Throwing Like a Girl, Twenty Years Later" (in *Body and Flesh*, ed. Donn Welton [Oxford: Blackwell, 1998]), and her piece "Pregnant Embodiment: Subjectivity and Alienation" (in *Throwing Like a Girl and Other Essays in Feminist Philosophy and Social Theory* [Bloomington: Indiana University Press, 1990]) remain singular as examples of both critiques of the presumptively male body in Merleau-Ponty and positive phenomenologies of specifically female embodiment. There also appears to be a new interest in using phenomenology for queer theory; see Sara Ahmed's volume *Queer Phenomenologies: Orientations, Objects, Others* (Durham: Duke University Press, 2006).

5. For an example of this kind of critique, see Grosz, *Volatile Bodies*.

6. For example, Janice Raymond's *The Transsexual Empire* (Boston: Beacon Press, 1979), reads the motivation for MTF transition to be sexual gratification, and, in particular, the sadistic sexual gratification of "becoming" a woman, a sadistic gratification that is, Raymond suggests, akin to rape.

7. J. Michael Bailey's *The Man Who Would Be Queen* (Washington, D.C.: National Academies Press, 2003) is one example of this trend. In an inversion of Raymond's theory, Bailey asserts that bodily transitions of "transmen" (by which he means MTF transwomen) is a result of their attraction not to the women that they want to become and thus supplant but to *themselves* re-imagined as women. The theory of "autogynophilia"—the term originates with Ray Blanchard—recasts the theory of a sexual attraction to oneself in a different scientific genre. This fetal androgen bath theory of transsexual development suggests that transpeople are "made" by exposure to the wrong kinds of hormones in utero and is regarded positively by

some transpeople (such as Anne Lawrence, a doctor herself), though rejected by most, in the same way that the "gay gene" or "gay brain" research is regarded positively by some homosexuals: a single, and resolutely biological, explanation of the "condition" means that its sufferer cannot be thought as morally culpable for her homosexuality or transsexuality, which is a biological, and thus ostensibly immutable, "fact." This recent discourse insisting on both the biological basis of trans and asserting that it is fundamentally a sexual obsession with oneself replicates with surprising faithfulness the concepts of inversion and homosexuality understood as a form of sexual narcissism that once dominated discourses on homosexuality. Though I'm interested in the structural similarities of these two misreadings, I don't want to suggest that transgenderism has replaced homosexuality in this regard, which would risk obscuring the fact that the narcissistic interpretation of homosexuality is still dominant in some circles.

8. The acronym LGBT demonstrates this conflation in its inclusion of transgenderism (and sometimes intersexuality in the case of LGBTI), with the other categories that denote sexuality rather than gender. For more on the sometimes uneasy relations in what Dean Spade has called the "LGB fake T" community, see Susan Stryker, "Transgender Theory: Queer Theory's Evil Twin," *GLQ: Journal of Lesbian and Gay Studies* 10, no. 2 (2004): 212–15.

9. Sandy Stone expresses both sympathy for this disengagement and doubt of its efficacy in "The *Empire* Strikes Back," in *Body Guards: The Cultural Politics of Gender Ambiguity*, ed. Kristina Straub and Julia Epstein (New York: Routledge, 1991). Joanne Meyerowitz's *How Sex Changed* (Cambridge: Harvard University Press, 2002) also explores accounts of early trans autobiographies in which the subject of sexual desire is either politely avoided or entirely disavowed.

10. For an extended consideration of this concept in philosophy and its particular implications for women, see Gail Weiss, *Body Images: Embodiment as Intercorporeality* (New York: Routledge, 1999).

11. Gayle Salamon, "Is There a Phenomenological Unconscious? Time and Embodied Memory in Merleau-Ponty" (unpublished ms.).

12. Sigmund Freud, *Three Essays on the Theory of Sexuality*, trans. James Strachey (New York: Basic Books, 1963).

13. Merleau-Ponty's commitment to ambiguity in his discussions of the body has frustrated even his least identitarian critics. This is, for instance, Derrida's chief quarrel with Merleau-Ponty as outlined in *On Touching—Jean-Luc Nancy* (Palo Alto: Stanford University Press, 2005).

14. For an extended consideration of the eye, the look, and their structuration of perception, as well as a challenge to Sartre's theorization of the gaze, see Merleau-Ponty's essay "Eye and Mind," in *The Primacy of Perception, and Other Essays on Phenomenological Psychology, the Philosophy of Art, History, and Politics*, ed. James M. Edie (Evanston, Il.: Northwestern University press, 1964).

15. For reflections on the iconic place of Brandon Teena within the trans movement, see Judith Halberstam, *In a Queer Time and Place* (New York: NYU Press, 2005). See also BRANDON (1998–1999), a multimedia collaborative project by Shu Lea Cheang, Jordy Jones, Susan Stryker, and Pat Cadigan commissioned by the Guggenheim museum and accessible at http://brandon.guggenheim.org. See also the "Queer Spectrality" chapter in Carla Freccero's *Queer/Early/Modern*.

16. Thomas Laqueur describes flesh as that which "shines through in its simplicity" in *Making Sex: Body and Gender from the Greeks to Freud* (Cambridge: Harvard University Press, 1992).

6

Trans Identities and First-Person Authority

Talia Mae Bettcher

Trans studies constitute part of the coming-to-voice of transpeople, long the theorized and researched objects of sexology, psychiatry, and feminist theory. Sandy Stone's pioneering "The *Empire* Strikes Back: A Posttranssexual Manifesto" sought the end of monolithic medical and feminist accounts of transsexuality to reveal a multiplicity of trans-authored narratives.[1] My goal is a better understanding of what it is for transpeople to come to this polyvocality. I argue that trans politics ought to proceed with the principle that transpeople have *first- person authority* (FPA) over their own gender; and I clarify what this means.[2]

Preliminaries

I distinguish the practice of gender and sex within mainstream culture and within trans-friendlier subaltern contexts.[3] When I talk about FPA over gender, I do not mean this exists in many of the powerful "worlds" hostile to transpeople.[4] I mean that in various trans-friendlier contexts different cultural practices have emerged that depart from more mainstream ones. In aiming to understand FPA with respect to gender and sex, I seek to provide a framework to describe this real-world shift in cultural practice.

Since I am speaking of mainstream and subaltern practices, I emphasize the cultural dimension in both realms. I take this to mean that gender and sex are woven into forms of life that reflect and regulate interactions. Within such contexts, words have relatively fixed meanings: Persons may not declare themselves teapots and thereby make it so. Nor may they, through sheer force of will, alter the meaning of words within determining cultural contexts. In advocating FPA over gender, I am discussing an already regulated cultural interaction rather than an "anything goes" or "because I say I am" doctrine.[5] My goal is to understand FPA as an ideal for that which already exists in less-than-politically-ideal practice, to help transpeople treat ourselves and each other better, and to offer it to those who also exist and struggle in various subaltern places, who do not know transpeople well but want to form meaningful friendships and political partnerships with (some of) us.

My other aim is to elucidate a particular form of transphobia, which I call the Basic Denial of Authenticity.[6] For example, an FTM who identifies as a "trans man" may find himself represented as "really a woman living as a man." One obvious feature of this denial of authenticity is that transpeople are identified in ways that are contrary to or even hostile to our own self-identifications. But a less frequently discussed feature is that such identifications are generally embedded within discourse about "appearance," "reality," "exposure," "discovery," and "deception." I show that from the perspective of trans-resistant culture, such forms of "reality enforcement" must be seen as deep violations of FPA, executed through sexually abusive techniques.

The chapter has four main parts. First, I examine the phenomenon of FPA; I argue against standard epistemological accounts of FPA in favor of one that emphasizes ethics. Second, I examine mainstream gender and sex practices; I argue that gender presentation communicates genital status and that often gender terms (such as "woman" and "man") are used to circulate information about genital status. In my view, these practices are sexually abusive. Third, I provide an account of (trans-friendlier) subaltern practices in which FPA over gender is instituted; I argue that in these contexts, a person's claim to a particular gender is determined by "existential identity" (that is, by *who* rather than *what* one is). Fourth and finally, I show how dominant practices of gender and sex constitute an assault on ethical FPA. Specifically, these practices deploy tactics of sexual abuse to raze the existential identities of transpeople. I conclude by reflecting on some of the political consequences of nontrans feminist theorizing about gender that does not take seriously the relationship between sexual abuse of and the assault on the ethical FPA of transpeople.

First-Person Authority: Epistemology and Ethics

What Is First-Person Authority?

Philosophers take FPA to extend to two selected groups of mental states: (a) fleeting, phenomenal states (such as pains and momentary thoughts), and (b) more durable mental attitudes *about* something (such as beliefs, fears, and desires). In its most basic (and largely discredited) form, FPA is taken as the "Cartesian" view that first-person awareness about such mental states is both immediate (i.e., basic, not derived or inferred) and incorrigible.

Associated with FPA is the notion of an *avowal*.[7] Present-tense first-person statements of the type "I am in pain" and "I want to go home" can be made both immediately (i.e., without external evidence) and incorrigibly. Thus, in avowing my wish to go home, I appeal to no evidence (noticing that I keep looking at the clock and tapping my foot); I say, "I wish to go home" without ado.

Much contemporary discussions of FPA take the rejection of this "Cartesian" view as its starting point. Certainly there appear to be (limited) cases in which we make mistakes about phenomenal states. Nonetheless, avowals of such states generally exhibit an immunity that many judgments do not. Consequently, it makes sense to regard the first person as an expert about her phenomenal states, even though she is not absolutely infallible (as a "Cartesian" might have it).

In attitudinal cases, FPA is less strong. A psychoanalyst (or even a close friend) can make an interpretation based on one's behavior (including one's pattern of avowing) that one does not hold an attitude which one consistently avows. In reflecting on one's brother, one may feel no sense of betrayal; one may avow one's love for and trust of him. Yet based on one's behavior, a psychoanalyst may come to the correct conclusion that one actually feels betrayed by him.

Though such avowals are not strongly immune to error, it has been thought that the first person is, all things being equal, in a superior epistemic position than a third person and that this is due to the way in which the first person ascribes psychological states to herself. In other words, even though attitudinal avowals are defeasible, the first person is supposed to retain some epistemic authority owing to the modality of first-person knowledge. Recent debate has concerned whether this epistemic advantage is a genuine cognitive achievement[8] or a mere artifact of general ways of speaking (our "grammar" in a suitably Wittgenstenian sense).[9]

An Argument against Epistemic First-Person Authority

In my view, FPA over attitudinal states is not constituted by a serious epistemic advantage in the way here supposed; rather, it is ultimately a kind of *ethical* authority. My argument is based on a dilemma: either epistemic accounts of FPA in attitudinal cases must make a claim about epistemic advantage that is not true a priori, or they must make a weaker epistemic claim and thereby fail to account for the actual phenomenon of FPA.

This alleged epistemic advantage is not supposed to derive merely from the fact that one is in a better position to secure knowledge about oneself (since one is always "around") but from the peculiarities concerning first-person perspective. In this view, interpretative cases that trump FPA must be exceptions to the rule. Yet this claim seems to me very controversial (if not patently false), given the degree to which denial, self-deception, wishful thinking, and unconscious attitudes are common (and detectable) in society. If I am right about that, it becomes unclear how first-person avowals could have any claim to epistemic authority.

According to some philosophical accounts, a complete failure of first-person knowledge can be ruled out a priori.[10] One might argue that a person with almost complete failure of first-person knowledge of attitudes could not be a rational agent.[11] Yet even if true, this is insufficient. Just because people are not chronically unreliable about their attitudes does not mean that they are highly reliable experts. If denial, self-deception, and wishful thinking are fairly common although not the rule, first-person *expertise* cannot be in play. In short: immunity to systematic fallibility is much weaker than even limited expertise.

Yet whether self-deception is fairly common but not the rule is an empirical rather than an a priori matter. So there is no basis for explaining the existence of first-person expertise or even the presumption thereof on an a priori basis. While we can grant that first-person knowledge about one's attitudes may be different from third-person knowledge, it doesn't follow that there is anything close to special first-person expertise secured by this modality of knowledge.

Yet if the epistemic account of first-person authority gives up on the stronger claim that the first person has a kind of expertise, and opts only for immunity to systematic fallibility, then it is no longer capable of explaining the phenomena. There remains something insightful about the "Cartesian" view that such avowals are incorrigible, about the description "authoritative" despite the preceding argument, and this *exceeds* the weaker view that the first person cannot be proven chronically unreliable. After all, there is a great distance between the avoidance of chronic unreliability and the full weight of authoritative discourse. I elucidate this fact in what follows.

Ethical First-Person Authority

Consider: after being profoundly shaken in therapy by the depth of one's own denial and failure to grasp the abiding attitudes that have governed one's life, it is still inappropriate to say when asked "Do you want to go home?" "In my opinion, yes. But I am hardly certain about that." The answer is humorous; in my view it is "out of order." One is expected not to merely state an opinion about one's desire, but to take responsibility for that desire. Were the response expressed with certitude, this wouldn't help: "Yes. Based on all the evidence, it's my contention that I do want to go home. Indeed, this hypothesis can be confirmed most conclusively."[12] The problem is not that one does not know what one wants. The problem is partially "grammatical": one has not answered the question properly. More important, the problem is ethical: one has not "staked a claim" by taking responsibility for a desire. No mere assessment of fact can constitute such an *act* of taking responsibility.

Obviously, the sheer fact that the first person cannot be systematically mistaken about their mental attitudes goes no distance in explaining this phenomenon of authority. Indeed, even if the first person *did* have a complete epistemic advantage, it is not clear that this would explain the phenomenon which seems largely ethical in nature. Given the failure of the epistemic account, and the salience of ethical considerations in case of first-person authority, I argue FPA should be understood strictly as an ethical phenomenon.

The meaning of "avowal" involves two related aspects. First, avowal concerns an *acknowledgement* as one might take responsibility for one's feelings. This exceeds mere judgment since it has special ethical force. Second, avowal often has the force of confession where concealment is presumed. Given the privacy of attitudes, it is unsurprising that there be a kind of guarantee involved in first-person avowals.

Now there are at least three related senses in which our attitudes are "private." First, we can often keep our attitudes to ourselves (if we don't act on them in public or blurt them out). Second, our attitudes are our "own business." Finally, our attitudes are private insofar as wrongful disclosure by another constitutes a violation. In saying this, I mean the way unauthorized disclosure of the contents of one's diary is an invasion of privacy or the capacity to read another's mind may constitute a violation of the right to privacy. So, there are at least two senses in which "privacy" is ethical in nature.[13]

This ethical privacy derives, in part, from the fact that we are responsible for our attitudes. I do not mean that they are always up to us in the sense that we have rational control over them. I mean one can be faulted for holding inappropriate, false, or irrational attitudes. Given that one is ethically responsible for one's attitudes, it makes sense that it is up to one to take responsibility for them by publicly avowing them (or not). Given that one can be held responsible for holding false, inappropriate, or irrational attitudes, whether one is "put on-the-line" ought to be one's decision alone. There are social consequences of avowing an attitude: it generates a social situation in which there will be specific reactions. It sets a chain of events into motion.

If this is correct, there is something to the idea that avowals are not reports of fact or at least not *mere* reports of fact. Using terms developed by J. L Austin, we can say there are two different kinds of illocutionary acts: the forces involved in first-person and third-person gender ascriptions, respectively, are different.[14] In publicly avowing an attitude, the first person has in some sense staked a social claim and certified a view about their mental life on which we can "bank." In avowing an attitude, one authorizes a view of one's mental life that is then fit for circulation. This may explain why avowals are taken to constitute such impressive evidence for third-person interpretations.

So the certifying function of a first person avowal is connected to ethical issues of privacy and ownership of one's own mental attitudes. This, in turn, is obviously connected to issues of autonomy. For example, it is unacceptable to coerce an avowal (where that avowal is taken to carry the same social and moral weight as one freely offered). Consider the domestic violence abuser who extorts the concession that his partner deliberately made the dinner too spicy to spite him.[15] The abuser has bullied an avowal where the victim either insincerely concedes or, more disturbing, sincerely recognizes the "truth" of what her victimizer presses. He takes this coerced avowal to stand as a genuine avowal of intention (and guilt). Even if the abuser's assessment is true, this is irrelevant to the most disturbing aspects of this case. He has secured an avowal through force and consequently taken his own assessment as itself authoritative with respect to his victim's attitudes: the victim's FPA is under assault.

Or consider a case in which a second person simply *tells* the first person with certitude what her attitudes are. For example, even if it is clear one wants to go home (one looks at the clock, taps one's foot), it is odd for one's date to announce, unprompted, "You want to go home now." To be sure, he might ask, "Do you want to go home? Because it seems like you do." He might even say, "It seems to me you want to go home." What seems problematic is the attempt to avow somebody else's mental attitudes on their own behalf, and there is the sense that if "You want to go home now" is not meant humorously, it is an attempt to control. Again, there is something that feels "ungrammatical." More important, there is an infringement on the first person's autonomy. The second person is inappropriately treating his own interpretive assessment as authoritative.[16]

Negotiations of Gender in Dominant Cultural Practices

An Argument against Definitional Accounts of Gender Concepts

In analyzing the semantic content of gender terms such as "woman," a first move is to follow the Oxford English Dictionary's definition of "woman" as "adult, female, human being." Here, "female" grounds the concept of woman in physical sex, leaving the exact meaning of "female" unspecified. The term "female," however, is hard to determine. The OED defines it as "belonging to the sex which bears offspring" (as opposed to "belonging to the sex which begets offspring"). Yet a person who cannot bear offspring can still belong to the female sex. On the basis of what criterion does this person "belong to the sex which *generally* bears offspring"?

Harold Garfinkel calls the everyday, pre-theoretical conception of sex *the natural attitude* and those who hold it, *normals*.[17] In this view, there are two naturally mutually exclusive, exhaustive, and invariant sexes, and membership within a sex is determined by genitalia. Presumably, genitalia and other aspects of the reproductive system are taken together without criterial distinction. In reality, however, while features such as genitalia, karyotype, and gonads generally coincide, it is unclear what to do in cases in which the features conflict. Which feature determines sex membership?

Even experts do not agree how to define sex. For example, Joan Roughgarden writes, "among animals that reproduce sexually there is near-universal binary between very small (sperm) and large (egg), so that male and female can be defined biologically as the production of small and large gametes, respectively."[18] Obviously this is a deflationary view, restricting binarism to gamete size, reducing sex to the sheer production of one or the other gamete. By contrast, genitalia, gonads, and karyotype all contribute to the determination of sex in Anne Fausto-Sterling's proposal of five sexes.[19] So it seems there are hard cases, and no meditation on the concept of "female" will yield a definitive answer.[20] Instead, it seems there are different discursive practices (legal, medical, scientific, everyday) in which the criteria for sex determination vary.[21]

One problem for a definitional account of "woman" is that the term "sex" does not itself seem very easy to define. A second problem is that this definitional account omits the cultural role of woman, and the conceptions and practices related to that role. We can imagine a world where the cultural roles normally assigned on the basis of sex are inverted: females dress "like men," males dress "like women"; stereotypical traits and behaviors are assigned to each group. Here, it isn't clear how to apply the terms "man" and "woman." Does physical sex or cultural role determine category membership? If this is a hard case (I believe it is), then cultural roles (and related practices and conceptions) must somehow be connected to the semantic content of gender terms like "woman."[22]

Second, consider adjectives such as "womanly," "manly," "girly," and the like. It seems as if they have cultural traits packed right into their meaning. When somebody says, "Well, no. That's a bit too girly for me, I'm afraid," we shouldn't expect them to be complaining about having to dig ditches. To be sure, one might argue that such adjectives really mean only "like a woman" and "like a girl" (where the current cultural facts are extraneous to the content). However, it does seem that in the case of the world imagined above, the very meaning of the word would have changed, if "girly" should be a good way to describe ditch digging. So it again seems that cultural roles assigned on the basis of sex are part of the semantic content. And this suggests that there is something wrong with this definitional account of gender.

An Argument against Family-Resemblance Accounts of Gender Concepts

One solution to both of these problems is to provide a Wittgensteinian family-resemblance account of gender terms such as "woman" according to which there are no determinable necessary and sufficient conditions for category membership but only multiple, overlapping features of similitude. C. Jacob Hale provides such an analysis, enumerating differently weighted characteristics that include cultural aspects of gender (such as mode of presentation, speech, occupation, leisure).[23] One benefit is the frame for the tension between dominant and resistant conceptions of gender without deflating the significance of resistant conceptions of gender: even if there is only one concept of "woman," the dispute can concern the different weighting of the various family-resemblance features.[24]

Yet one difficulty with this account is the underestimation of the difference between features taken to determine category membership and other aspects that go into an understanding of what a woman is. While it is true that the latter must have some sort of involvement in semantic content of gender terms, the involvement seems different in kind rather than different in mere degree of weight.

One argument for this is that when the natural attitude prevails, physical sex strictly determines the application of gender terms such as "woman." While an individual may fail to live up to prevailing cultural role, this will not undermine her status as female. Instead, she will simply be assessed negatively for failure to conform to standards of excellence. In cases in which she fully adopts the cultural role of man, she will be regarded as a woman pretending to be a man. Thus there is not merely a difference in weighting sex and conformity to cultural role. There is a difference in *kind* of semantic contribution made to category terms: sex determines individual category membership; role, while involved in normative assessments, does not.

Another argument for the centrality of sex is based on the recognition that "adult, human female" is a standard dictionary definition of "woman." While we can question dictionary definitions, it remains that defining "woman" by appeal to sex is a well-established cultural practice. According to Hale, the view that there is a sharp feature (sex) to distinguish men and women is part of the "natural attitude," and his own Wittgensteinian analysis is intended, in part, to point to the inadequacy of that attitude.[25] However, as Hale no doubt recognizes, in many cultural contexts, the meanings of gender terms are partially determined by such practices and attitudes. So an analysis of the meaning of the term within such contexts requires an analysis of the attitudes and related practices.

As a consequence of the preceding arguments, I distinguish between a gender term's definition and its underlying metaphysical conceptions. By the latter, I mean much of what is captured in family-resemblance style analysis. Robust with cultural content, conceptions are normative accounts of what a woman (or man) is. They include sex characteristics and also features that are purely culturally determined. I recognize multiple conceptions (paradigms or exemplars) per category, as well as considerable variability in metaphysical conception as negotiated in different power-stratified contexts. Thus not all conceptions need to be stereotypical: they can involve opposition to stereotypes.[26]

Yet how should we understand this notion of "definition"? On the face of it, the definition "female, adult, human being" *really does seem right*. Indeed, it seems as perfect a definition as one might have ever wanted. The reason for this is that the concept "woman" has two built in *contrasts*. It contrasts with man, and it contrasts with girl. Moreover, it's clear that as a consequence of these two contrasts, it can be used to convey specific information about sex and information about adulthood. Indeed, the OED even *lists* these contrastive uses. So the only answer I can think of why "woman" has such a nice definition is just this: because "woman" is frequently *used* to convey information about sex and because it is frequently *used* to convey information about adulthood, it acquires such explicit contrasts. In other words, it seems to me that the uses must ultimately explain the appearance of a definition, rather than the definition itself explaining the uses.

Gender Presentation Is Genital Representation

As a consequence of the preceding considerations, I move to an account of the gender terms in specific contexts (the illocutionary force, in particular) as central to an analysis of how physical sex is constituted as the defining feature of category membership. My starting point is the Basic Denial of Authenticity. Consider a case in which an MTF is taken to be "really a man disguised as a woman." This juxtaposition between gender presentation and (presumed) "biological sex" inscribes an appearance or reality contrast. This contrast is the basis for the representation of transpeople as deceivers which figures frequently in cases of transphobic violence and attempts to blame the victim ("He tricked me! I didn't know that was a really a man!").[27]

In my view, gender presentation literally *signifies* physical sex.[28] If it is true that transpeople who "misalign" gender presentation with sexed body are deceivers or pretenders, then those who "correctly" align presentation with body tell the truth. Thus, there is a representational relation between gender presentation and sexed body. In previous work, I argued this representational relation is part of a larger nonverbal system of communication that works to facilitate manipulative and rape-excusing heterosexual sexuality, as well as underwriting racial oppression.[29]

In claiming that gender presentation signifies sexed body, I mean it signifies *genital status*.[30] I believe genital status has a fundamental role to play in determining physical sex that is not shared by other possible features such as karyotype. I do not deny the role such notions play in more sophisticated discussions of sex or in cultural practices of sex determination. I do affirm that there is a fundamental semantic relationship between gender presentation and genital status not shared with karyotype, and this relationship plays a crucial role in fixing the natural attitude about genitalia.

Clothing serves a "concealing" function. By "hiding" the body, the contrast between clothing and body is immediately implicated in the notions of *exposure* and *revelation*. This function is connected to taboos against nudity in public space and the demarcation of certain body parts as private. Yet it is precisely because genitalia are marked off as sexually private that they require available representations in public. If this is correct, the status of genitals as the "truth" flows from their required public concealment (which necessitates public signs).[31]

Because of the preceding, genital status is distinct from all other features involved in sex or gender attribution: Genitalia are specifically designated "private" and "concealed" by genital-representing clothing in public space.[32] In this way, genital status as essential determinant cannot be fully separated from constituting the "private reality" of sex, where this "reality" derives force through contrast with gender appearance. In other words, the role of genital status as sex determinant is a function of its being gender *referent*: "concealed" and signified by gendered attire.[33] So, it is little wonder that "shocking exposures" of transpeople as "really a so and so" are often so heavily sexualized. Indeed, forced genital exposure is a distinctive form of sexual abuse that occurs frequently in cases of transphobic harassment and even murder.

This illuminates a question that many transpeople have had asked to them in inappropriate situations: "Have you had *the* surgery?" To a large extent, this is a more polite way of asking about genitalia. No wonder people are curious. They're used to *knowing*. This points to how terms like "man" can function as gender presentation. In locutions like "That's really a man," the word "man" circulates information about genital status. It occurs in a situation in which the explicit circulation of genital information would be inappropriate.

While genital status is the signified of these terms (i.e., the core information circulated), this signification occurs against the background of social taboo. "Man" and "'woman" function as a code or euphemistic replacement for restricted discourse, just as "darn" replaces "damn." The pragmatic meaning of "man" and "woman" when deployed in these contexts is determined, in part, by social restriction based on the appropriateness of sexual discourse. The categories circulate information about genital status insofar as they function as euphemistic replacements for the restricted discourse.

Indeed, it seems to me that the very salience of sex as definitive with respect to woman and man *derives* from the underlying practices of circulating genital information through gender terms and gender presentation. While I don't claim to fully defend the view here, if the centrality of genital status in the natural attitude is determined by its role as the concealed referent of gender presentation, and if the natural attitude (which privileges genital status) is in some way basic to other discourses about sex, then it follows that sex as determinative of woman/man category membership flows from the mundane system by which gender presentation communicates concealed genitalia.

To briefly support the claim that the natural attitude is basic, I observe that since the natural attitude is bound up with everyday sensibilities, and more deeply the very communicative relation between gender presentation and genital status that informs our mundane interactions in the world, it seems inevitable that the natural attitude maintains a "visceral reality" in face of the abstracted discourses that play little role in guiding such interactions. Indeed, given the degree to that legal, medical, and scientific discourses are deployed within restricted professionalized settings, it seems likely that "theoretical" accounts of sex will seem disconnected from "the real world." Indeed, there may be ways in which the natural attitude can "infect" the more theoretical ones through individuals who adopt sophisticated discourse intellectually, while maintaining the natural attitude at a visceral level; or through "normals" who borrow technical terms in order to support the natural attitude.[34] It is little surprise that, as Hale argues, specialized discourses generally attempt to maximally preserve aspects of the natural attitude as consistent with their specialized aims.[35]

Negotiations of Gender in Resistant Cultural Practices

If part of the function of clothing is to secure one's right to privacy, it is unclear why one should not have a right to privacy about one's genital status. And if we grant that posing questions to strangers like "Do you have a penis?" is harassing, it is unclear why coded questions requesting the same information aren't likewise. Given this, a case can be made that the system of genital disclosure through gender presentation and gender terms is itself invasive. Given that failures to disclose inevitably lead to condemnation and even violence, systematic disclosures of genital status are culturally mandated. Given the preceding, it follows that this system of forced genital disclosure is sexually abusive.

Trans politics must require that bodily privacy be expanded to include information about genital status. Gender presentation may not be taken to communicate genital status; terms such as "woman" may not be deployed to circulate genital information. This is necessary to undo the mechanisms that construct transpeople as deceivers or pretenders. Consequently, the shift in meaning of gender terms concerns not merely the "pure semantics" of the terms but a shift in force (i.e., the kind of illocutionary act involved in the utterance "I am a woman"). In particular, while metaphysical conceptions of men and women may remain stable, the practice of circulating genital information and the semantic correlate of distinguishing men and women on the basis of sex must be altered.

What Subcultures?

In my experience in Los Angeles, there are many subcultures that could be described as "trans." I move in several communities that intersect in grassroots activism, bringing together some FTM people (typically self-identified FTMs or transmen), MTF people (typically self-identified MTFs or transwomen), other transpeople (typically self-identified as genderqueer). The confluence mixes disparate people and involves complex intersections of race, class, and religion.

While these interactions, for various complex reasons, aren't politically ideal (as I point out below), in them gender presentation is not understood to communicate genital status but, instead, indicates how persons want to be treated. Individuals' self-identifications are generally accepted at face value. Often identity terms (*transman*, *genderqueer*) do not have well-specified, fixed definitions. While there may be some general background set of related, negotiated conceptions that provide general content to the notions, there is no clear set of criteria that determine range of application.[36]

When I say these interactions aren't "politically ideal," what I have in mind is that even in these subaltern contexts, some interactions continue to reflect mainstream transphobic attitudes. I mention two examples. First, despite the fact that gender presentation isn't taken to communicate genital status, the importance of genital status has not been abolished. Sometimes transpeople inquire about somebody else's status inappropriately and freely circulate information without consideration. Second, it is a sad, peculiar fact that some MTFs (who have no difficulty referring to each other with appropriate pronouns) when first learning to interact with FTMs can't or won't transfer the practice. Perversely, it takes time and education for this confusion to be rectified.

Private Attitudes, Private Body

Having briefly discussed the resistant contexts I have in mind, I move to examine self-identifying locutions such as "I am a woman" in a trans-friendlier context. In doing so, I understand these locutions as inevitably resistant to dominant cultural practice. So suppose that the following question is posed to a trans person: "Are you a man or a woman?" Such a question, in a dominant context, is generally a coded question about genital status. Moreover, since the answer is often already supposed to be known, the question is less an inquiry than a demand that this person be held accountable for concealed genitalia; it is a demand that they "own up."

There are curious analogies with self-knowledge about attitudes. An acknowledgement is demanded. And people generally know what genitals they have. Since people don't walk around naked, others do not have sensible access to others' bodies. And it is really (ethically) up to the individual whether others have access to one's body in this way. Consequently, the means by which others learn about one's genital status are indirect (mediated through the communicative function of gender presentation or the circulation of the euphemistically deployed gender terms). So, the anticipated confession ("I am really a man") is closer to an avowal of one's mental attitudes than one might have thought. It is a coded avowal of one's genital status.[37]

The analogy breaks down since, while direct access to bodily "privates" falls within the moral authority of the first person (in dominant culture), information about genital status does not. While it us up to the first person whether her private thoughts are shared with others, it is not up to her whether her genital status is shared. On the contrary, genital declaration through gender presentation is socially mandated. While an avowal is demanded, it is not an avowal that is connected to FPA. It is analogous to a forced avowal of guilt.

Self-Identity Determines Gender: Some Objections

When the transperson answers "I am a woman," she cannot be understood to avow concealed genital status. To be sure, this is how "he" will be understood by many. But one who is interested in hearing will recognize that this is not (or at least not merely) a misleading avowal of genital status. It may, instead, be understood as resistant *refusal* to disclose genital status.[38] The deeper question is: How is it to be understood as more than a refusal? The first thought is that it is an avowal of self-identity. This seems promising since, while genital status is not amenable to the philosophers' notion of FPA (which applies only to one's mental attitudes, not one's physical traits), one's self-identity is as follows: if self-identity is a set of beliefs about oneself, FPA applies in such cases in a straightforward way. In this view, self-conception provides the criterial basis for category membership.[39]

There are difficulties, however. First, there is a theoretical problem. If believing one is a woman replaces genital status as sole determinant of membership, there are difficulties concerning an account of what it is to believe one is a woman. Is it to believe one possesses the special feature making one a woman? If so, to believe one is a woman is to believe one believes one is a woman. And now we seem to have some problem of circularity or regress.[40] In practice this means that the criterion is virtually unintelligible.[41]

There are also problems in providing an accurate account of actual subaltern practices. The account of FPA in terms of self-conception isn't broad enough to cover cases in which transpeople self-identify for various political reasons rather than on the basis of beliefs about oneself. Somebody might self-identify as a transwoman and yet refuse to self-identify as an MTF, not because she believes she is one and not the other but because she approves of certain political terms and objects to others. Since FPA is culturally recognized in such cases, an account is needed that goes beyond FPA over beliefs about what one is.

Moreover, many transpeople believe that we are men, women, or something else for particular reasons: we have accounts of why we believe what we do. Yet in the account proposed, the only reason for thinking that one is a woman is the fact that one thinks that one is a woman. But *why* does one think that one is a woman?

This connects to a deeper problem: no room is allowed for disputes about the criterion for category membership—it is fixed as *self-identity*. Yet transpeople *do* have metaphysical disputes about what makes a woman a woman and a man a man; these disputes don't always centralize the notion of self-regarding beliefs. So it isn't clear how stipulating self-conception as determinant of category membership accommodates this phenomenon. On the contrary, it seems that the correct account is one that fails to provide *any* defining feature of category membership and thus leaves it open for cultural dispute.

Existential Self-Identity

To address these concerns, I point to the perplexity a non-trans-friendly person may experience when a transperson (who does not look at all "like a woman") announces she is a woman. One can understand that her conceptions of woman may be roughly similar to one's own. Here, however, concepts like "woman" have become contestable like concepts like "genderqueer." There is a background set of related conceptions of womanhood without any definition that provides necessary and sufficient conditions.

Yet, if she is not avowing genital status, what is she doing and why? Indeed, since gender presentation is no longer taken to communicate genital status, this ignorance does not merely concern what she is doing with words, it concerns all gendered behavior and self-presentation. This suggests that in order to understand, one must with some degree of deference acknowledge the transperson as better positioned to answer such questions.

Self-identification may not necessarily indicate something deep about the person's self-identity. It may reflect political choices made for tactical reasons. In general, one does not know in advance what a person's reasons are for self-identifying and gender presenting. Yet an account of the reasons would render intelligible the person's behavior, and reasons for acting are plainly subsumable under FPA. Thus we have the beginning of an account how FPA over gender is conferred.

The background reasons for acting also inform how the success of the self-identification is to be assessed. When somebody engages in the political act of category-claiming, the question whether she has made a true statement isn't germane. Rather, if there is any defeasibility, it concerns whether this action reflects a genuine political commitment. This can be assessed through the conformity between the person's overall intelligibility-conferring narrative with their overall pattern of actions.

Of course, when somebody is self-identifying in order to make a true statement about herself, this is because a particular gender term is taken as part of her identity. Here, I distinguish between metaphysical and existential self-identity. By metaphysical self-identity, I mean a self-conception that answers the question "What am I?" It involves an overall picture of the world (including categories such as men and women) in which one then locates oneself. By existential self-identity, I mean an answer to the question "Who am I?" where this question is taken in a deep sense. Thus, while "Talia Mae Bettcher" is an answer to the trivial question "Who am I?" it is not an answer to the profound question "Who am I, really?" The question, when taken in full philosophical significance means: What am I about? What moves me? What do I stand for? What do I care about the most?[42] Unlike metaphysical self-identity, existential self-identity is not a *conception* of self. Rather, the fact that one holds all of the beliefs that one holds (true or false, self-regarding or not) goes into the set of facts that determines "who one is, really." Much of one's attitudes, values, and commitment go likewise into making this determination.[43] This falls under the reach of FPA.

The contrast between metaphysical and existential identity is reflected in the difference between the questions "What is a woman?" and "What does it mean to be a woman?" In the spirit of the second, there is a way in which a person can truthfully claim "I am a woman" before any sort of transition *at all*. Similarly, "teacher" and "philosopher" can constitute valid answers to the question "Who am I?" even if one has never been employed as a teacher or a philosopher and, indeed, hasn't spent much time teaching or philosophizing. Perhaps one is an unactualized teacher who has never had the chance to be "who one really is." Admittedly, these issues are deep and may not be perfectly transparent to the first persons themselves. I do not wish to require that deep philosophical reflection is necessary to confer minimal intelligibility on gender self-ascriptions. I do mean that regardless of self-reflection, people are partially guided by what is important to them, which is where existential self-identity is situated.

There are several reasons for employing existential rather than metaphysical self-identity in an explanation of FPA over gender. The latter involves a broad conception of men and women more generally and, consequently, risks running into conflict with the self-conceptions of others. However, it is generally assumed in community interactions that one's self-identity need not be taken to invalidate the self-identity of another, despite a difference in metaphysical views about gender and sex. Existential self-identity involves no such conflict.

Moreover, metaphysical self-identify requires a person's self-identifying claim be false in case they fail to live up to their metaphysical conception or the conception is itself false. For example, if one believes some neurological state makes one a woman and it turns out one lacks this state, it follows one is not a woman. However, it is generally assumed in community interactions that the truth or falsity of a person's self-identifying claim does not stand or fall on such issues. More deeply, metaphysical self-identity places FPA at the wrong level. Whether one conforms to various conceptions of womanhood (which include physical features) is not something open to FPA. One does not, therefore, have FPA over being a woman but only over one's *believing* one is a woman.

Finally, existential rather than metaphysical self-identity illuminates the centrality of reasons in conferring intelligibility on a person's act of self-identifying. One's understanding of what is important is fundamental to one's reasons for acting, and so one's existential self-identity is the anchor of the narrative. While metaphysical narrative can include behavior-governing norms (e.g., I am a woman, I must gender present and self-identify in these ways), it does not explain why these norms should be taken seriously. Only a final appeal to one's existential self-identity can explain this motivation; only an existential self-identity is essentially bound up with reasons for acting.[44]

In defending this view, I don't mean transpeople lack metaphysical self-identities. One can certainly believe one is a woman when believing one conforms to some of the related conceptions of womanhood. Indeed, it is difficult to pull apart metaphysical self-identity from beliefs about one's existential identity. After all, the belief one is a woman may be a belief about both what one is and who one is. My claim is that existential self-identity is far more useful in explaining community recognition of

FPA over gender. It is not whether one conforms to the characteristics one takes to be germane that matters, it is what those beliefs show about "who one is." Understanding the avowal as a statement grounded in existential self-identity involves understanding it within the context of other areas of importance for the first person. This will probably involve the importance of body, and the importance of one's personal history of relatedness to gender, body, and sex. It will also probably involve the significance of the question "What does it mean for me to be a woman?" to one's interpretation of one's past and one's projects for the future. The claim that one is a woman will be true in case womanhood is part of "who the person is, really" and false if it is not. The consequence of this is a person is only a "gender deceiver" on the condition that they misrepresent "who they are, really" rather than if they refuse to indicate their genital status. For in this context, gender presentation does not *represent* anything at all. Rather, its significance is to be understood within the context of the person's reasons for acting and, more specifically, their understanding of who they are.

First-Person Authority Revisited: Knowledge and Power

Situated Knowledge and the Subaltern

In jettisoning practices that connect gender terms to fixed criteria for application, such terms become more like those used for mental attitudes. Words like "anger" are defined in terms of object, cause, and effects; synonyms or closely related attitudes are mentioned. However, there are no clear criteria determining whether a person has a particular attitude. To be sure, there are behaviors that count as evidence. But no symptom is so strong that it cannot be trumped by other considerations. Much depends on a broader understanding of the person (her history of attitudes, her current attitudes, etc.). In effect, third-person assessments of mental attitudes (and gender self-identities) are interpretative in nature. For example, one's self-identification as woman will fail if one does not do so for political reasons about which one is serious, or because womanhood is not part of "who one is, really." Such assessments, however, are not easily determined. They are a matter of complex interpretation.

So caution is required. A person unfamiliar with trans-friendlier contexts approaches avowals of identity in extreme ignorance. I say this not merely because she lacks sufficient acquaintance to provide an interpretation (unlike a close friend) but, more important, because she lacks the cultural resources to identify evidence for or against an interpretation. Suppose an MTF has facial hair (stubble) which she hasn't bothered to shave in several days. Somebody unfamiliar with MTF realities may construe this as sloppiness or lack of care. By contrast, somebody acquainted with the realities of some MTFs will understand she may have had to let her hair grow out for electrolysis.

In addition, metaphysical conceptions underlying terms such as "woman" place constraints on what counts as acceptable interpretations. Yet, despite the overlap between the meaning of gender terms in mainstream and subaltern contexts, there may be sufficient variation to undermine interpretive capacity. "Woman" cannot be completely abstracted from other relevant gender terms that are especially salient in some trans-friendlier contexts, such as "genderqueer," "FTM," and "transwoman." One who does not have a grasp of these latter concepts cannot have a sufficient grasp of the semantic content of "woman" and "man" to be able to assess interpretations of avowed gender.

There is a kind of epistemic authority here. It is not an authority deriving from the way in which a first person knows certain facts about herself. Rather, there is sufficient cultural variability between dominant and resistant contexts that one unacquainted with resistant context is incapable of interpreting self-identifies. Thus, the first-person epistemic advantage is one shared by those who are likewise participants in the culture and speakers of the language. However, to the degree that these contexts involve complex intersections of multiple worlds, there is a more systematic danger of *anyone* making easy assumptions about expertise in interpreting attitudes and behavior across worldly intersections. Such presumption risks arrogance that violates ethical FPA and therefore warrants considerable humility, caution, and attention even among those who think they know their way around.

Despite this ignorance, many from dominant contexts approach transpeople as if they themselves were experts. This sense of expertise is based largely on ignorance of subaltern realities. The expertise concerns only the status of genitalia and its importance in determining the truth of sex and gender. One way this kind of "expertise" can be flexed is through exercises of "clocking people" by drawing on morphological cues (e.g., adam's apple) to make assessments about genital status ("Hey, that's really a man!"). Yet such displays of "expertise" are violations of a transperson's ethical FPA. In order to show this, I move on to consider analogies between invalidations of trans identities and invalidations of women's subjectivity in cases of sexual assault.

First-Person Authority and Rape

To be sure, when a woman's refusal to have sex is disregarded, this may not seem to usurp the woman's first-person authority but an overlooking of her wishes: It is rape. Yet rape is "justified" in particular ways. And when it is justified by an assessment of the victim's attitudes, it is also a violation of FPA. I say this since the ideological assessment is taken as sufficiently authoritative to justify acting against the avowed attitudes of the first person.

Consider the myth that "her mouth says no, but her eyes say yes." One narrative underlying this view is that *no means yes* or, more plainly, that a woman's refusal to have sex isn't a *real* refusal but a coy flirtation. While, thanks to feminist intervention, this is less pervasive, this myth remains salient. A man who disregards a woman's refusal on the basis of this ideology about what women intend to be communicating acts as if his own assessment about her attitudes were authoritative. He demonstrates a lack of respect for the authority of a woman's explicit avowals.

On the face of it, this may not be clear. Sometimes people speak insincerely, and we understand what they mean. One might sarcastically avow in response to the question "Do you want to go out for dinner?" "Nah. I want to stay home alone and eat crackers." If one's partner made reservations for two on the grounds that the avowal wasn't serious, or even that the avowal meant the opposite of what was explicitly said, this would hardly constitute an assault on FPA.

What is important about *no means yes* is that it was (and is) sufficiently pervasive that no room was (and little room is) afforded a woman to avow her intention not to have sex. This is to say that there was no (and is little) allowance made for genuine avowals. This suggests not an assault on the social recognition of ethical first-person authority but the complete absence of it in the first place. In this case, however, it is not merely that men failed (and fail) to respect women's avowals as authoritative by treating their own assessments as authoritative. It is that women had (and in some case still have) no such socially recognized ethical authority to declare their sexual disinterest to begin with. Instead, "knowledge" of women's intensions and desires was strictly (and still is to some degree) ideological in nature.[45]

First-Person Authority and the Basic Denial of Authenticity

Let's now consider the denial of trans FPA. Some women are ideologically taken to deliberately communicate sexual interest through the use of playful refusal. Analogously, since gender presentation and gender terms are taken to communicate genital status, one who "misaligns" presentation and description with genital status is viewed as deliberately deceiving.

In both cases, there is no room for genuine avowal. A "no" means "yes," and a "yes" means "yes": it is impossible for a woman to say "no" and mean it. Given the assumptions that people generally intend to use words to communicate according to standard rules, there is no room in the dominant context for her to *intend* to refuse; a legitimate "no" is not an available to her.

Similarly, gender presentation and gender terms are taken to communicate genital status. This is enforced through violence and other morally objectionable means; persons who do not conform are viewed as liars. This seems inevitable, since if one understands the relationship between gender presentation and genital status (and therefore how others will interpret one's presentation) and one knows one's own genital status, it seems to follow that one intentionally misleads when gender-presenting is in "misalignment" with genital status.

When the intention to deceive isn't attributed because the transperson is "out," s/he is seen as confused about the basic facts. At its most extreme, this amounts to the view that s/he is mentally ill. Transpeople have been historically relegated to objects of investigation, where any capacity to avow has been disabled under the socially recognized authority of the medical scientist. Here no room is allowed for any genuine avowals; speech is taken as mere evidence for the authoritative interpretations of experts.[46]

A less extreme view is that s/he is in some way childlike, clueless about the realities of the world. As a child might approach her mother with a toy stethoscope around her neck and say, "Look, mommy, I am doctor!" so, too, a transperson may be seen as confused about the difference between reality and pretense. While playing along, "the adult" knows this person is confusing pretense with reality; she knows something the "child" does not. Thus, a mental attitude is attributed. S/he is taken to confuse pretense with reality (despite the fact that transpeople know full well how they are viewed by others).

Overall, what is annihilated is not merely the resistant refusal to disclose genital status but one's very reasons for acting and possibly the profound significance of gender presentation and self-identification to the transperson herself. There is no room for such reasons or self-identifications in this situation. Instead, the claim "You are really a man" has a similar force to "You want to go home now" insofar as it denies trans reasons for acting. The former seems worse than the latter, however, for at least two reasons. First, "You are really a man" is an abusive claim about genitalia. Second, this claim silences a transperson's avowal of existential self-identity. Together, we find utilization of sexual abuse to raze a person's sense of who she is at the deepest level. To the extent that such verbal violations are backed up by physical violence and sexual assault, they are like the assault on FPA found in cases of sexual and domestic violence.

Moreover, the authoritative force of such verbal violations is supported by the many forms of sociality that govern mainstream contexts. The authority to determine gender flows from the overall cultural conception and organization of gender, quite similar to cases in which avowals of sexual disinterest either have the force of avowing sexual interest or count for nothing. Since these denials of FPA are ideologically driven and institutional in nature, it is little wonder the possibility for trans resistance emerges only within subaltern contexts.[47] Any work for altering practices within dominant contexts amounts to undermining those social practices that preclude our subjectivity there.

Concluding Remarks: Trans and Feminist Theory

Sandy Stone's intention was to end monolithic accounts of transpeople by opening up possibilities of multiple trans-authored stories. In this essay, I attempt to stay true to her vision by articulating what it is for transpeople to come to voice. In elucidating the transformation of the high-risk game of circulating information about genital status to the social conferral of ethical first-person authority on transpeople, I hope to have shown that the basis for such authority resides in the ultimate priority of ethical considerations over metaphysical and epistemological ones.

In addition, this essay yields important results for nontrans theorizing about gender. Deployments of terms such as "woman" and "female" are political acts even within the context of theorizing. To be sure, there are truths about bodies. Yet such truths can be expressed without the notion of sex. And once this notion is deployed within the context of the natural attitude, one has engaged in discourse that depends on the communicative system of genitalia as gender referent. Unsurprisingly, in everyday discourse, "female" and "male" are often used as *synonyms* for "woman" and "man." While specialized discourses many promise a purer, technically restricted use of terms, the broader context remains salient. Given this inevitable "tarnish," it is a political question whether using expressions like "physical sex" is wise, unless grounded in practices that afford FPA.

From a trans perspective, deployment of gender and sex terms is highly political, and accounts that reach verdicts about the appropriate (metaphysical or political) deployment of gender categories without attending to trans voices erases trans subjectivities. As I have previously argued, feminist and trans theory and politics are scarcely at odds.[48] So any nontrans feminist theorizing engaged in this erasure would have to ignore the intersections. From a trans perspective, such theorizing would be threatening; the authoritative determination of gender category application only reinstates the contrast between appearance and reality (with politically determined group membership replacing genital status as "reality"). Such theorizing could support the very gender and sex communication system that promotes, facilitates, and justifies violence against women.

As I also hope to have shown, however, there are deep similarities between violations of FPA in sexual violence against women and in denials of trans self-identity claims. One important theme is the connection between intimate (sexual and mental) gender violation and resistant selves. In this essay, therefore, I continue the project of outlining some common ground for antiracist trans and feminist theorizing, as well as for authentic personal empathy and mutual comprehension.

NOTES

Thanks to Susan Forrest, Ann Garry, Jacob Hale, Maria Karafilis, and Laurie Shrage for their helpful suggestions, criticisms, and insights.

1. Sandy Stone, "The *Empire* Strikes Back: A Posttransexual Manifesto," in *Body Guards: The Cultural Politics of Gender Ambiguity*, ed. J. Epstein and K. Straub (New York: Routledge, 1991), pp. 280–304.

2. Here, *MTF* refers to individuals assigned male at birth whose gender presentation may be construed female, and *FTM* refers to individuals assigned female at birth whose gender presentation may be construed male. *Transperson* applies to FTMs and MTFs alike, as well as some people who present gender not easily intelligible. I do not attribute identity.

3. As I argue, in mainstream contexts the sex–gender contrast involves an abusive system by which the private sexual body is represented through gender presentation, while in trans-friendlier contexts this is not present in the same way or to the same degree. This raises deep worries about uncritical deployments of the concept "sex." See "Concluding Remarks" in this essay.

4. María Lugones, "Playfulness, 'World'-Travelling and Loving Perception," *Hypatia* 2, no. 2 (1987), pp. 3–19, reprinted in Lugones, *Pilgrimages/Peregrinajes: Theorizing Coalition against Multiple Oppressions* (New York: Rowman and Littlefield, 2003).

5. There are important limitations to my approach. What counts as mainstream or resistant is informed by blended aspects of domination. For example, in analyzing mainstream gender and sex, I focus on English discursive practices. It isn't obvious to what degree my analysis applies to other languages. More generally, gender and sex practices vary culturally, and the ones that I discuss prevail in the United States. Again, it is not clear how far my analysis extends; at least to the degree to which these practices are exported, a colonial dimension

may be attributed to them. And there are contexts involving resistance in one aspect but not another. There are trans-friendlier worlds only friendlier for white transpeople and racially resistant worlds oppressing transpeople of color. As my account fails to fully address such complexity, it is inherently limited.

6. Talia Mae Bettcher, "Appearance, Reality, and Gender Deception: Reflections on Transphobic Violence and the Politics of Pretence," in *Violence, Victims, and Justifications*, ed. Felix Ó Murchadha (New York: Peter Lang, 2006).

7. Following Crispin Wright, I distinguish "phenomenal avowal" and "attitudinal avowal" (Crispin Wright, "Self-Knowledge: The Wittgensteinian Legacy," in *Knowing Our Own Minds*, ed. Crispin Wright, Barry C. Smith, and Cynthia Macdonald [New York: Oxford University Press, 1998], pp. 13–45).

8. In Richard Moran's view, epistemic authority is grounded in one's authorship of attitudes. Attitudes are "up to the agent," as exemplified by making up one's mind. In deliberating, one reflects on attitudinal objects rather than the attitudes about them (hence immediacy). The entitlement to knowledge derives from the rational demand that one "be able to make up one's mind and have it count for something." Moran's account has the advantage of answering the problem discussed in the following note (Moran, *Authority and Estrangement: An Essay on Self-Knowledge* [Princeton: Princeton University Press, 2001]).

9. Crispin Wright defends this position. A more skeptical view maintains there is no self-knowledge at all. "Cartesianism" involves a *perceptual model* of self-knowledge. If this model is rejected, then a mystery is generated: if avowals are *immediate*, what could ground them, short of experience?

10. Wright, "Self-Knowledge," p. 41.

11. For Wright, people cannot be chronically unreliable in avowing their attitudes owing to the constraints built into the very truth-conditions of psychological ascriptions (ibid.).

12. Moran makes a similar point: it is a demand of rationality that a person be able to state her attitudes as the result of deliberation (Moran, *Authority and Estrangement*, p. 24).

13. There are cases of avowal that do not seem to involve anything especially "private." Consider, for example, that one is asked to choose between two items in a catalogue: "Which one do you prefer?" The answer "I prefer this one" does not really seem to involve the confession of something especially private. Indeed, there is a way in which the entire reference to one's attitudes can be eliminated in the exchange. Nonetheless, it seems to me clear that the issue of *autonomy* remains important.

14. J. L. Austin, *How to Do Things with Words* (Cambridge: Harvard University Press, 1962). A *locutionary act* involves saying something; an *illocutionary act* of doing something *in* saying something (e.g., warning); a *perlocutionary act* of doing something *by* saying something (e.g., alarming). The latter is determined by the effect caused in a speaker, while the former is determined by convention. The *illocutionary act* is the *force* of the locutionary act. I follow Judith Butler's work in drawing on the work of Austin in gender and queer theory (Judith Butler, "Critically Queer," in *Bodies That Matter: On the Discursive Limits of "Sex"*[New York: Routledge, 1993], pp. 222–43). While I do not have the space to provide a contrast between our views, I do offer comments at notes 27, 30, 37, and 44.

15. I owe this example to Susan Forrest.

16. Even in cases in which there is no avowal of private attitudes involved (see note 13), the attempt of a second person to avow on the first person's behalf would be "ungrammatical" and controlling.

17. Harold Garfinkel, *Studies in Ethnomethodology* (Oxford: Polity Press, 1957), pp. 122–33. See also Suzanne Kessler and Wendy McKenna, *Gender: An Ethnomethodological Approach* (New York: Wiley, 1978), pp. 113–14; Kate Bornstein, *Gender Outlaw: On Men and Women and the Rest of Us* (New York: Routledge, 1994), pp. 45–51; and C. Jacob Hale, "Are Lesbians Women?" *Hypatia: Journal of Feminist Philosophy*) 11, no. 2 (1996), pp. 94–121.

18. Joan Roughgarden, *Evolution's Rainbow: Diversity, Gender, and Sexuality in Nature and People* (Los Angeles: University of California Press, 2004), p. 26.

19. Anne Fausto-Sterling distinguishes herms ("true hermaphrodites"), ferms ("pseudo-hermaphrodites"), and merms ("male pseudohermaphrodites"). These three, plus male and female, yield five sexes. Her proposal is intended as a political-social intervention (Anne Fausto-Sterling, *Sexing the Body: Gender Politics and the Construction of Sexuality* [New York: Basic, 2000]).

20. Ibid., p. 4. See also Jennifer McKitrick, "Gender Identity Disorder," in *Establishing Medical Reality: Essays in the Metaphysics and Epistemology of Biomedical Science*, ed. Harold Kincaid and Jennifer McKitrick (Dordrecht: Springer, 2007), 144–45.

21. Hale, "Are Lesbians Women?" p. 132.

22. Hale provides a related argument (ibid., p. 112).

23. Ibid. Cressida Heyes offers a similar account in *Line Drawings: Defining Women through Feminist Practice* (Cornell: Cornell University Press, 2000), pp. 83–96. See also McKitrick, "Gender Identity Disorder."

24. Hale leaves open the possibility that there are multiple concepts of woman.

25. C. Jacob Hale, "Leather Dyke Boys and Their Daddies: How to Have Sex without Men and Women," *Social Text* 52/53 (1997), pp. 223–36, at p. 223.

26. This account is similar to a family-resemblance analysis since there are overlapping features linking different metaphysical conceptions of woman. However, analyses that abstract these features cannot account for the way different features work together in specific conceptions of womanhood to yield normative assessments.

27. Butler starts with the heterosexist conceit that queer presentations of gender (e.g., butch and femme) are imitative of the original (i.e., heterosexuality). I start with the transphobic conceit that transpeople are deceivers or pretenders. The latter doesn't concern an original or imitation of a contrast between gender appearance and sex reality.

28. *Gender presentation* means not only gendered attire but also gesture, posture, manner of speech, and socially interactive style. *Sexed body* means physical characteristics such as genitals, breast tissue, facial and body hair, fat distribution, height, bone width, and so forth. I intend for this distinction to admit of blurriness.

29. Talia Mae Bettcher, "Evil Deceivers and Make-Believers: On Transphobic Violence and the Politics of Illusion," *Hypatia: Journal of Feminist Philosophy* 22, no. 3 (Summer 2007), pp. 43–65.

30. For Butler, while gender is taken as expressive of an internal psyche, the unity of the substance is performatively constituted through acts of repetition or citations of gender norms: the subject is the effect rather than the cause of gender. For me, the relationship between gender presentation and genitalia (rather than "the subject") is communicative (rather than expressive or performative) in nature. Although I *do* think that the existence of this relationship itself is what constitutes genitalia as the reality of sex, I do not think that gender presentation brings about this status as signifier through repetition.

31. For further discussion, see Bettcher, "Evil Deceivers and Make-Believers." However, even there my discussion is incomplete. In my view, these issues are deep: they connect in very important ways to the very notion of a person. I do not have space to develop these themes here.

32. Buttocks and female breasts are coded private, so more complexity is required. There are different grounds for privacy besides the sexual one, and there are degrees to which body parts are regarded as private. I do not develop the significance of grounds for privacy (given in background ideology) in this essay. The themes here are connected to the ones mentioned in the preceding note.

33. The split between presentation and genitalia provides a basis for the distinction between sex and gender. This is not to claim that sex is the unconstructed substrate of constructed gender. Rather, the possibility of distinguishing sex and gender is the product of the cultural fact that gender functions as the representation of concealed referent. The denial of a sex/gender distinction needs to admit the possibility that that very sex/gender distinction is part of the social construction.

34. Sometimes "karyotype" is deployed to defend a modified natural attitude where surgically constructed genitalia are artificial and genital status is determined by birth genitalia (Bettcher, "Evil Deceivers and Make-Believers").

35. Hale, "Are Lesbians Women?" p. 103.

36. I believe there are important lessons here for applications of philosophy of language to trans community contexts, and perhaps for philosophy of language more generally. Since this is not central to my agenda in this essay, I do not further develop these themes here.

37. For Butler, such self-identifying claims performatively constitute oneself as a particular kind of subject (within an identity category). I suggest that such claims can involve other functions such as circulation of genital status.

38. In some cases there might be a disclosure of genital status. Suppose our transperson has had genital reconstruction surgery. Then she may be taking up the standard way of disclosing genital status. Thanks to Susan Forrest for this point.

39. The reason the philosophical notion of FPA concerns mental states is that it primarily concerns epistemology. The view is that a first person can have a special knowledge over her own mental life that does not extend to physical traits. While she might be better acquainted with the latter than anybody else, she does not have a special kind of epistemic access in the same way that she seems to have a special access to some of her own mental states. This special access is captured in the notion of "immediacy" discussed above. However, if my argument that FPA ought to be understood principally as an ethical (rather than an epistemic notion), then there is also a way in which FPA can be expanded to include one's body as well. In both cases, one has certain personal rights of privacy (over bodily and mental information), and the attempt to deny or undermine these rights constitutes a violation of FPA.

40. McKitrick, "Gender Identity Disorder," pp. 140, 142.

41. I owe this point to Hale. More generally, discussions with him have stimulated and informed my thinking about difficulties related to gender self-conception and the use of gender self-conception in determining gender category membership.

42. This position is similar in spirit to Hale's suggestion that self-conceptions be put to the side in favor of political and ethical values (C. Jacob Hale, "Tracing a Ghostly Memory in My Throat: Reflections on Ftm Feminist Voice and Agency," in *Men Doing Feminism*, ed. T. Digby [New York: Routledge, 1998], pp. 99–129; reprinted as chap. 3 in this volume).

43. Naomi Zack discusses connected issues in "Race, Life, Death, Identity, Tragedy, and Good Faith," in *Existence in Black: An Anthology of Black Existential Philosophy*, ed. Lewis R. Gordon (New York: Routledge, 1997), pp. 99–109.

44. For Butler, resistance emerges from the possibility of variation in acts of repetition. She specifically commends the use of gender to make explicit its inherently imitative quality. I see resistance in new trans practices of FPA over gender, which are free from the abusive circulation of genital status.

45. Rae Langton and Jennifer Hornsby defend a related position (Rae Langton, "Speech Acts and Unspeakable Acts," *Philosophy and Public Affairs* 22, no. 4 [1993], 229–330, Jennifer Hornsby and Rae Langton, "Free Speech and Illocution," *Legal Theory* 4, no. 1, [1998], 21–37). In their view, pornography silences women by disabling the illocutionary force of a woman's "no." An objection is the concern that if there is no genuine refusal, there can be no genuine rape. Another objection is that the Hornsby/Langton position assumes that a genuine refusal requires that the "uptake" of the speaker's intent on the part of the hearer (Alexander Bird, "Illocutionary Silencing," *Pacific Philosophical Quarterly* 83 [2002], pp. 1–15). In my view, the issues run deeper than the disabling of refusal: they concern the disabling of a woman's first-person authority over her own mental states. More correctly, rather than suggesting a "disabling," I suggest that as a matter of social convention (quite independent of an individual's interpretation) women's avowals of sexual disinterest were and are broadly not allowed insofar as the force of "I don't want to have sex" was and is conventionally taken as a playful act, if anything at all. From this, it does not follow that the daily rapes that constituted normal sex were not real rapes. Rather, they were not rapes within the dominant ideology. This is why I represent the view that "no means no" as political intervention rather than as an observation. This is suggestive of the ways in which "subjects" are "constituted" by cultural practices. I do not pursue the point here.

The issues are deeply bound up with race. To put it crudely, the institution of *no means yes* within a game of flirtation has applied historically to white women more predominantly. Contrast this with racist representation of black women as "Jezebels" (who never say no). To the extent that black women's "avowals" have historically been disregarded entirely on the basis of an ideology that depersonalizes, there is a more radical denial of first-person authority that is instituted on the basis of a racist ideology. For more, see Patricia Hill Collins, "The Sexual Politics of Black Womanhood," in *Black Feminist Thought: Knowledge, Consciousness, and the Politics of Empowerment*, 2nd ed. (Routledge: New York, 2000), pp. 123–48. In this essay, I have not developed these issues in any depth. They connect in important ways to the connection between privacy of the body and the notion of personhood (alluded to in note 32). This is a much larger topic that needs the full space of an independent article.

46. The analogy with racist depersonalization is clear here.

47. Lugones represents oppression as inescapable within the dominant ideology: resistance emerges through consciousness of one's existence in multiple worlds (Maria Lugones, "Structure, Anti-Structure: Agency under Oppression," *Journal of Philosophy* 87, no. 10 (1990), pp. 500–507, reprinted in María Lugones, *Pilgrimages/Peregrinajes: Theorizing Coalition against Multiple Oppressions* (New York: Rowman and Littlefield, 2003).

48. Bettcher, "Evil Deceivers and Make-Believers."

7

Queer Breasted Experience

Kim Q. Hall

One of the great achievements of feminist theory and activism is its critique of the patriarchal medicalization of the female body, a critique that bears some similarity to the critique of the medical model by disability studies, queer theory, and both queer and disability rights movements. From the perspective of feminism, queer theory, and disability studies, medical models have made visible, categorized, observed, pathologized, and exerted control over the body in ways that have been harmful for all marginalized groups. For example, just as feminists have criticized the medical community's patriarchal distortions of female bodily processes (such as pregnancy) and female anatomy (such as the vagina), disability studies asks us to rethink how disability has been marked by the medical model as bodily anomaly in need of correction or cure. Similarly, queer theorists critique the medical model's diagnosis of transgender bodies as the product of Gender Identity Disorder: a patriarchal characterization of transgender bodies as "abnormal" bodies due to their failure to conform to binary gender norms.

In their criticisms of medical distortions of "normal" female anatomy and physiology, feminists have increased awareness of how female bodily experience is mediated by patriarchal medical discourse. In place of these patriarchal medical narratives, feminist theorists and health care practitioners emphasize the need for women to feel proud about what they contend is natural to female bodies. For instance, in writing about breast health, Dr. Susan Love points out that feeling comfortable and acquainted with one's breasts enables women to better monitor their own breast health and eases entrance into puberty for young girls:

> Little girls should be encouraged to know their breasts, so that when the changes of puberty come about, they can experience their growing breasts with comfort and pride, and continue to do so for the rest of their lives. Most of us have not been raised

that way, however, and it's often hard for an adult woman to begin feeling comfortable with her breasts. Yet it's important to become acquainted with your breasts—to know what they feel like and what to expect from them. No part of your body should be foreign to you. (Love 2000, 25–26)

To a certain extent, Love is right, and her book undoubtedly continues to help many women become better-informed advocates for their own breast health. Still, there is something that troubles me about her discussion, especially the last sentence: "No part of your body should be foreign to you."

What troubles me is an assumption that I argue also informs many feminist efforts to reclaim and reconfigure female breasted experience on women's own terms: namely, the assumption that the body with which one is born is unambiguously one's own and that oppression is the only thing that prohibits this realization and, hence, a more healthy self-concept and embodiment. On the one hand, some feminists argue that prioritizing the lived connections between one's female body and the world (that is, female bodied experience) can forge a path out of alienation from one's body and hence one's self. From this perspective, a feminist project is for women to reclaim their breasts as important parts of their selves. But what are the implications of this feminist project of reclamation for female-bodied people who identify as men and who experience their bodies as male?[1] If not all female-bodied people understand and experience "their" breasts as central to their being in the world and identity, what are we to make of a feminist project of reclamation of alienated female body parts?

I seek to explore these questions in the context of feminist writing about breast cancer and female-to-male transsexual mastectomy. As I see it, the central issue regarding breasted experience, surgery, and identity is not whether the desire for prosthesis, breast reconstruction, or mastectomy is a result of false consciousness, which previously has been *the* question for many feminist theorists who have pondered this issue. Instead, the issue is more complex and involves grappling with the following questions: If, following Judith Butler, the sexed body (like gender) is a discursive construction, in what sense, if any, do women *have* breasts? Moreover, what does it mean to assume that breasts (or other so-called female body parts) are indicative of true *female* sex? What does it *mean* to say that no part of one's body should be foreign to one's self? And if there is a part of one's body that is experienced as foreign to one's self, why should the assumed solution be reacquainting oneself with and learning to love the alien body part? In the course of considering the significance of these questions, I propose Audre Lorde's *The Cancer Journals* as not simply a feminist model for women who are making decisions about breast cancer treatment but as a way of thinking about bodies, embodiments, and identities that troubles and crosses the boundary of binary gender, as well as about the creative possibilities of queer spaces that are essential for the emergence of unruly bodies. While gendered bodily experience is certainly mediated by hegemonic discourse, it is also mediated by lived experience in alternative communities, communities that form part of the horizon of possible gendered bodily experience and identity.

Rather than merely describe and critique forms of oppression experienced by women and female-to-male transpeople, I want to turn my attention to how a queer crip² feminist approach to sexed and gendered embodiment points to possibilities of resistance and creativity. Instead of focusing on how our bodies *are* our selves, I consider how we *make* our bodies our selves and, and in the process, move toward a more inclusive and transformative feminist politics of the body. Specifically, I reflect on what many take to be an unquestionably female bodily experience—namely, breasted experience—in order to question the idea that breasts provide a metaphysical ground for defining women. Far from being irrelevant to the lives of real women, as many critics contend, I hope to show that raising questions about the relationship between being a woman and having breasts attempts to conceptualize sex and gender in ways that take account of real people whose bodies and experiences defy the assumption of dualistic sex and gender (FTM transpeople, female-bodied men, butch lesbians, bois, leatherdyke daddies, etc.).

Given my argument in this essay against the biologization of sex and gender identity, my use of terms such as *female-bodied man* might appear contradictory to some. In other words, does my use of this term imply that transmen have a true sex after all? This term may indeed point to a need for new sex and gender concepts to reflect queer identities and embodiments. Nonetheless, my use of female-bodied men in this article is not intended as a claim that there is a true sex that underlies queer efforts to create and live new gendered and sexed identities and bodies.

Further, the term *female-bodied man* is used by some (although not all) transmen to describe their sense of their own identity. It is important to acknowledge that not all terms are considered accurate or adequate by all transpersons. While some transmen might have no problem with the term *female-bodied men*, others might object to the notion that "female-bodied" accurately represents their lived bodily experience and identity. Some transmen also use the term *biomen* to distinguish between their male identities and those of men who were marked as male at birth and subsequently recognized and socialized as boys who will become men. In all cases, I think it is extremely important for theorists to acknowledge and respect the names individuals in marginalized communities choose for themselves, especially given oppressed groups' experiences of being named by others, often to their detriment. Many trans activists and theorists critique the term "transsexual" for this reason, just as many gay and lesbian theorists have critiqued the term "homosexual." So, on the one hand, it's important to acknowledge that this term accurately captures some people's trans bodily experience. As C. Jacob Hale (1997) points out, terms for queer identities and embodiments have been and continue to be forged within queer communities, and within those communities queers are creating new modes of bodily being and relationship, along with the terms that seem to best capture their identity and experience in a given historical moment. Equally important, I believe, is the need to acknowledge, as Judith Halberstam (1998) does, that so-called biomen do not own masculinity or maleness. There are, in fact, myriad, emerging ways of living one's maleness and masculinity. Thus, I use terms such as *female-bodied people* and *female-bodied men* to highlight the inadequacy of binary understandings of sex and gender for understanding body parts and their relationship to sex and gender identity.

My approach draws on the work of scholars such as Michel Foucault, Judith Butler, Jacob Hale, and Simi Linton, who point to the role of non-dominant communities in the reconfiguration of one's embodied self. Foucault, for instance, argued that what the gay liberation movement needed was an "art of life," by which he meant an ethics and politics of becoming, of creating our bodies, communities, relationships, and selves (Foucault 1990, 163). Foucault's emphasis on the creative, transformative potential of queer communities and politics is echoed in Judith Butler's claim that norms of identity and embodiment make possible certain ways of life while simultaneously excluding others, and in order for feminist politics and theory to be transformative, it must be based on an ethics and politics of becoming, open to the ongoing process of gender transformation within queer communities. Feminists must, according to Butler, "expand our capacity to imagine the human" (Butler 2004, 228). Regarding gendered embodiment, I contend, queer disability perspectives have much to bring to a feminist project that expands our capacity to imagine male and female bodies beyond a binary and reproductive model.

Histories of Making Sex

Numerous scholars have revealed how the meaning of sexual difference has shifted historically, and their revelations have profoundly influenced feminist theorizing about the sexed body. For instance, Londa Schiebinger offers evidence that the female skeleton came into being between 1730 and 1790 with the first drawings of them in Europe (Schiebinger 1989, 191). Obviously, this does not mean that there were some bodies with no skeletons prior to the eighteenth century! Shiebinger's point is in the eighteenth century, science and medicine strove to show that sex difference permeated the body, that differences between male and female bodies could be found not only in genitalia but also in the blood, musculature, and bones (ibid.). There was an effort to show that every part of the body was evidence for its sex.

In his book, *Making Sex: Body and Gender from the Greeks to Freud*, Thomas Laqueur provides a history of sexual difference and shows how what many now assume to indelibly mark the body as either male or female has not always been perceived as bodily evidence for sexual difference. Sexual difference, he contends, became a fact about the body only when it became politically important to provide evidence to justify the subordination of women in society (Laqueur 1990, 10). The "one sex" model perceived all sex characteristics as shared between men and women, even if they were distributed differently; sex itself only emerged as an ontological category in the eighteenth century (6, 8). In the nineteenth century, the belief that sexual difference could be seen even on the microscopic level was established. The more minute the bodily evidence, the more real and distinct the differences between the sexes.

Lest we be tempted to think such musings are simply the result of poor or outdated scientific method (rather than ideological assumptions that inform the practice of the science of sex itself) the search for the truth of sexual difference in the body persists today. One example is the ongoing effort to distinguish between "male" and "female" brains. Recently (in 2006), I watched a documentary about sex differences and the brain that aired on PBS. The subject of the documentary was a study of five women and five men who were placed in certain situations such as competitive go-cart driving, unexpected conversations with a taxi driver, watching a news program, and changing a diaper. The self-identified men and women were observed as they conducted themselves in these situations and later asked questions about what they had done. In one particularly troublesome scene, the men and women were asked to watch the same news program but in sex-segregated rooms. There were two news anchors on the program: one man and one woman. After the program, both groups were asked to report what they had heard. Not one single man could remember what the anchorwoman had said. All they could remember were various details about her appearance such as her breast size, her age, and her attractiveness. By contrast, they were able to remember various pieces of what the male reporter had actually said. In contrast, the women were able to report some of what both the man and woman had said. The documentary concluded that these differences in response to the news program are rooted in biological, not social, differences between men and women.[3]

In their critiques of the science of sexual difference, neither Laqueur nor Schiebinger denies that there are physical differences between bodies. Instead, they question what it means to understand the differences as unmediated markers of true sex. From their point of view, something much more than mere description of what is seen is occurring; they observe that in the attempt to describe those bodily attributes that most differentiate between male and female bodies, medicine and science have ignored the wide spectrum and complexity of anatomical and physiological variation, the ambiguities found within what is understood to be male and female. By drawing the boundary between the sexes in such as way as to heighten differences between males and females, medicine and science have, for the most part, erased those complexities within sex categories that challenge the very ground for distinction between them.

In her book *Hermphrodites and the Medical Invention of Sex* Alice Dreger shows how efforts to naturalize sexual difference have depended on the pathologization and elimination of the "questionable" body—namely, the intersex body. Even our efforts to draw the boundary between males and females on the basis of chromosomal or hormonal make-up are fraught with complexities that make it difficult to justify a binary understanding of sex as biologically, rather than ideologically, based. Regarding hormones, Dreger points out:

> [T]he "sex" hormones don't divide simply into two kinds, "male" and "female." Men and women produce the same kinds of hormones, though usually in different relative quantities, but we know that all girls' and women's bodies do not uniformly produce a single, identifiable "feminine" cocktail of hormones, nor do all boys and men produce a single, identifiable sort of "masculine" cocktail. (Dreger 1998, 7)

And, more to the point of my concern with breasts, while many consider breasts to be a marker of the female body, it is no clear matter at which point a breast becomes a properly female breast. There are, for instance, self-identified men who have breasts that are more full than the breasts of many self-identified women. And there are female bodies that do not have breasts.

Making Our Bodies Our Selves

Ultimately, the relationship between the body and one's self—or, specifically, the relationship between the body and gendered identity and experience—is, I contend, best understood as a process in which we make our bodies our selves. Sex (by which I mean our understanding of anatomical and physiological differences as male and female) is not the ground that ultimately settles the matter of gender identity. It is, rather, gender that makes sex intelligible. Of course, I am not the first person to make this latter claim. Indeed, this essay locates itself in the midst of a long-standing feminist debate about whether there are really women and men, female bodies and male bodies. What I hope to add to this discussion is an understanding of how questions about the materiality of sex do in fact arise, as have the best feminist analyses, from real embodied experiences in the world. Those feminists who have argued against Butler's contention that sex, like gender, is a product of discourse argue that such a claim offers little that can help women in the "real world." Some go as far as to say that feminist efforts to question the materiality of both sex and gender, and in particular to denaturalize sex, ultimately undermine feminist activism to improve the lives of all women and girls. If there are no women, such feminists claim, how is it possible to make visible a pattern of women's oppression and to mobilize women in the interest of feminist liberation?

Most recently, Linda Alcoff claims that there is a way to provide "an objective basis" for sexed identity that does not reproduce essentialist conceptions of women. She argues for a distinction between biological determinism and a lived relationship to biological possibility that will be different for women and men. She identifies the difference between women and men in terms of "their different relationship of possibility to biological reproduction, with biological reproduction referring to conceiving, giving birth, breast-feeding, involving one's own body" (Alcoff 2006, 172). Alcoff stresses that female biological possibility does not mean that all women can or should reproduce; her point is that being female is determined by the fact that females are expected to use their bodies in reproduction in ways that males are not (172). It is the historically contingent social, political, and economic forces of these expectations, rooted in perceived biological possibility, that establish the ground of real sexual difference according to Alcoff.

Alcoff's account is interesting, and she agrees that feminists should "develop a hermeneutics of suspicion in regard to what looks natural" (171). However, when considered from the perspective of trans embodiment, her claim that there are female and male horizons of experience grounded in biological sexual difference does not account for the experiences of female-bodied and male-bodied people who do not contend with expectations in ways that she describes. Writing about his experiences as a transman in leatherdyke communities, Hale emphasizes how queer embodied identities are made possible through a queer community discourse that exceeds theoretical discourse: "These community discourses sometimes reflect rich and subtly nuanced embodiments of gender that resist and exceed any simple categorization into female, male, woman, man, and thus into homosexual, bisexual, and heterosexual" (Hale 1997, 223). For Hale, participation in leatherdyke communities disrupts dominant understandings of body parts, such as genitals, that are assumed to settle the question about what sex a person really is and whether one's body is male or female (230). Hale understands sadomasochism as a "gender technology" enabling a transformation of one's embodied self, and claims, "who I 'really' am is a matter of social/cultural facts about my categorical locations; there is facticity here, but it is not natural or essential and is continually changing as culturally available categories change and as I change relative to them" (229).

Similarly, writing about the transformative potential of disability communities, Simi Linton contrasts demarcations of disability and able-bodied in the rehab center, where patients were disabled and staff were not, with those in the Center for Independent Living (CIL) (Linton 2006, 50). The CIL, for Linton, was "a universe" where everyone had a significant impairment and that bustled with business and noise. It was "a disability underground" where dominant meanings of disability were subverted (50–51). Foucault on the art of life and self, Butler on the transformative openness of the human, Hale, and Linton—all illuminate the creative force of queer crip feminist communities, a force that enables the reconfiguration and transformation of the meaning of one's body parts and functions and their relation to one's self.

Queer Breasted Experience

Audre Lorde once dreamed of an army of one-breasted women descending on the U.S. Congress, demanding adequate funds and information for breast cancer prevention: an army of one-breasted women outraged at breast cancer, responding to an undeclared war against women. Lorde raged against the invisibility of women who had survived or who were in the midst of their struggle with breast cancer, an invisibility conditioned as much by the wearing of a prosthesis to hide a mastectomy as by the absence of prevention information. As she opted not to wear a prosthesis, Lorde searched specifically for the dykes, the black lesbian feminists with breast cancer, but found no role models. In admirable characteristic fashion, Lorde transformed the silence, pain, and anger she experienced into *The Cancer Journals* (1980) in an effort to deconstruct and reconstruct her experience with breast cancer and mastectomy and hopefully provide a model for black lesbian feminists and dykes in general who would have to wage their own battles with breast cancer. To be sure, the most immediate concern for Lorde as she recorded her experiences in her journal was to find a way to inhabit her new, one-breasted body.

Since Lorde, some such as Diane Price Herndl have critiqued what they perceive to be essentialist feminist critiques of surgery. Contrary to Lorde, Herndl chooses breast reconstruction and, in the process, critiques Lorde's decision to forgo prosthesis as based on a notion of a natural body that must be accepted without technological alteration. Arguably, Lorde's one-breasted body is also a body shaped by technology; however, the purpose of this essay is not to speculate about whether feminists should or shouldn't opt for reconstructive surgery or prosthesis. In her interpretation of Lorde's decision to remain visibly one-breasted, Herndl criticizes what she perceives to be Lorde's equation of breast reconstruction or prosthesis with a desire to be a conventionally feminine woman who succumbs to treating her body as an aesthetic object (Herndl 2002, 145). I suggest that it is, in fact, possible to understand Lorde's choice to remain visibly one-breasted as something other than a choice to identify with a natural, unaltered, essential female body. Both Lorde and Herndl made decisions to make their bodies their selves; and they made these decisions based on embodied experience and identity shaped within the context of different communities. I'm interested in what Lorde's account reveals about the possibility and meaning of queer breasted experience, a possibility that I believe has been overlooked in feminist accounts of breasted experience.

Other feminists such as Iris Marion Young[4] have critiqued both the failure to understand how mastectomy damages a woman's subjectivity and how attempts to hide a post-mastectomy body represent conformity to a patriarchal standard of how female breasts should appear and function. Breasts, like vaginas, are frequently assumed to be a common denominator uniting women across differences of age, class, ethnicity, nationality, and sexuality. To be a woman is to be female-bodied, and to be female-bodied is to have breasts. In her essay, "Breasted Experience: The Look and the Feeling," Young offers a phenomenological analysis of breasts and female subjectivity. She argues that, given the centrality of breasts to women's experiences of themselves and their bodies as female, women in a significant sense *are* their breasts (Young 2005, 204). The ability to make one's own body an unfamiliar and despised object is what Young takes to be one of the many ways in which patriarchy profoundly harms women. Because women are their breasts, the objectification of them (a move epitomized for Young in breast augmentation surgery) is an assault on women's subjectivity, a subjectivity that necessitates being able to be in one's body and to experience that body as one's own. Interestingly, Young makes an exception for breast-reduction surgery, a surgery that she argues is based on women's subjective experience of their bodies to the extent that its presumed purpose is to relieve back pain and other discomforts that can accompany having large breasts. Alternatively, she contends that the decision to enlarge breasts is based on satisfying male desire, an experience of one's breasts as objects.

Further, it is the development of breasts, along with the onset of menstruation, that signals the sexual maturity of females in western sociocultural contexts. And, as Young observes, it is precisely this fact that contributes to many young women's feelings of discomfort, embarrassment, and horror at the development of their breasts. While Young doesn't mention this, these feelings can be even more intense for many butch lesbians and female-to-male transpeople.

What I find troubling about Young's account of female breasted experience is her assumption, like Love's, that all female-bodied people will somehow be liberated, less alienated, if they learn to love their female bodies as they are, unless those bodies cause physical discomfort. Such an assumption ignores the complex relationship between gender identities and sexed bodies and the embodied experiences of many intersexed people, butch lesbians, and transmen. That female-bodied people may feel ambivalent about their breasts or not understand their breasts as an unambiguous part of their selves is not the result of individual pathology; it is a consequence of living and forging an identity in a society that recognizes only what it can see and, in the face of incongruence, seeks to normalize the body by enforcing symmetry between gender and the body.

Young's essay, "Breasted Experience," is the only attempt with which I am familiar to offer a phenomenology of breasted experience, and my own efforts here owe a great debt to Young's groundbreaking work. There is, however, an important difference between Young's approach and the one I propose here. Namely, Young offers an account of gendered embodiment that assumes a ground of biological sex; whereas I am considering a phenomenology of sex in which biology offers no unifying ground. There is in Young's essay, as well as in the work of many other feminists, an underlying assumption that all female-bodied people are women in ways that are either problematic or unproblematic for them. The problem is this assumption fails to acknowledge that not all people who are medically classified as having female bodies perceive and experience their bodies as female.

Many transmen describe their presurgery bodies as male and contend that sexual reassignment surgery made it possible for others to recognize the male bodies they've always experienced as their own. Henry Rubin writes that transsexual men

> "fail" to recognize parts of their body as their own. For transsexual men, this includes the insistent ignorance of breasts and female genitalia or the fantasization of a penis and scrotum. Transsexual men know that they have female bodies. They are not psychotic. They merely ignore the features of their bodies that do not conform to their body image. (Rubin 2003, 29)

While Rubin describes the phenomenology of female-to-male trans embodiment as characterized, in part, by conscious disregard of those body parts that are taken as signs of "femaleness," other transmen describe their experience as one in which the corporeal itself is resignified and transformed by their male body image. In this sense, the failure to recognize a transman as male is experienced as a failure to be seen at all, not a failure to recognize alternative meanings one has given to one's body.

In his collection of female-to-male (FTM) portraits, Loren Cameron highlights the marginalizing effects of the insistence of focusing on particular visible and invisible sexed body parts (genitalia, breasts, ovaries, chromosomes, etc.) while ignoring the transman's experience of his body as male. In the section titled, "Distortions," Cameron presents three self-portraits framed by a cacophony of accusations and distortions of his experience. Examples of these messages include "You're just a dyke with a beard"; "Why can't you just be a butch"; "You still look female to me"; "Where's your dick"; and "You're not a man: you'll never shoot sperm" (Cameron 1996, 28–31). These messages surround photographs of a tattooed, muscular, and bare-chested Cameron looking progressively sad, defiant, and just plain perplexed and fed up. These portraits highlight the extent to which assumptions that the biological body with which one is born settles the question of gender identity and embodied sex do not come close to understanding how Cameron experiences his own body and gender identity. The accusations assume that sex is a property of bodies that ultimately defines one's gender identity, no matter what transmen may think of their own bodies. Thus, feminists who are critical of Butler's challenge to the category "woman" point to what they contend are ultimately definitive biological "facts," such as the capacity of the female body to become pregnant, menstruate, and breast feed, whether or not that capacity is ever realized (Alcoff 2006). These proclamations treat the sexed body as if it is a fixed, stable truth about the gendered self and ignore how our corporeal selves are created within communities.

When feminist theorists assert the fixed and foundational nature of biological sex, they by default conceptualize trans experience as a pathological denial of reality. Rather than having Gender Identity Disorder, one is characterized as having "Sex Identity Disorder." By contrast, understanding trans embodied experience is understanding how sex in general is best understood as an "attribution" rather than a fixed biological reality that enables the body to do some things and prohibits it from doing others. Disability studies scholars have made a similar point about disability. Rosemarie Garland-Thomson writes, "Disability... is an attribution of corporeal deviance—not so much a property of bodies as a product of cultural rules about what bodies should be or do" (quoted in Herndl 2002, 154). In making this claim, disability scholars aren't failing to acknowledge bodily impairment and the fact that some bodies are unable to do things that others can. Their point is that impairment and disability aren't best understood as bodily facts; they are better understood as attributions in a context of bodily norms. Moreover, these attributions shape our embodied experiences whether we're perceived as disabled or not. Having a body with two arms matters only when having two arms is made necessary for participation in public life, but it need not be necessary. Similarly, having a body with the capacity to lactate matters only when conformity to the norm of "biological sex equals gender" is made necessary for participation in public life, but it need not be necessary.

Breasts are certainly read as visible signs of female identity , so much so that, in our society, the appearance of "larger-than-normal" breasts on male bodies is considered abnormal and an occasion for medical intervention. In his discussion of male bodies with breasts, Sander Gilman points out that of the breast-reduction surgeries performed each year, a significant number are performed on men to correct what is perceived to be the gendered bodily abnormality known as "gynecomastia" (woman-breast) (Gilman 1999, 260). Gynecomastia is attributed to body building (especially if it involves the use of steroids) and some intersex conditions. Breasts on what are perceived to be male bodies are considered abnormalities that must be surgically "corrected" because they challenge heteronormative, patriarchal norms of gendered bodily dimorphism and a two-sexed society, norms which specify that females have breasts and males do not (259–60).

In the face of the use of surgery and therapy to force unruly bodies into compliance with the norms of gendered embodiment, what are queer crip feminist theorists to make of the fact that while mastectomy for women with breast cancer and men with gynecomastia is covered by insurance, insurance does not cover bilateral mastectomy for transmen? As Jamison Green and other transmen have pointed out, transmen experience the presence of breasts on their presurgery bodies in much the same way as men experience what society characterizes as excessive breast tissue on male bodies. Green notes that surgery and hormone treatments didn't make his body a male body. His body was always male. Surgery and hormones simply made it possible for others to recognize his body and identity (Green 2004, 91–92). Many transmen and transwomen have challenged those who criticize sexual reassignment surgery (SRS) as an ultimate form of conformity to traditional notions of gender. As Henry Rubin contends, body modification for transmen is not necessarily body mutilation or conformity. Instead, it is an attempt to achieve "intersubjective recognition" (Rubin 2003, 173). Though not all have mastectomies, breast removal is a highly desired surgery for ftm transpeople. For many transmen there is a sense of betrayal by the body into which they were born, and it is only through surgical alteration that their bodies can become their selves (Green 2004; Rubin 2003). Without such surgery and hormone therapy, the male identities of transmen will not be recognized; such recognition, Rubin argues, "is the intersubjective principle that guarantees social integration and shared moral principles, as well as individual authenticity" (Rubin 2003, 14). While I am highly suspicious of any claim to individual authenticity or a core self, I think Rubin's principle of intersubjective recognition is useful for a queer crip feminist perspective on identity, breasted experience, and breast surgery.

We make our bodies our selves in the context of communities of support and recognition; because our participation in those communities changes us, it also changes our bodies, even what dominant culture assumes to be an unchanging, biological fact about our bodies—our sex. To the extent that an erotic community of women played a significant role in Lorde's decision not to wear a prosthesis, Lorde's decision is rooted in queer desire. As she becomes acquainted with her new postmastectomy body, Lorde is reminded of a lover who died of breast cancer; she recalls touching her lover's mastectomy scar. On the eve of her own mastectomy, Lorde remembers Eudora, her lover in Mexico years earlier:

> I remember the hesitation and tenderness I felt as I touched the deeply scarred hollow under her right shoulder and across her chest, the night she finally shared the last pain of her mastectomy with me in the clear heavy heat of our Mexican spring. I was 19 and she was 47. Now I am 44 and she is dead.
>
> Eudora came to me in my sleep that night before surgery in that tiny cold hospital room so different from her bright hot disheveled bedroom in Cuernavaca, with her lanky snapdragon self and her gap-toothed lopsided smile, and we held hands for a while. (Lorde 1980, 35)

It is this experience that enables Lorde to look down at her own scar and to see her flesh, to experience this changed body as her body. Lorde does not present her choice as the only possible feminist choice. Instead, she writes, "I think now what was most important was not what I chose to do so much as that I was conscious of being able to choose, and having chosen, was empowered from having made a decision, done a strike for myself, moved" (33). Similarly, queer communities are places where the male bodies of transmen are recognized and where it is possible to choose to create one's body and one's self, where one can strive "for that which doesn't yet exist and about which we cannot know how and what it will be" (Foucault quoted in Halperin 1995, 206).

Throughout *The Cancer Journals* (and her writing generally), Lorde emphasizes movement, change, the never-ending process of self-awareness and transformation. As she struggles with breast cancer and difficult but necessary decisions, Lorde is reminded that she and all who are oppressed were never meant to survive and that in this circumstance survival itself is a form of resistance. She writes, "Growing up Fat Black Female and almost blind in america requires so much surviving that you have to learn from it or die" (Lorde 1980, 40). It is the litany, "we cannot live without our lives" (Barbara Deming quoted in Lorde 1992, 205–6) that characterizes Lorde's strategy as a queer crip feminist strategy of resistance, a strategy that entails creating spaces of queer recognition, spaces in which queer subjectivity is made possible and nourished.

"I am who the world and I have never seen before," writes Lorde (1980, 48). She chooses to celebrate her asymmetrical body, a choice made possible in a real and imagined space of one-breasted lovers, friends, and the women she has not yet met. Similarly, some transmen make choices that make their bodies more reconizably male to others, choices made possible by counterhegemonic horizons of sexed and gendered embodiment and identity often found in queer communitites. These are spaces of queer recognition—the recognition of the selves, bodies, relationships, and families we choose, not those into which we were born. Those bodies will be variously gendered, functioning, and appearing. Lorde's "rage to live" is fueled by her desire for and experiences with queer bodies and spaces in which recognition is not contingent on conformity to gender binary norms and medical models. It is a desire for spaces in which subjects are able to achieve intersubjective recognition through an ongoing life project of deconstructing and reconstructing (of grappling with) identities and embodiments, of grappling with unknowns and queer possibilities. For, in the end, queers cannot live without their, and other, queer lives.

NOTES

I thank Beth Carroll, Jill Ehnenn, and Laurie Shrage for their useful comments on earlier drafts of this paper.

1. As Laurie Shrage points out in her contribution to this volume, the fact that "men" can have "female" body parts like breasts challenges societal assumptions that breasts are "female" and that bodies are only "male" or "female."

2. My use of the term "crip" is informed by its recent reclamation by scholars in disability studies such as Carrie Sandahl. In her essay, "Queering the Crip or Cripping the Queer? Intersections of Queer and Crip Identities in Solo Autobiographical Performance" (2003), Sandahl points to many commonalities between "crip" and "queer." For instance, both terms have been used as pejoratives against disabled people and LGBT (lesbian, gay, bisexual, trans) people, and both have been reclaimed as terms of pride by some disabled people and some LGBT people. Both "queer" and "crip" signal critiques of normalizing tendencies in various theories and policies regarding disabled people and LGBT people, even when those theories and policies are supported by people who are disabled or LGBT. In other words, "crip" and "queer" signify a resistance to the normal, and both are necessarily contested categories as opposed to self-evident descriptions of identity (26–27).

3. Evolutionary psychologists also posit the evolved biological—and, hence, natural and inevitable—nature of gender differences. One of their favorite examples seems to be what they

contend are evolved sex differences in mating strategies (e.g., men's preference for youth and beauty in women). For evolutionary psychologists, gender is ultimately sex. For examples, see David M. Buss (1994); Steven Pinker (2002); and David N. Stamos (2008). Pinker and Stamos, in particular, are highly critical of feminist theorists who disagree with biological explanations of gender. For an excellent feminist critique of the popularization of evolutionary psychology's understanding of sex and gender difference, and evolutionary psychologists such as Pinker who lambaste "gender feminists," see Martha McCaughey (2008). For an excellent critique of the "science" behind evolutionary psychology, see Robert C. Richardson (2007).

4. My thinking about sex and gendered embodiment owes a great debt to the work of Iris Marion Young. Young contributed so much to feminist thinking about the body, and feminist philosophy will miss her voice. My title is obviously a variation of her "Breasted Experience" essay, and it is my hope that my thoughts about queer breasted experience constructively build on the groundbreaking insights of her phenomenology of female embodiment.

WORKS CITED

Alcoff, Linda Martín. *Visible Identities: Race, Gender, and the Self.* New York: Oxford University Press, 2006.

Buss, David M. *The Evolution of Desire: Strategies of Human Mating.* New York: Basic, 1994.

Butler, Judith. *Undoing Gender.* New York: Routledge, 2004.

Cameron, Loren. *Body Alchemy: Transsexual Portraits.* San Francisco: Cleis, 1996.

Dreger, Alice Domurat. *Hermaphrodites and the Medical Invention of Sex.* Cambridge: Harvard University Press, 1998.

Foucault, Michel. *The History of Sexuality: An Introduction.* Vol. 1. Trans. Robert Hurley. New York: Vintage, 1990.

Gilman, Sander. *Making the Body Beautiful: A Cultural History of Aesthetic Surgery.* Princeton, N.J.: Princeton University Press, 1999.

Green, Jamison. *Becoming a Visible Man.* Nashville, Tenn.: Vanderbilt University Press, 2004.

Halberstam, Judith. *Female Masculinity.* Durham, N.C.: Duke University Press, 1998.

Hale, C. Jacob. "Leatherdyke Boys and Their Daddies: How to Have Sex without Women or Men." *Social Text* 15, no. 3–4 (Fall/Winter 1997), 223–36.

Halperin, David. *Saint Foucault: Towards a Gay Hagiography.* New York: Oxford University Press, 1995.

Herndl, Diane Price. "Reconstructing the Posthuman Feminist Body Twenty Years after Audre Lorde's *The Cancer Journals.*" In *Disability Studies: Enabling the Humanities,* ed. Sharon Snyder, Brenda Jo Brueggemann, and Rosemarie Garland-Thomson. New York: Modern Language Association of America, 2002.

Laqueur, Thomas. *Making Sex: Body and Gender from the Greeks to Freud.* Cambridge: Harvard University Press, 1990.

Linton, Simi. *My Body Politic: A Memoir.* Ann Arbor: University of Michigan Press, 2006.

Lorde, Audre. *The Cancer Journals.* San Francisco: Aunt Lute, 1980.

———. "Need: A Chorale for Black Women's Voices." In *Undersong: Chosen Poems Old and New,* rev. ed. New York: Norton, 1992.

Love, Susan M. *Dr. Susan Love's Breast Book,* 3rd ed. Cambridge, Mass.: Perseus, 2000.

McCaughey, Martha. *The Caveman Mystique: Pop-Darwinism and the Debates over Sex, Violence, and Science*. New York: Routledge, 2008.

Pinker, Steven. *The Blank Slate: The Modern Denial of Human Nature*. New York: Penguin, 2002.

Richardson, Robert C. *Evolutionary Psychology as Maladapted Psychology*. Cambridge, Mass.: MIT Press, 2007.

Rubin, Henry. *Self-Made Men: Identity and Embodiment among Transsexual Men*. Nashville, Tenn.: Vanderbilt University Press, 2003.

Sandahl, Carrie. "Queering the Crip or Cripping the Queer? Intersections of Queer and Crip Identities in Solo Autobiographical Performance.," *GLQ: Journal of Lesbian and Gay Studies* 9, no. 1–2 (2003), 25–56.

Schiebinger, Londa L. *The Mind Has No Sex? Women in the Origins of Modern Science*. Cambridge: Harvard University Press, 1989.

Stamos, David N. *Evolution and the Big Questions: Sex, Race, Religion, and Other Matters*. Malden, Mass.: Blackwell, 2008.

Young, Iris Marion. "Breasted Experience: The Look and the Feeling." *On Female Body Experience: Throwing Like a Girl and Other Essays*. New York: Oxford University Press, 2005.

8

Changing Race, Changing Sex

The Ethics of Self-Transformation

Cressida J. Heyes

Analogical Minefields: What Is Changing Sex Like?

First published in 2006, "Changing Race, Changing Sex" was one of those articles that comes out of the backchat at conferences and in bars. It was a response to a tendency among feminists who are relatively far from trans politics to wonder why people don't change race, how feminists should respond if they did, and whether this (putatively critical) response could be transposed to the much more well-trodden ground of changing sex. At a time when "transgender" is a ubiquitous term of art within feminist theory, the analogy can function as a Trojan horse for skepticism about transsexuality: rather than risking censure by arguing outright that sex change is politically regressive, critics would rather imply this by asking, rhetorically, "Well, what would you say to a transracial?" A lot of this wondering never seemed very well grounded to me: people *do* "change race," even if they don't have a psychiatric diagnosis to explain it. I don't exactly know the best response as a feminist to such changes—real or imagined—and I'm not sure one response would cover all eventualities. Most of all, the idea that sex and race necessarily function in the same ill-defined constructionist way does a great disservice to the long and complex histories of the categories as we have inherited them. The article, then, tries to flesh out these intuitions in a philosophical voice, showing that race and sex yield different possibilities that we all negotiate but none of us can dictate.

The discourse of individual authenticity—especially as it is mediated through biomedical models in psychiatry—seems to have gained pace in many of the ways I implied toward the end of "Changing Race" (when I alluded to the idea that if extreme racism can become a psychiatric disorder, then "transracialism" might be only one step behind). Reflecting this trend, since "Changing Race, Changing Sex" came out, I have also published a book in which I talk about how transsexuality rests in part on a similar model of the authentic inner self as one increasingly used to justify having cosmetic surgery. I felt rather politically uncomfortable, however, including analyses of transgender politics and cosmetic surgery in the same monograph, and my introduction gestured toward this discomfort without really addressing it.[1] Yet it is hard to deny that cosmetic surgeries and trans surgeries are mutually implicated, even if one pulls back from the conclusion that sex reassignment simply *is* a set of cosmetic procedures.[2] They have an intertwined institutional history in medicine, use many of the same techniques, and are performed by surgeons with basic training in the same subspecialty, for example. Both effect changes to the body's soft tissues in the name of ameliorating psychosocial distress. Many defenders of the right to change sex, however, make the same kind of too-casual analogical move I challenged in "Changing Race." Sex reassignment is *not* cosmetic surgery, they aver, because it is, variously, medically and psychologically necessary, central to personal integrity and mental health, outside history and driven by a universal struggle, and motivated by a kind of suffering beyond the control of the individual. Cosmetic surgery, by implication, must be a self-indulgent luxury, instrumentally undertaken, driven by fad and fashion, peripheral to individuals' well-being, and frivolously self-interested.[3] That this is an implausibly univocal and facile view of the psychology of cosmetic surgery is apparent. It is not apparent, though, what would be argued if the disanalogy were more carefully spelled out.

Noticing this, therefore, I started to write a familiar sort of article about how trans surgeries and cosmetic surgeries compare and contrast, in which I pointed out that most attempts to analogize or disanalogize them are undertheorized, serving only rhetorical purposes rather than making any convincing case. In a more constructive vein, I also wanted to say something about the way this analogy should be handled so that it respects the complex realities of each phenomenon, while also developing a political position I could stand behind. Thus this new essay quickly took on a form highly reminiscent of "Changing Race, Changing Sex." Looking back, my avowedly selective history of race and sex stressed certain discontinuities, but a different inflection might have made them look much more alike. My own anxieties about defending changing sex by making it seem *unlike* anything else linger in the text. This only became evident when I found myself oddly reluctant to point out how interconnected trans and cosmetic surgeries are and how disanalogies by trans activists often demean cosmetic surgery recipients. Perhaps I risk inverting rather than avoiding the ad hoc reasoning for which I criticized Janice Raymond. That is, I argue backward from the conclusion that changing sex is *exceptional* (especially in being distinct from practices that are considered more obviously vulnerable to feminist critique), to the premise that analogy x, y, or z is unjustified.

This move mirrors a larger political trend among transsexual activists, if not among transgender theorists (a controversial but, I would argue, real distinction that correlates in interesting ways with one's position on analogical arguments).[4] The former are directly concerned with, among other things, protecting and expanding legal rights and access to health care for transsexuals, including those who do sex work, are living with HIV/AIDS, or are in poverty. Especially for these populations, medical and social services are, where they exist at all, vulnerable to political retrenchment.[5] In this light, endorsing the psychiatric model of transsexuality (in which a diagnosis of Gender Identity Disorder is followed by supervised guidance using the WPATH standards of care) serves a strategic function, no matter how convinced (or not) one is of its ethical or epistemological adequacy.[6] A common—although contingent—underpinning of the psychiatric model is an understanding of transsexuality as an organic pathology the universal cause of which will eventually be found. On this view, while the *expression* of gender disorder may of course vary by cultural context (or historical epoch), its underlying nature remains constant and the remedy remains individual. Under current regimes of truth, this general form of explanatory model is perceived to get more uptake from health care systems and in the law than any feminist constructionism or libertarian demands for freedom of choice could hope to garner.[7]

I don't endorse the model of gender and the self on which the diagnosis of Gender Identity Disorder is typically founded for reasons both philosophical and political, and I don't think defending biological essentialism for strategic reasons is guaranteed to have the positive effects that some advocates seem to believe. Eve Sedgwick famously remarks that to believe any particular causal origin story for homosexuality—including that homosexuality is "natural" or "biological"—will inoculate us against homophobia is to seriously underestimate the latter's multiple origins and strategies, as well as its power to survive in the face of contradiction. My suspicion is that the same is true of transphobia (a neologism badly in need of theorizing) and that advancing the view that transsexuality is a biomedical "disorder" will have mixed and unpredictable political consequences that currently emerge against the backdrop of a ubiquitous prior desire to eradicate gender ambiguity and perceived inauthenticity.[8] Nonetheless, theorists of transgender—especially if we are ourselves cisgendered[9]—have a responsibility to think hard about the consequences of our writing for trans people, as well as how our own identities inform our accounts. There is also clearly a lot of work to be done in spelling out just how the *refusal* of analogy—making transsexuality always exceptional—might be linked to essentialist models, and how to theorize in ways that are both philosophically precise and politically responsive to the exigencies of trans-oppression. Some questions I am left with, then, include the following:

What investments do cisgendered people like me have in treating transsexuality either as "just like" some other phenomenon we think we understand or as exceptional—unlike anything we might recognize? How are these two responses related?

How is the impetus to treat transsexuality as exceptional conceptually connected to biomedical psychiatric models?

Does defending a biomedical psychiatric model (or refraining from attacking it) actually lead to positive political consequences in particular cases? Positive for whom? At what cost? To whom?

What is the connection between strategizing for trans rights and employing explanatory models one believes to be true?

Every year when I teach an introductory course in feminist philosophy, I see individual women and men drastically rethinking their previous understandings of gender and race and of their own place in a gendered and racialized world. Often as a part of this rethinking, we struggle over what an ethical life amounts to; *ethical*, that is, in the sense of being responsive and responsible to one's relation to others and to the work one does on oneself.[10] To talk in this way of the self as, at least in part, self-making presumes another set of questions about the very possibility of changing oneself. So, for example, feminists are not only interested in establishing who to count as "women" with regard to some already foundational definition but also in troubling and transforming the definition itself—in part through changing ourselves.

To address these simultaneously ontological and ethical questions, we need to ask what makes it possible to change one's identity—and not just incrementally within a defined category (e.g., as by becoming a more assertive woman through feminist consciousness raising) but also more drastically. Specifically, what are those people who "change sex" undertaking, and what makes sex into the kind of thing that can be changed? How is changing sex different from "passing"—the phenomenon central to the histories of both race and sex, in which one is read as, or actively pretends to be, something that one avowedly is not? It is in light of questions like the above that my interest in identity categories extends to asking: What makes a particular facet of identity into something the individual *can* transform? And what implications do answers to this question have for all our ethical lives?

These questions also invite reflection on how we think about the relationships among different identity categories. In particular, it is by now an orthodoxy in feminism that race and gender are always mutually implicated in individual phenomenology and social group analysis and that the most politically responsible thinking will fully incorporate both without assuming that either can be isolated from the other. It does not follow, however, that race and gender are always *analogous*—that is, that any conceptual analysis of gender applies straightforwardly to race, and vice versa. (I call this "the analogy thesis.") As I show, some feminists have invoked the analogy thesis in ways that serve only to elide the very different histories of these two categories. That is, a certain analytic treats gender, race, sexuality, and other identity categories as identical building blocks for theory by assuming their equivalence.[11] When this occurs, authors typically transpose ontological and ethical conclusions they may have drawn based on one context directly onto another. This is precisely the phenomenon, however, that accounts of mutual constitution were intended to avoid. Thinking through how gender and race work together, therefore, may actually be hampered by assuming the analogy thesis.

These two problematics—the possibilities for individual identity transformation and the limits of analogy—come together in the questions: Why are there "transsexuals" but not "transracials"? Why is there an accepted way to change sex but not to change race? I have repeatedly heard these questions from theorists puzzled by the phenomenon of transsexuality. Feminist thinkers, in particular, often seem taken aback that in the case of category *switching* the possibilities appear to be so different. Behind the question is sometimes an implicit concern: Does not the (hypothetical or real) example of individual "transracialism" seem politically troubling? And, if it is, does not the case of transsexuality merit equivalent critique?[12] Or, conversely, if one accepts transsexuals as people with legitimate demands (e.g., on medical resources or single-sex spaces), then would one not also be committed to accepting the putative transracial in analogous ways? Understanding the ontological constraints and possibilities with regard to transforming one's identity is, I suggest, a project that should accompany ethical evaluation of those transformations. Under what circumstances is it (un)ethical to leave behind a gender or racial group with which one has once been affiliated? This question is, again, especially pressing for radical thinkers who endorse the claims that race and gender taxonomies are internally hierarchical and constituted through relations of oppression, domination, and normalization. Changing one's identity under these circumstances will surely always be linked, however tenuously, to consideration of the larger political and cultural milieu in which such changes are advantageous or disadvantageous, complicit with oppressive norms or resistant to them.

To illuminate these larger questions, in this essay, I first provide three examples of the analogy thesis in feminist thinking about race and sex change, each of which draws ethical conclusions about individual motivation, political strategy, or public policy, premised on the assumption that race and sex change are equivalent phenomena. None of these accounts considers the genealogy of each category as significant to contemporary possibilities. I next offer a descriptive analysis that highlights different norms at play in contemporary North American understandings. Sex–gender, I argue, is essentialized as a property of the individual's body, while race is essentialized with reference to both the body and ancestry. This analysis, I conclude, shows politically significant disanalogies between the categories and reveals the importance of genealogical accounts of race and sex in thinking ethically about changing ourselves.[13]

The Transracial Analogy

Why is it now considered legitimate to change one's *sex*, but not one's *race?* Why don't we have "transracials"? Here, in brief, are three textual examples of feminists whose theories answer these questions by assuming or arguing that changing sex and changing race must be analogous processes (and that, consequently, sex and race are analogous categories). In all three cases, implicitly or explicitly, race and sex end up divorced from their histories in ways that oversimplify and decontextualize the ethical possibilities and dilemmas that face agents working within the constraints of larger social group systems.

First, a bold version of the analogy thesis is advanced by Janice Raymond in the introduction to the 1994 edition of her notorious book *The Transsexual Empire.* Originally published in 1979, this text contains not only a critique of the then-incipient medical practices that institutionalize transsexuality but also an indictment of male-to-female (MTF) transsexuals themselves for their alleged appropriation of women's identities and bodies. Reading MTF transsexuality as another way for men to make women their property and to dictate gender norms, Raymond launches a critique of patriarchal psychiatry and of MTF transsexuals as perverse patriarchs. She uses what she sees as the contrast between gender and other social hierarchies, including race, age, and class, to make her political critique. Transsexuals, she claims, are anomalous in relying on a psychiatric diagnosis to explain their gender identity conflicts. For those dissatisfied with their raced, aging, or impoverished status, it is much more evident that what is required is not personal transformation to satisfy the white, young, rich individual within but, instead, political action to end oppressive taxonomies or inequalities. She asks, "Does a Black person who wants to be white suffer from the 'disease' of being a 'transracial'?" and claims, "there is no demand for transracial medical intervention precisely *because* most Blacks recognize that it is their society, not their skin, that needs changing."[14]

A second example: the Michigan Womyn's Music Festival has a policy of allowing only "womyn-born womyn" onto its land, and MTF transgendered people are officially barred from entering the festival. In order to avoid masculine women being challenged on their gender, however, the organizers have a "don't ask, don't tell" policy that allows some MTFs who are able and willing to "pass" as genetic women to attend. Bonnie Morris, in her adulatory book *Eden Built by Eves*, vacillates between perspectives but ultimately opposes the inclusion of MTF transsexuals in the Michigan Womyn's Music Festival, arguing that "the celebration of female life and energy that is festival culture seems mocked by the inclusion of men who have *selected* female identity; they are not, to use Alix Dobkin's phrase, *survivors of girlhood*." Ruefully citing lesbian activism in support of transinclusion, Morris asks rhetorically, "Is it not possible for there to be one event, one annual festival, intended for women born female? One does not see any 'transracial' persons demanding entry to Michigan's Womyn of Color Sanctuary. But this analogy angers some activists."[15] Here the section trails off; Morris is apparently unwilling to explore why the analogy might deserve a critical response and, much like Raymond, is content to let her rhetorical version of the transracial analogy stand on its implicit merits.

Both Raymond and Morris are working in a radical feminist tradition hostile to the institutions of transsexuality (and to MTF transsexuals themselves). In particular, they oppose the idea that an MTF transsexual can ever really "count" as a woman, including for the purpose of defining and defending the boundaries of women-only spaces; in their minds, then, MTFs are really only "passing" as women. How this claim is parsed within feminist politics and debates about the nature of women's shared identity is a complex question I discuss elsewhere.[16] However, the abbreviated invocation of the transracial analogy in these contexts has the rhetorical effect of dismissing transsexuals as capricious or appropriative, without doing the political theoretical work of explaining why changing race and changing sex are relevantly different or similar for the ethical purposes at hand. In this respect, the texts fit well with Cass Sunstein's observation that most cases of analogical reasoning contain "an unarticulated supplemental judgment" that is necessary to make the analogy but not explicitly defended.[17] In this case, the judgment is that race and sex are analogous for the purposes of comparing the motivations and politics of individuals who change their identities—a comparison also based on false claims (such as that there are no medicalized interventions on racial identity) and dubious inferences about individual behavior (that the acceptance or refusal of transition is based on transparent political evaluation of its benefits and drawbacks).

In a far more nuanced treatment of the analogy, third, Christine Overall seeks to make some unarticulated judgments explicit by exploring the if-then statement, "if transsexual surgery is morally acceptable...then transracial surgery should be morally acceptable." Addressing those "inclined to accept the antecedent and reject the consequent," Overall presents and then argues against eight possible reasons for the ethical rejection of transracial surgery (which she suggests is at present perhaps hypothetical, with the familiar exception of Michael Jackson).[18] In effect, she is arguing the inverse of the position that Raymond and Morris imply: the latter suggests that because "transracial" would *not* be considered an intelligible or ethical subject-position, "transsexual" should be subject to the same political critique. Overall, by contrast, argues that if feminists in particular *accept* transsexual body modification, then we must in the interests of consistency endorse embodied race change (with whatever similar justifications).

Despite their evident political differences, both positions incorporate the claim—implicitly in the cases of Raymond and Morris—that sex and race are analogues. This assumption, however, operates at a high level of generality: "Either both sex and race are inherent fixed characteristics, or, more plausibly, both are socially constructed and socially acquired or ascribed," writes Overall.[19] The latter is a widely accepted claim among feminists, certainly, but the precise nature of the construction, acquisition, or ascription in question might be different in the two cases. In other words, both race and sex are constructed, but are they constructed in the same way? Overall's work is admirably clear in anticipating and rejecting potential arguments for treating transracialism from transsexuality, yet she offers no positive account of the ways in which race and sex are the same kinds of identity categories for the purposes of making a *transition*. She tends to divorce race and sex from their discursive locations and histories, whereas location and history, I argue, set up different possibilities for the subject seeking to change her embodied identity. Overall's argument operates on the basis of, a number of hypotheticals: for example, "physical identities are changeable; thus, transsexuals seek to change their public physical identity in crucial ways. "(Some regard themselves as 'always already' having the identity with which they aspire to make their physical body congruent.) The same would be possible for the transracialist."[20] Would it? This argument needs to be made with some attention paid to the actual institutions engaged in racial body modification and the ideologies of racial difference on which they draw.

A corollary of the hypothetical voice is an approach that treats history as irrelevant to ethics. For example, Overall bases her ethical argument on the premise that "it is hard to see how the transracial case would be different from transsexual medical interventions, except for the fact that there is a history of 'sex change' surgery but not yet for 'race change' surgery."[21] This "except," then, erases more contextualized approaches to understanding sex and race, as well as the implications such approaches might have for ethical thinking. Yet to the extent that the creation of particular subjectivities is a necessarily historical process, in which certain possibilities become sedimented by years of social practice, sex and race have emerged looking rather different. What possibilities, then, have been worked into the discourses political philosophers thinking about transrace and transsex have inherited? When we talk about changing sex or race, what do—or could—we mean?

Changing Race

"Race is socially constructed," claims virtually every philosopher writing on racial identity—by which they usually mean that there are no necessary or sufficient physical criteria (especially genetic criteria) that can determine an individual's membership in a racial category.[22] Instead, the somewhat diverse taxonomies of race that western countries have inherited are contingent on ideologies developed in a colonial age. Claims about popular understandings of racial membership must be located in a context (and my context in this essay is contemporary North America), for the rules of race change as the national, cultural, and historical milieu changes. For reasons beyond the scope of this article, the thesis of the social construction of race seems to have had relatively little impact on folk beliefs about how racial identity works or on the power of racism. Thus, considering what it would mean to "change race" is a question that operates on different levels: philosophers of race are likely to think about this in ways that are significantly different from more widely shared intellectual inheritances. Let me, then, trace three North American contexts in which an individual might be said to change race: the legal context (where a specific jurisdiction's rule-governed norms for determining race are in play), the social context (where intersubjective perceptions of affiliation, community, and self-identification operate), and the context of body modification (where physical racial signifiers matter). My goal is to show how beliefs about the kind of thing race *is* shape the possibilities for race change. In particular, I show that the belief that an individual's racial identity derives from her biological ancestors undermines the possibility of changing race, in ways that contrast with sex–gender.

In jurisdictions where individuals are assigned to a racial-ethnic category (a practice now much less widespread than the ubiquitous assignment of legal sex), these assignments are often contested by individuals who feel an "error" has been made, resulting in a legal change of race. In the notorious 1982 Phipps case, Susie Guillory Phipps applied to the state of Louisiana to have the racial classification of her birth records (which labeled her "black" on the basis of one or more African great-great-great-grandparents) changed to white. Although she lost her case, the law was overturned, ironically leaving behind the even more stringent "one-drop rule," on the basis of which everyone with *any* African ancestry at all is black.[23] Examples like this one are the darlings of the critical race literature, showing the sometimes absurd lengths that racial states will go to in order to maintain a semblance of coherence for legal race classifications (and their segregationist implications). Within these legal frameworks race is explicitly and uniformly tied to ancestry: the "race" of any particular individual is derived from the racial classification of her forebears (in accordance with different rules in different jurisdictions, to be sure), and hence changing race requires an inquiry into family history to ascertain whether the rules have been correctly applied in the particular case.

Second, changing one's race can also sometimes arguably be achieved by moving in or out of relationships, neighborhoods, social class groups, or cultural practices, affecting one's perception by others and one's sense of oneself. Think of the famous

English *voyageur* Archibald Belaney who "went native" and lived for many years as "Grey Owl" in the northern Canadian wilderness, becoming a native icon invariably photographed in aboriginal garb, or of Philip Roth's character Coleman Silk—a light-skinned African American man who for most of his life passes as Jewish. To make a wholesale transition in this way requires a more radical divorce from a differently racial (or ethnic) past. Linda López McAlister, in "My Grandmother's Passing," tells the gripping story of her Mexican American grandmother's lifelong struggle to pass as an Anglo lady. Born María Velarde in a Texas border town, Mary Douglas (as she became known) married a wealthy Anglo and spent the last fifty years of her life in an entirely white milieu. Yet, McAlister points out, her grandmother did not successfully pass as Anglo due to her accented English and dark skin—but she apparently thought she did. Thus, when McAlister describes her to a friend as "Mexican," her grandmother is so offended that she never speaks to her again: "my unpardonable sin was to reveal what she believed was a secret, even though it was not, thereby outing her, even though she wasn't really passing, except in her own mind."[24]

Notice that McAlister uses the language of "passing" in telling this story, which she distinguishes from identity transition: "To pass implies that you are successfully fooling people into believing that you are something you are not. But there is a world of difference between successful passing and *being* the new identity. For one's identity actually to change you have to go beyond successful passing and become someone different from who you were."[25] For her grandmother's ethnic identity actually to change, McAlister suggests, she would have to have complete amnesia for her language and culture of origin. In fact, on McAlister's own account, both Archie Belaney/Grey Owl and María Velarde/Mary Douglas are more properly described as passing than as individuals who have changed race, because one cannot change one's family of origin or one's ancestors—although one can, of course, disavow them. Racial identity is in these social contexts, too, commonly understood as *narrative*: my race does not exist only in the moment but depends on my heritage, which will be scrutinized if my racial identity comes under question.

Indeed, passing is a phenomenon so central to the history of race that it is constitutive of racial meanings and hence the possibility of race changes. Anyone who attempts a race change is vulnerable to the charge that she is trying to pass, no matter what her avowed intentions are. This observation makes Overall's circumscription of her argument question-begging: "I am not concerned here with the phenomenon of passing....Nor am I interested in the phenomenon of compulsory assimilation, in which social pressures force individuals, through self-presentation to appear to become members of another race, whether they want to or not."[26] Transracialism, I suggest, cannot be understood outside the historical frame in which racial crossing has typically been a matter of political expediency or survival, any more than changing one's sex can be understood apart from the apparatus of transsexuality, which, as I argue, in turn mitigates (even if it does not dispel) the specter of gendered passing.

Heritage and morphology thus interact in complex ways to capture racial meanings. Legal racial reclassification is usually only available to a certain subset of phenotypically ambiguous individuals—the suitably "mixed" mixed-race child, or the very light-skinned African American, for example. Had Susie Phipps had exactly the same ancestors, but through a trick of the gene pool not *looked* white, she would have had a weaker legal case. If "transracialism" simply means changing one's *legal* race, then there are numerous precedents; but while these say something about the application of rules of inheritance to particular cases, they do not imply that legal "race change" is open to anyone who cares to pursue it. Similarly, the social negotiation of racial identity is circumscribed—although not entirely dictated—by the body's visual cues. Mary Douglas was not entirely convincing in part because of her dark skin, while Grey Owl apparently worked hard with dyes to keep his hair black and his skin red. These visual cues, in turn, are not independent of racial hierarchy (and the history of passing): because whiteness maintains the privilege of neutrality, the pale-skinned can in theory have almost any mixed heritage, while nonwhite markers tend to overdetermine racial reception. This explains why Mary Douglas's appearance contributed to her being an unconvincing Anglo, while her granddaughter, whose "skin is white, not olive," can exercise greater control over whether she is perceived as all-white or part-Chicana.[27] Thus, the individual work of changing one's intersubjective recognition depends on a complex combination of self-presentation, social context, and embodiment. A certain amount can be achieved without changes to the flesh, and for some individuals noncorporeal markers may be enough. For others, however, the characteristics of a racialized body will tend to overdetermine identity, whatever other changes they make.

Third, then, people do (despite Raymond's and Overall's different skepticisms on this point) inflect their race through changes to their bodies. Most obviously, there are many cosmetic modifications—from hair-straightening treatments, to rhinoplasty, to eyelid surgery, to skin-lightening creams. Stated motivations for choosing these procedures, as things stand, rarely include "I want to become truly white" (or even, "I've always felt I was a white person trapped in a person of color's body"). Such claims are somewhat implausible, first, as I have shown, because race is taken to be *inherited* in a way that sex is not. The claim that "I've always known I was really white inside" is unpersuasive in part because it implicates others; if one's immediate forebears are not white, the claim risks being unintelligible. In part as a consequence, second, this ontology does not have an institutional psychiatric apparatus behind it. With race inhering *both* in the body and in ancestry, and transracialism lacking a diagnostic mechanism, the marketing of race-altering body modifications cannot play to individual essence to the extent that sex change can.

On the contrary, purveyors of racialized body modifications must seek to undermine the notion that making oneself look less like other members of one's racial group (including, perhaps, one's biological family) is disloyal. Products and surgeries must be advertised to attract appropriate consumers; having drawn in their customers, vendors must then actively deny that making use of their services constitutes race treachery. The surgical rhetoric uses bland counterassertion even when confronted with procedures to transform characteristics that are only incongruent if a racial identity itself is aesthetically illegitimate.[28] Promotional information for Asian eyelid surgery, for example, rejects the claim that it will westernize the surgical candidate. Instead, surgeons claim, the creation of a double eyelid crease is intended to make the eye more "objectively" attractive, or more like other, more attractive Asian eyes, to improve the "overall appearance" or "harmony and balance" of the face, or even to make it easier for women to apply eye makeup.[29] Those who seek out an "ethnic" nose job are represented not as whitening their image but as seeking to correct malproportioned features and express their individuality;[30] cosmetic surgeons sell the procedures with talk of "enhancing ethnic beauty" rather than creating Caucasian uniformity; advertising for skin-lightening creams mostly focuses on its success in treating "patchy" pigmentation or unsightly "age spots," despite the fact that many products also come in "whole body" formulations.[31] The popular commodification of racially inflected body modifications often rests on the ideology of diverse individual self-expression rather than (as with sex change) on ideologies of psychological identity.

There is actually remarkably little contemporary research that delves more deeply into the complex motivations of people of color who elect to change their appearance along what might be thought of as racialized lines, although race is central to the history of aesthetic surgery.[32] Individuals who undergo cosmetic procedures have diverse rationales, and it is perhaps a conceit—or a projection—of a white interpretive stance to think that all body modifications undertaken by people of color are motivated exclusively by a desire to look white.[33] In this light, Overall's remark— echoed in many other analyses—that "Michael Jackson...has had surgery on his cheekbones, eyes, chin, and nose in order to make his face less 'Black'-looking, and more 'white'," attributes individual motivation in the absence of any real inquiry.[34] We assume that Jackson's transformations are in the service of whiteness because our cultural imagination is so systematically organized around the desirability of whiteness that we cannot imagine any other psychology for him. Race is defined through ancestry; racial transformation is commonly read as passing; hence the body modifications of individual people of color can only exemplify that they are dupes of whiteness. The ideology of individuality comes into play, therefore, to deflate the charge of racial treachery or masquerade when a product or procedure implicated with racial morphology is being sold.

Changing Sex

The possibilities for and constraints on changing race could be almost infinitely detailed through historical and contextual work; here I have just shown how three key moments rely on appeals to the genealogy of the individual to establish racial essence. How are the possibilities for changing sex–gender similar or different? First, unlike race, all western jurisdictions insist that their citizens have a legal sex. Almost all official documents—driver's licenses, passports, birth certificates, and so on— bear the information "male" or "female," and this has consequences for other legal rights (in particular, in most jurisdictions, the right to marry). To change one's legal sex requires medical documentation that the appellant is "really" the sex they aspire, legally, to be. The force of this "really" is not, as with race, an inquiry into whether the rules of inheritance have been correctly applied but, rather, an investigation into the nature of the individual, especially the nature of her or his sexed body. Although successful legal race change entails correcting a mistake without altering the individual, successful legal sex change requires medical intervention to make the person's body match the label.

Like race, one can shift one's gender by changing social context or self-presentation. Dressing differently, moving differently, using (or not using) cosmetics, adopting certain friends or joining certain communities, can all have consequences for gender identity. This can be a matter of degree: if a Chicana can sometimes seem more Anglo, then adopting a butch haircut and wearing dress pants and a button-down shirt can make a woman seem less feminine (if not quite a man). Gender offers a wide range within the two categories man and woman, and everyone will at some point (whether deliberately or not) incrementally shift their gender identity. Again, there is a rich history of passing here that partly constitutes the meaning of such transitions, and traditions of gendered performance (in the Butlerian and literal senses) inform our reception of gender change. Some transgendered persons do cross to the "other" gender, or blur the lines between woman and man, without ever undertaking surgery or hormone treatments.

Moving not just within a gender category but decisively between woman and man, however, including through transforming the sexed body, engages a complex institutional medical apparatus of psychiatrists, endocrinologists, and surgeons engaged in the business of diagnosing transsexuals in North America with Gender Identity Disorder (GID) and effecting sex change—including legal sex change. Exactly which medical procedures are required to effect the latter is often legally vague (especially in the case of female-to-male [FTM] transsexuals).[35] Sex chromosome patterns cannot be altered, but with certain measures, (including vaginoplasty, phalloplasty, testicular implants, mastectomy or breast implants, facial feminization surgery, hormones, or electrolysis) all male and masculine persons can be made (more) female and feminine, and vice versa. (Of course, vice versa is a rather different matter, as the current results for surgical phalloplasty [construction of a penis] are poor, and many FTMs forego genital surgery. On the other hand, ironically, FTMs are often seen by others to be more convincing men than MTFs are as women.) An abundance of autobiography, memoir, and documentary attests to this experience and aspiration, which has come to structure many transsexual lives and has entered into popular understandings of gendered possibilities. Any individual with the means may opt to change their racialized body for whatever reasons they choose, and mounting a legal challenge to one's racial classification is open to anyone (although, as I have suggested, unlikely to succeed if the right ancestral and phenotypical conditions are not met). However, the medical apparatus of sex change (the precondition for legal reclassification) is available only to certain kinds of person—those who suffer from the condition of GID.[36]

This is the most noteworthy contrast between the histories of race and sex: transracialism is not (yet) a mental disorder. GID is in the *Diagnostic and Statistical Manual* (*DSM*) of the American Psychiatric Association (4th edition)—the bible of categories of psychopathology that uses diagnostic criteria to define the mentally disordered (and to make judgments about health insurance coverage and eligibility, and suitability for treatments, including sex reassignment surgery):

> There are two components of Gender Identity Disorder, both of which must be present to make the diagnosis. There must be evidence of a strong and persistent cross-gender identification, which is the desire to be, or the insistence that one is, of the other sex (Criterion A). This cross-gender identification must not merely be a desire for any perceived cultural advantages of being the other sex. There must also be evidence of persistent discomfort about one's assigned sex or a sense of inappropriateness in the gender role of that sex (Criterion B).[37]

The diagnostic criteria continue at some length, explaining typical behaviors and desires of girls, boys, adolescents, and adults with GID. The picture that holds this diagnosis captive is that of an essential difference in certain persons, biological in origin or nurtured by childhood relationships (or both), but nonetheless having its locus and causal origin in the individual, who then interacts with (rather than being made possible by) her society.[38] Because one's identity as a man or woman (or boy or girl) is, within the essentialist framework that organizes dominant views of GID, conceptually separable from anyone else's gender, a transition can be made without a necessary contradiction with others' identities. More specifically, one's identity as a boy or girl is not taken to mimic one's ancestors—I am not a woman just because my mother is a woman. In terms of the actual content of gendered relationships, of course, one's personal history (e.g., the kind of gendered person my mother is) is deeply significant to the kind of woman or man one will become. As I and many others have argued, gender *is* narrative and relational rather than essential, and hence changing gender often does challenge the identity of others—we just lack a vernacular for describing the phenomenon.[39] However, the history of biological essentialism with regard to individual sexed character exerts a powerful force here, in ways that avoid attention being drawn to the social context of gender as a relation rather than a substance. Susie Phipps was required to assemble extensive information about her ancestors in order to make her case that she was really white, but the person who seeks to change legal sex must show to the state's satisfaction that the new classification is appropriate to his *individual* psychological and physical condition.

Gender Identity Disorder thus has no obvious equivalent in the context of race: one cannot be diagnosed with any mental disorder specifically pertaining to confusion about one's racial identity. However, in arguing that race and sex have similar genealogies, Ladelle McWhorter suggests that for race there exists "the theoretical possibility ... that deviant racial identities could be altered by scientific means."[40] She has in mind nineteenth- and twentieth-century eugenic public policies that aimed to bring "primitive" racial groups up to the developmental level of Europeans—the residential school system for First Nations children, for example. Science has been less preoccupied with changing deviant racial identity in individuals than in populations (whereas both sexuality and gender have, historically, been the targets of normalization at the level of personal identity). Today, an ongoing media skirmish has mooted the idea that *racism* in its more virulent forms constitutes a mental illness and deserves a place in the *DSM*.[41] Although media treatments are critical—typically offering "for and against" debates—the growing plausibility of the idea that racism could be a mental illness marks, to my mind, the conceptual crawl of psychopathological accounts of human experience from sex–gender and sexuality, where the discourse is well established, to race, where the primary focus has hitherto been control of populations.

Why has this trend not gained more rapid purchase? To understand *why* transsexuality stands out as deeply connected to disease models, we need both a broader understanding of the history of gender and sexuality and a careful evaluation of how that history confronts individuals. "Sex," "gender" (and "sexual orientation") have come to be thought of as core ontological differences attaching to individuals, organized through binary schema. One simply *is*, essentially, either male or female, and concomitantly man or woman (and heterosexual or homosexual, depending on the relation of sexual object choice to biological sex). This schema, while in some moments resistant to any crossing of categories, has a history that simultaneously creates conditions of possibility for "mistaken gender" understood as a biological or pathological phenomenon. As Toril Moi recounts, "the distinction between sex and gender emerged from a concern with individual identity. At its inception [in the 1950s and 1960s], the distinction medicalizes 'sex' and turns 'gender' into a purely psychological category."[42] Indeed, the way that changing sex has been institutionalized in the postwar western world has, I would argue, come to be constitutive of what sex *simpliciter* means, just as the rather longer history of passing constitutes race. Combine this historical account with the still-pervasive dualism that construes sexed bodies as inert machines, animated by the gendered mind, and it becomes clear how a quest for an authentic identity could lead to changing the individual's body.

Despite this institutionally powerful history, there is no simple mapping between an internalization of the GID diagnosis and the desire to change one's sex. Nor is it the case that GID diagnosis is supported by all transgendered people (some want to get rid of the category, drawing the analogy with eliminating homosexuality as a mental illness[43].) Recent work on the history of transsexuality reveals the increasingly powerful grip of medical experts on discourses of sex and gender in the latter half of the twentieth century; but it also exposes how this labeling from above managed to repress an extraordinary diversity of autobiographical accounts and political organizing by loosely grouped gender nonconformists, some of whom agreed with aspects of medical opinion, but others of whom were entirely opposed to the idea of a mental illness diagnosed by gender deviance.[44] Arguably, it has only been since the 1990s that an organized transgender movement has generated sufficient communal resistance to enable a shifting of the balance of power back toward politicized accounts of gender nonconformity. Importantly, a useful rhetoric in this move has been that of the right to individual self-expression—the same discourse that often rationalizes racial body modification. For transgendered people, the right to individual self-expression without diagnostic overdetermination transgresses an established norm, enabling a kind of resistance that, paradoxically, the norm itself may have made possible. In the context of racial body modification, the language-game of individual self-expression, however, has been thoroughly (albeit contingently) colonized by normalizing practices—expressing one's true self is almost always achieved through conformity, in other words.

Finally, once GID became established—a process at once culture-driven and the local decision of a small coterie of psychiatric experts—it produced its own subjects. Once a disorder is in place, complete with diagnostic criteria, any individual who wants the clinical responses the disorder commands—for whatever reason—has a motivation to conform to the criteria. This is a well-known phenomenon among adult transsexuals in the case of GID, who read medical literature and use social networks to find out what kind of self-descriptions and behaviors are required to gain access to hormones, surgeries, or services. Quite disparate experiences and aspirations are thus erased and homogenized into a single category.[45] And there are powerful social motivations for participating in medical procedures that will make sexed bodies more or less legible to others, even if one is critical of GID: while many mixed race people often face a certain level of intrusive curiosity or skepticism about their racial identity, gender-ambiguous individuals face extraordinary levels of social discomfort and aggression. Gender limbo seems almost uninhabitable, while a consistent identity as a gender at odds with one's sex requires extraordinarily careful self-presentation and interaction.

The Ethics of Self-Transformation

This exercise in comparing and contrasting possibilities for race and sex change reveals the complexity and distinctiveness of the genealogies of race and sex themselves. It illustrates that both categories are undergirded by a plethora of sometimes contradictory ontological assumptions, and they maintain their social meaning not because they are philosophically coherent labels that fit with unified political perspectives but because they are slippery, ad hoc, and available to serve various rhetorical purposes, depending on social contexts that are themselves in transition. It also undercuts one element of feminist handling of the analogy thesis—namely, the suggestion (implied or explicit) that race and sex change can be considered equivalent without further argument, including for ethical purposes.

None of us is at liberty to become any kind of person we want, and to align oneself with a particular identity formation is a necessarily intersubjective activity. Especially in cases of labels such as "woman" or "black," there will often be a larger tension between what Ian Hacking calls "the vector of labeling from above" and "the vector of the autonomous behavior of the person so labeled."[46] If we think that what we expect of agents, ethically speaking, is enabled or constrained by what it is actually possible for them to be and do (and here I just assert that it should be), then any discussion of the ethics of gender and racial identity must be sensitive to the range of actually available possibilities for sustaining and transforming oneself. The actions of individuals, now and in the future, will be constitutive of new norms of racial and gendered identity. The institutions and practices of transformation I have alluded to create a certain room for maneuver between overdetermination and individual freedom, oppression and resistance, opacity to oneself and transparency.

In the case of race change, a language of fidelity to one's heritage vies with popular insistence on individual autonomy, which, in turn, mystifies conformity to norms of racialized beauty. Thus, for example, Michael Jackson—a powerful symbol, but a very diffident spokesman for his own ethics of the self—is caught between these discourses. He is African American and expected to perform his allegiance to his black roots and to black culture; he is making himself over into his own aesthetic vision, a unique image that just happens to make him look more white than black. None of these discourses is unproblematic, yet, paradoxically, it is the unresolved conflict between them that may function to preserve a conceptual space for ethical engagement. In the absence of a single commonsensical (and ideological) explanation for why someone would change their racialized body as Jackson has, the very ambiguity of the act presses us toward investigating individual motivations and relations of power.

In the case of sex change, medical discourse has a historically contingent but nonetheless forceful hegemony that posits wanting to change sex as a disease of the individual, not a cultural condition, best explained by features inhering in individuals rather than by intersubjective accounts and reference to structures of power. Radical feminists have rightly been quick to challenge this model, as Raymond and Morris both did in my earlier examples. These critics, however, push too hard in the opposite direction: those who change their sex (and thereby deny their XX or XY heritage, so to speak) are either traitorous or appropriative. Their motivations are entirely in the realm of the political and can never be justified in feminist terms. But this position inverts rather than challenges the very same problematic attitude to the individual that it sought to undercut. On a particular psychiatric view, those who suffer from GID are victims pulled along by an inherent mental disorder; but a contrary feminist position risks portraying them as Machiavellian architects of the gender landscape. The rhetorical deployment of the transracial analogy against transsexuals thus tends to attribute political naivete or (self-)deception to those who seek to change sex (and equally problematically praises those who maintain a stable racial identity for their ability to distinguish individual capitulation from challenges to systemic oppression).

Few, however, would claim that transsexuals are part of a systemic conspiracy to maintain sex–gender dichotomies, or that no one who has changed sex is aware of the oppressive consequences of sex–gender systems. Indeed, some of the most powerful political writings on the constraints of western gender systems on individual freedoms come from transgendered commentators.[47] It seems implausible to suggest that anyone would go as far as to change sex only because they self-consciously aspire to appropriate or benefit from a novel gender identity, while people of color knowingly and unanimously resist race change because they share an analysis of its role in sustaining racism. Furthermore, my examples suggest that many people do disavow (parts of) their racial heritage and change their racial reception to find or accommodate themselves to a new niche in a racialized and racist world.

Instead of attributions of transparency and equivalence, feminist thinkers need to pay closer attention to context in making ethical diagnoses. Only a fully contextualized account that recognizes the different ontologies of race and sex will be adequate to the task of ethically evaluating race and sex change, including by drawing the kinds of policy conclusions that Overall articulates. Perhaps more important, this argument points toward a richer ethics that reflects on the decisions *all* gendered and racialized subjects with commitments to feminist politics face about self-presentation and transformation from within a space marked out by full appreciation of our conditions of possibility.

NOTES

This essay was previously published in *Journal of Social Philosophy* 37, no. 2, Summer 2006, 266–282. © 2006 Blackwell Publishing, Inc. I would like to thank members of the "Sexual Difference and Embodiment" workshop at McGill University (especially Alia Al-Saji, Marguerite Deslauriers, Penelope Deutscher, and Laurie Shrage), audiences at the University of Melbourne, Keele University, and University College Dublin, David Kahane, and three anonymous referees for their helpful comments on earlier drafts of this paper.

1. Cressida J. Heyes, *Self-Transformations: Foucault, Ethics, and Normalized Bodies* (New York: Oxford University Press, 2007)

2. The categories "trans surgeries" and "cosmetic surgeries" are both capacious and internally diverse, which contributes to the difficulty of theorizing this particular analogy. Sex reassignment surgery (actually a set of procedures that may include vaginoplasty, labiaplasty, orchiectomy, clitoroplasty, etc. in MTFs, and phalloplasty, inserting testicular implants, or metoidoplasty for FTMs) is the archetype for trans surgery, but the category also includes breast augmentation, tracheal shave, facial feminization, and male chest construction. Cosmetic surgery is a contested term that can include breast augmentation, facelift, rhinoplasty, breast reduction, liposuction, and so on.

3. Critics also charge that cosmetic surgery is all these things and that trans surgeries are just the same, as well as various other kinds of comparisons or contrasts, but the most common claim, and the one I focus on, is that trans surgeries and cosmetic surgeries are disanalogous along these axes.

4. David Valentine, *Imagining Transgender: An Ethnography of a Category* (Durham, N.C.: Duke University Press, 2007).

5. Viviane Namaste, *Sex Change, Social Change: Reflections on Identity, Institutions, and Imperialism* (Toronto: Women's Press, 2005).

6. The World Professional Association for Transgender Health (WPATH, formerly known as the Harry Benjamin International Gender Dysphoria Association, Inc. [HBIGDA]) is a professional organization devoted to the understanding and treatment of so-called gender identity disorders.

7. I don't mean to suggest here that the *only* reason anyone might have for endorsing a psychiatric model is strategic. Clearly, many experts endorse it because they believe it is the best scientific explanation for transsexuality, and many transsexual people endorse it because it offers a plausible rationale for their lived experience.

8. Eve Kosofsky Sedgwick, *Epistemology of the Closet* (Berkeley: University of California Press, 1990, 40–44). Here there is a possible comparison with debates in feminist theory around so-called strategic essentialism, as well as with debates about whether biomedicalizing mental disorders in general might reduce stigma. For her insights into the latter that will form her doctoral dissertation project, I am grateful to Angela Thachuk.

9. Cisgender: identifying with a gender that matches one's initial assigned sex; someone who experiences hir gender as consonant with hir socially assigned gender. This increasingly popular term is backformed from "transgender," where "trans" means crossing or changing, while "cis" means the same as, on the same side as.

10. This usage of "ethical" clearly has roots in both existential and Foucauldian philosophy; it is not an ethics that takes a stand in relation to consequentialist or deontological ethical theories, although the questions raised in this essay have connections with virtue ethics.

11. The distinction between sex (biological maleness and femaleness) and gender (socially constructed masculinity and femininity) has no obvious analog in the case of race, where both embodiment and social role are captured by the same ambiguous term. In this essay, I follow popular usage and mostly talk about changing "sex" rather than "gender," although the kind of transformation I am discussing confounds the sex–gender distinction. Thus, I occasionally use the term "sex-gender" when I want to reinforce that both embodiments and intersubjective presentation are at stake. It also is worth noting a different elision between race (historically variable taxonomies that in contemporary North America typically include internally diverse categories such as white, black, Asian, Hispanic, and First Nations) and "ethnicity"—one's affiliation with a certain cultural or ancestral group not necessarily coterminous with race ("Irish American," "Jewish," "Vietnamese Canadian," etc.). Some ethnicities have, at various times, been thought of as races (e.g., Jews), while different ethnic groups have crossed between racial categories as their local status changes. In this essay, I use examples and arguments that capture popular understandings of "race" in contemporary North America, but the slipperiness of the concept again causes race sometimes to run into ethnicity.

12. The terms "race change" and "transracialism" also appear in a related literature that investigates the historical and contemporary phenomena associated with racial masquerade, mixing, and interculturality in the United States. See, for example, Susan Gubar's book *Racechanges: White Skin, Black Face in American Culture* (New York: Oxford University Press, 1997), and Leon E. Wynter. *American Skin: Pop Culture, Big Business, and the End of White America* (New York: Crown, 2002).

13. I use the term "genealogical" here in its Foucauldian sense, to imply a critical history of a particular identity formation that shows the contingency of our current self-understandings and encourages us to "think ourselves differently."

14. Janice Raymond, *The Transsexual Empire: The Making of the She-Male* (New York: Teacher's Press, 1994 [1979]), xvi; emphasis in original. For an extended consideration of Raymond and other feminist accounts of transsexuality, see Cressida J. Heyes, "Feminist Solidarity after Queer Theory: The Case of Transgender," *Signs* 28, no. 4 (2003): 1093–1120.

15. Bonnie Morris, *Eden Built by Eves: The Culture of Women's Music Festivals* (Los Angeles: Alyson, 1999), 173 (emphasis in original) and 173–74.

16. Heyes, "Feminist Solidarity."

17. Cass Sunstein, "Analogical Reasoning," in *Legal Reasoning and Political Conflict* (Oxford: Oxford University Press, 1996), 73.

18. Christine Overall, "Transsexualism and 'Transracialism,'" *Social Philosophy Today* 20, no. 3 (2004): 184 and 185.

19. Ibid., 185–86.

20. Ibid., 186.

21. Ibid., 190.

22. This orthodoxy deserves more parsing than I can manage here; it has also been challenged in recent debates. See the web forum on "Is Race Real?" at http://raceandgenomics .ssrc.org/ (accessed February 11, 2006).

23. As summarized in Adrian Piper, "Passing for Black, Passing for White," in *Passing and the Fictions of Identity*, ed. Elaine K. Ginsberg (Durham, N.C.: Duke University Press, 1996), 251.

24. Linda López McAlister, "My Grandmother's Passing," in *Whiteness: Feminist Philosophical Reflections*, ed. Chris Cuomo and Kim Q. Hall (Lanham, Md.: Rowman and Littlefield, 1999), 23.

25. Ibid., 24.

26. Overall, "Transsexualism and 'Transracialism,'" 184.

27. López McAlister, "My Grandmother's Passing," 21.

28. Eugenia Kaw, "'Opening' Faces: The Politics of Cosmetic Surgery and Asian American Women," in *Many Mirrors: Body Image and Social Relations*, ed. Nicole Sault (New Brunswick, N.J.: Rutgers University Press, 1994), 241–65.

29. Quoted from the "Frequently Asked Questions" page of the website of one of the most prominent West Coast plastic surgeons performing Asian blepharoplasty: http://www .asianeyelid.com/ (accessed May 10, 2005).

30. Diana Dull and Candace West, "Accounting for Cosmetic Surgery: The Accomplishment of Gender," *Social Problems* 38, no. 1 (1991): 59.

31. Amina Mire, "Skin-Bleaching, Poison, Beauty, Power, and the Politics of the Colour Line," *Resources for Feminist Research* 28, no. 3/4 (2001): 13–38.

32. For example, Sarah Lucile Eichberg, "Bodies of Work: Cosmetic Surgery and the Gendered Whitening of America," Ph.D. diss., University of Pennsylvania, 2000; Eugenia Kaw, "Medicalization of Racial Features: Asian American Women and Cosmetic Surgery," *Medical Anthropology Quarterly* 7, no. 1 (1993): 74–89; Kaw, "'Opening' Faces"; Sander L. Gilman, *Creating Beauty to Cure the Soul: Race and Psychology in the Shaping of Aesthetic Surgery* (Durham, N.C.: Duke University Press, 1997).

33. Kathleen Zane, "Reflections on a Yellow Eye: Asian I(Eye/)Cons and Cosmetic Surgery," in *Talking Visions: Multicultural Feminism in a Transnational Age*, ed. Ella Shohat (Cambridge, Mass.: MIT Press, 1998), 164.

34. Overall, "Transsexualism and 'Transracialism,'" 184.

35. Viviane K. Namaste, *Invisible Lives: The Erasure of Transsexual and Transgendered People* (Chicago: University of Chicago Press, 2000), 235–63.

36. It is possible to obtain sex-reassignment surgery (SRS) with minimal psychiatric evaluation if one is willing to travel (e.g., to Thailand) and to pay out of pocket, although all "reputable" surgeons will insist on a psychiatric diagnosis and letters of recommendation from other medical practitioners before performing genital surgeries.

37. American Psychiatric Association, *Diagnostic and Statistical Manual of Mental Disorders*, 4th ed. (Washington, D.C.: American Psychiatric Association, 2000), 576. The criteria do not explain how one might separate a cross-gender identification derived from "perceived cultural advantages of being the other sex" from any other kind, although this is surely a project that—even if one believes a priori that it is possible—requires extraordinary epistemic skill.

38. For a detailed critique of this diagnostic language, see Ellen K. Feder, "Disciplining the Family: The Case of Gender Identity Disorder," *Philosophical Studies* 85 (1997): 195–211; and Judith Butler, "Undiagnosing Gender," *Undoing Gender* (New York: Routledge, 2004), 75–101.

39. See Cressida J. Heyes, "Can There Be a Queer Politics of Recognition?" in *Recognition, Responsibility, and Rights: Feminist Ethics and Social Theory*, ed. Robin Fiore and Hilde Lindemann Nelson (Lanham, Md.: Rowman and Littlefield, 2003), 59–71.

40. Ladelle McWhorter, "Sex, Race, and Bio-Power: A Foucauldian Genealogy," *Hypatia* 19, no. 3 (2004): 48.

41. This story was pursued by ABC's *Nightline* in a 2001 documentary, in a 2004 episode of *Law and Order* when a defendant characterizes his racism as a mental illness to bypass a murder charge, and by Canadian TV news in 2003, among many other examples. For a psychiatric defense, see Alvin Poussaint, "They Hate. They Kill. Are They Insane?" *New York Times*, August 26, 1999.

42. Toril Moi, *What Is a Woman? and Other Essays* (Oxford: Oxford University Press, 1999), 21–22.

43. For example, Riki Ann Wilchins writes: "To get [sex-reassignment] surgery, you have to mount what I call an Insanity Defense. *I can't help myself, it's something deep inside me, I can't control it.* It's degrading.... In a civilized society, wanting what you want and getting help should not require you to accept a psychiatric diagnosis, produce a dog-and-pony show of your distress, and provide an identity to justify its realness" (Riki Ann Wilchins, in *Read My Lips: Sexual Subversion and the End of Gender* [Ithaca, N.Y.: Firebrand, 1997], 191–92). By contrast, Viviane Namaste argues against the "conservative" consequences of this position on the grounds that removing GID from the *DSM* will eliminate SRS from health insurance coverage (Viviane Namaste, "Addressing the Politics of Social Erasure: Making the Lives of Transsexual People Visible," interview in *New Socialist Magazine*, at http://www.newsocialist.org/magazine/39/article04.html (accessed February 14, 2006).

44. Joanne Meyerowitz, *How Sex Changed: A History of Transsexuality in the United States* (Cambridge: Harvard University Press, 2002), chs. 6 and 7.

45. Namaste, *Invisible Lives*, 190–234.

46. Ian Hacking, "Making Up People," in *Reconstructing Individualism: Autonomy, Individuality, and the Self in Western Thought*, ed. Thomas C. Heller Morton Sosna, and David E. Wellbery. (Stanford, Calif.: Stanford University Press, 1986), 234.

47. For example, Kate Bornstein, *Gender Outlaw: On Men, Women, and the Rest of Us* (New York: Vintage, 1995), and Leslie Feinberg, *Trans Liberation: Beyond Pink and Blue* (Boston: Beacon, 1998).

9

Artifice and Authenticity

Gender Technology and Agency in Two Jenny Saville Portraits

Diana Tietjens Meyers

As a gender variant visual artist I access "technologies of gender" in order to amplify rather than erase the hermaphroditic traces of my body. I name myself. A gender abolitionist. A part time gender terrorist. An intentional mutation and intersex by design, (as opposed to diagnosis), in order to distinguish my journey from the thousands of intersex individuals who have had their "ambiguous" bodies mutilated and disfigured in a misguided attempt at "normalization." I believe in crossing the line as many times as it takes to build a bridge we can all walk across.

Del LaGrace Volcano, September 2005

Taking this deft self-description as a point of departure, I reflect as a feminist philosopher on feminist artist Jenny Saville's portrait of its author, Del LaGrace Volcano, together with a Saville self-portrait as a cosmetic surgery patient.[1] In this study of *Matrix* (1999, oil on canvas, seven feet by ten feet) and *Plan* (1993, oil on canvas, nine feet by seven feet), I analyze how Saville's artistic practice conveys differential agency in these two paintings and draws out the implications of these findings for the philosophy of personal identity and action.

Before I can proceed to my principal concerns, however, I must defend classifying *Matrix* and *Plan* as portraits, for neither Saville nor Volcano accepts this label. Saville explicitly eschews it: "I am not interested in portraits as such. I am not interested in the outward personality. I don't use the anatomy of my face because I like it, not at all. I use it because it brings out something from inside, a neurosis" (quoted in Mackenzie 2005). To counter Saville's disavowal of self-portraiture, it is worth pointing out that

155

the most renowned portraits do not purport to be solely about the "outward personality," nor do they gratify their subjects' narcissistic needs. Rembrandt's self-portraits (1620–1669) and Velázquez's *Portrait of Pope Innocent X* (1653) are paradigmatic examples of one strand of western portraiture. Rightly or not, such works are widely venerated for capturing the essential character—the inner being—of the sitter. In this genre, the face is the focus of attention because the face is presumed to reveal character. Posture, gesture, clothing, jewelry, and tools merely denote the sitter's social standing and occupation. The mind is the locus of selfhood, and the face is the public side of the interior self. Hence the body and even the sitter's location in social space are subsidiary. Saville's images certainly penetrate her subjects' subjectivity in the requisite way and to the requisite degree. But, in my view, her work surpasses the baseline standard, for she does what might be dubbed "whole-person portraiture." She represents her subjects' faces, as the conventions demand, but she exceeds the requirement that a portrait perspicuously render its subject's face by also representing her subjects' distinctive bodies stripped of garments and accouterments.

Bursting the boundaries of western portraiture, *Matrix* and *Plan* are portraits that give the body equal if not prime billing.[2] These works are premised, so to speak, on the proposition that the self is no less corporeal than mental. As a whole-person portraitist specializing in nude, anatomically unorthodox bodies, Saville is able to convey what I call the psychocorporeality of selfhood: the intertwining of cognition, affect, and desire in the constitution of intelligent, embodied subjects.

In the western tradition, the nude and the portrait have long been mutually exclusive genres. Archetypal nudes, such as Botticelli's *Birth of Venus* (ca. 1485) and Titian's *Venus of Urbino* (1538), idealize their models and claim to capture female corporeal perfection—that is to say, no one in particular and no body at all. There is a strand of western portraiture that is akin to the tradition of the nude. In these works, the painter glorifies the subject—say, by representing an emperor as a god. But Saville's nudes always deviate from accepted beauty ideals, and the *Matrix* and *Plan* figures are highly individualized. Never catering to her subjects' vanity, Saville's images bring sexuality to portraiture and suffuse bare bodies with personality and agency.[3] After you've seen Saville's work, conventional portraiture may look incomplete, even superficial, by comparison.

Volcano is ambivalent about his relationship to Saville's image of him:

> I don't feel like this painting [*Matrix*] is a portrait of me. I simply provided the raw material. No one needed to know who the body actually belongs to. Yet the act of writing this piece locates it absolutely within the realm of the personal. This requires and allows me to own it in a way that is not comfortable, rather than disown it, which would be more so. (1999)

I concede that Saville's titles preserve the anonymity of her subjects, which is at variance with the usual proper name labeling of portraits. Moreover, Saville speaks of creating "a landscape of gender" and "landscapes of the body" as opposed to portraits (Schama 2005; Mackenzie 2005). I grant that Saville's facture is seductive enough to induce viewers to forget the specificity of Volcano's humanity and become absorbed in the canvas's brilliantly orchestrated interplay of colors and textures. Still, I disagree that no one needs to know who posed for *Matrix*.

I'm sure that reading Volcano's texts and viewing his photography, especially his self-portraits, enriched my understanding of *Matrix*. Whatever the virtues of formalism, it's clear that relevant background information—for example, about Volcano's genetic inheritance, his struggles against body hatred, and his embellishment of his body—heightens sensitivity to artworks. If more needs to be said, comparing *Matrix* with *Passage*, a 2004–2005 Saville painting that portrays an anonymous transgendered, intersexed person, confirms that she does not treat Volcano as the personification of transgendered, intersexed people. On the contrary, Saville particularizes the *Matrix* and the *Passage* figures, and she gives a layered, nuanced account of each of her courageously exposed models.

My disagreement with Volcano notwithstanding, it is necessary to be mindful of Saville's mediating point of view. She readily acknowledges that ideas animate her art and that her reading in feminist theory infuses her thinking (Schama 2005; Gayford 1999). Moreover, she is fascinated by medical technologies of corporeal manipulation. All of Saville's work to date is directly concerned with corporeity, much of it with gender, the body image, and the dynamics of agentic power and disempowerment.

Matrix and *Plan* are exemplary Saville works, and they raise the two questions that this chapter addresses:

1. Why aren't sex-reassignment treatments analogous to elective cosmetic treatments that are popular with U.S. women, including breast augmentation, liposuction, and dermabrasion?
2. What is the role of the body and the body image in transgendered identity and agency?

Because Saville's paintings convincingly represent lived human bodies—subjectivized, agentic corporeity, as distinct from inert, objectified flesh—they provide an invaluable aid to reflection on these issues. Her sympathetic engagement with stigmatized bodies helps to reconfigure the standard gestalts of the human body that viewers typically carry with them and thus to convert fear and disgust into empathetic attention if not appreciation and understanding.[4] Based on my account of the pathos of *Plan* and the agentic vitality of *Matrix*, I argue that conceiving the agentic subject as a rational deliberative capability that uses a conjoined body as the instrument of its will is not conducive to understanding the agency of transgendered people. If, instead, agentic subjects are viewed as embodied subjects and embodiment is understood as a locus of practical intelligence, the agency of transgendered individuals becomes intelligible.

Impaired Agency and Medical Technology

It would be irresponsible to comment on *Matrix* before placing it in the social context from which I view it. To some extent, my U.S. context overlaps with Saville's British context. In both countries, countless nontransgendered girls and women suffer grievously because of disparities between their body images and culturally ubiquitous beauty ideals, and this suffering is coupled with gale-force commercial and interpersonal pressures to "solve" these problems by resorting to a medical fix.[5] In the

United States, the soaring popularity of breast augmentation as a sixteenth birthday or high school graduation present for girls and the "mommy makeover"—a menu of postnatal procedures to lift sagging breasts, tighten the vagina, and siphon off extra pregnancy weight—attest to the virulence of this blight (Boodman 2004; Singer 2007). The U.S. insurance industry and the British National Healthcare Service deem reconstructive procedures elective unless they are prescribed to remedy a diagnosed psychiatric or other medical condition. Whereas health insurance commonly covers breast implants after a mastectomy, it does not pay for breast augmentation sought for personal aesthetic reasons. In the United States, most patients or their families foot the bill for cosmetic treatments.

Saville got to know this medicalized gender climate while observing a New York City cosmetic surgeon at work and incorporated what she learned in a number of her subsequent paintings. It is fitting, then, to begin with one of the bluntest and most poignant of these works, *Plan* (figure 9.1).

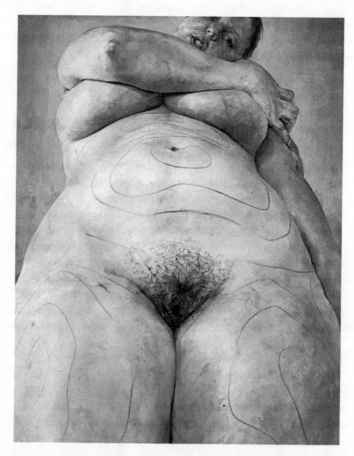

Figure 9.1. *Plan.* © Jenny Saville. Courtesy Gagosian Gallery, New York.

Plan

Jenny Saville used her own face and body for the figure in *Plan*—a towering frontal nude of a pre-op liposuction patient after she has been prepped for her procedure. That *Plan* is a portrait of the artist marked by an aesthetic surgeon and ready for sculpting is not its sole irony. The pre-op inscriptions span most of the figure's body. Except for a single horizontal line traversing her lower belly, the principal markings consist of four sets of concentric, irregularly spaced, wobbly circles. The crude target patterns look as if they had been drawn by a sloppy artist using a magic marker, not a twenty-first-century surgeon using sterile tools. These epidermal drawings turn the figure's surface into a topographic map of a flawed terrain. The sculptor-cum-surgeon's corrective labors will produce a geography that satisfies current taste in the lineaments of female flesh. The notional post-lipo map has a more level, more symmetrical, presumably more pleasing design.

Approaching this tall, vertical painting, you immediately register huge thighs topped by a mass of pubic hair. Your eyes travel up the torso, and the last thing you notice is a face. Either you are looking at a foreshortened standing figure seen from a kneeling position or a foreshortened prone figure seen from a point just above the figure's knees.

The perspective exaggerates the size of the thighs, accentuates the pubic area, and shrinks the size of the head. Indeed, the tiny head is tilted at a painful angle straining to cram itself inside the picture frame but doesn't quite succeed. The figure's knees and calves are cropped, and her inscribed torso and thighs nearly fill the canvas. The offending, targeted central body is the subject of this work. Doubly symbolic, the target patterns represent both the objectification of the figure's body and the subjugation of this body.

Many other details of this work reiterate the themes of body alienation and defeated agency. The geometry of the painting doesn't settle whether the figure is lying on an unpolished steel gurney or standing against a dull gray background. Although no platform is delineated, the distribution of the volumes of the figure's body suggests a flaccid body lying flat rather than a tensile body holding itself erect.[6] The seemingly prone position of the figure heightens the sense that she is at the mercy of demands and processes that are beyond her control.

Not only does Saville's foreshortening minimize the size of the figure's head, the horizontal line of the figure's right arm partially occludes it. The cropping and marginalization of the head notwithstanding, the face Saville depicts is haunting. The complexion is bluish grey—colors of injury, stupor, dismay, and sorrow. The lips slightly part as if a cry has just been emitted or a plea is about to be uttered. The eyes gaze down toward the viewer, yet they seem to be staring at nothing. This face is a study of helplessness and silent supplication. The spatial obscurity of the figure's head, the forlorn, plaintive expression on her face, and her blank eyes read as signs of diminished agency compounded by desolation.

Still, this figure is clearly doing something—she is trying to protect herself. Between the dense whorls of her marron pubic hair and her head are huge mammary mounds. Trying to conceal them and perhaps reacting to the chill of the clinic as well, the figure wraps her thick right arm around her chest and clasps her fingers tightly to the opposite shoulder. Although the arm hides her nipples, its weight squashes her breasts, making them appear more conspicuous because they bulge down toward the viewer. This desire for concealment prompts her to glue her gargantuan thighs together. Trying to make herself as compact as possible, she simultaneously tries to defend her genitals from prying eyes and instruments.[7] Her effort is wasted, however, for no one can will herself to shrink, and she'll soon be under anesthesia. *Plan* does not echo the demure gestures of feminine modesty that typify classic female nudes. It shows end-game gambits that cannot succeed—piteous, futile, defensive gestures.

Cruelly exposed as she is, *Plan*'s nude is naked and agentically neutralized. Despite the evident tension in the fingers gripping her shoulder and between her thighs, no defined musculature—no sign of agentic potency—is anywhere to be seen. The greyish creme pallor of the figure's skin and dirty tan and bruise-blue passages that define the volumes of her limbs and torso cement this body's inertness. The woman-patient that Saville portrays has compressed herself as much as she can short of self-inflicted implosion. All the agency that is left to her is to ante up and hand herself over to the medicalized beauty industry. Desperate and out of options, she is doing just that. *Plan* is sympathetic to her plight but vehemently denies that she is an exemplar of postfeminist agency.[8] Saville represents a desexed victim who gives the lie to the ideology of choice and liberation through medicine.

Cosmetic surgery has been a vexed topic in the feminist art world at least since Orlan began performing episodes of *The Ultimate Masterpiece: The Reincarnation of St. Orlan* before art audiences in 1990. It remains contentious among feminists to this day.[9] The best that can be said for it is that hiring these services may be the "best solution under the circumstances" for some women (Davis 1991, 31). I have no doubt, though, that as a rapidly and noticeably aging woman, it is incumbent on me not to dye my greying hair, botox out my wrinkles, or lipo away my cellulite. I don't pretend to be immune to the blandishments of the industries clamoring for my patronage. However, I don't believe in fabricating an illusory simulacrum of eternal youth or runway beauty, and I believe strongly in resisting the infliction of unachievable and insulting standards of feminine attractiveness.[10] Like Saville, I regard the alternative as agentically disenfranchising.

Transgendered Bodies and Medical Technology

There are no "after" images among Saville's paintings of female figures—no pictures of smiling post-op women feeling great because they look so great. There's a post-op head—looking battered with ugly stitches around her ear and a tube protruding from her mouth—but no happy outcome images (*Knead* 1994, oil on canvas, sixty by seventy-two inches). The reverse is true of Saville's paintings of transgendered, intersexed people—*Matrix* and *Passage*. These works are by no means banal "satisfied customer" images, but they do not depict disowned, subjugated bodies. They depict defiant corporeity and sexual agency.

Other philosophers incisively analyze how dominant gender norms and the medical establishment constrain the agency of transgendered people (e.g., Nelson 2001, 125–35; Butler 2004, 75–101). To obtain access to pharmacological or surgical technology, transgendered individuals are each obliged to construct a version of their life stories that coincides with a stock script: "From the beginning, I've felt like a man trapped in a woman's body (or vice versa), and I've always preferred acting in masculine (or feminine) ways." Perhaps this template and the diagnosis of gender dysphoria that it licenses actually fit the lives of some transgendered individuals. They certainly don't fit everyone's. Any inquiry into the agency of transgendered individuals must acknowledge the adverse impact of the institutionalized regimentation and pathologization of transgender in western societies. But I won't rehearse objections to these repressive practices, for Saville's artwork doesn't recapitulate them. Instead, it provides a glimpse of agentic possibilities that a transgendered person may seize in the teeth of a hostile social context.

If you are heterosexual, nontranssexual, and nonintersexual, and if you suppose that normalized schemas for human bodies are not deeply entrenched in your psyche, you'll (very probably) come away from Saville's *Matrix* or *Passage* disabused of your beliefs about your own open-mindedness and comfort zone. Here is art critic Suzie Mackenzie (2005). exclaiming about *Passage*: "Penis and breasts all at the same time. It's electric, it's like wow! To see something in a way you have not looked at it before." She might as well be naively reacting to a carny "freak show" or transported into the mind of a child confronted by the "primal scene." Art criticism is usually couched in more measured, analytic terms. To my own chagrin, when I saw *Matrix* and *Passage* in New York exhibitions, I latched onto the question of how the models came to have the anatomical configurations Saville depicts, and I took some pains to find out.

In interviews, Saville outlines the biomedical interventions that gave rise to her models' bodies. She supplies this information without being asked to. Why? Her observations about cognition and history in relation to gender and corporeity answer the question:

> I'm painting Del LaGrace Volcano at the moment—an intersex person who's been taking testosterone for three-and-a-half years. Del's body fascinates me as it represents a human form proceeding through a self-initiated process of body transition. He/she is a mutational body with gender defying body parts. You want to push Del's body into a category of male or female but can't—he/she is in a process of becoming. (Gayford 1999)[11]

And:

> With the transvestite [depicted in *Passage*] I was searching for a body that was between genders. I had explored that idea a little in *Matrix*. The idea of floating gender that is not fixed. The transvestite I worked with has a natural penis and false silicone breasts. Thirty or forty years ago this body couldn't have existed and I was looking for a kind of contemporary architecture of the body. I wanted to paint a visual passage through gender—a sort of gender landscape. (Schama 2005, 126)

Clearly, Mackenzie's discombobulation and my prurient curiosity about the genesis of these bodies are symptoms of our purblind investment in dual conceptions of properly gendered bodies, no doubt shored up by simplistic assumptions about biological naturalness. Our resulting suspicion of the artificial and presumed ability to ferret it out must be dispelled if either *Matrix* or *Passage* is to be interpreted with any insight whatsoever. In the interest of space, I confine myself to exploring *Matrix*.

Matrix

"I grew up believing I was a walking monstrosity, not quite female, not really male, fat ugly and unworthy of anyone's gaze" (Volcano 1999). Because the resemblance between this remark and many self-descriptions given by nontransgendered girls and women who suffer from body-image problems is unmistakable, I focus on the contrasts between Saville's nude portrait of Volcano and her nude self-portrait as a liposuction patient. In particular, I ask what sort of agency she bestows on Volcano's body in *Matrix* (figure 9.2) but withholds from her own in *Plan*.

As I've said, Volcano had been actively cultivating his intersexed body for three years before he posed for *Matrix*.[12] But the painting isn't about how Volcano came to be endowed as he is—his reconciliation to being intersexed and his enlisting of medical services to accentuate his body's "hermaphroditic traces." The painting is about the amplification of his agency that results from his acceptance of his body and his use of male hormones. Volcano avers that his project is to mobilize "technologies of gender," as distinct from technologies of anatomy. Characterizing himself as a "gender abolitionist," he assigns himself the role of embodying a "bridge we can all

Figure 9.2. *Matrix.* © Jenny Saville. Courtesy Gagosian Gallery, New York.

walk across" (2005). He's a nonpareil humanist activist, and Saville's painting keeps faith with his self-understanding.

A nude portrait befits Volcano because his body is the vehicle of both his art and his politics. Both *Plan* and *Matrix* show figures of colossal proportions—vast expanses of flesh. As in *Plan*, the *Matrix* figure is prone, but unlike in *Plan*, a cushioned platform is inserted beneath the *Matrix* figure. Whereas *Matrix* presents a well-supported individual, *Plan* presents one with no visible means of support, nothing to sustain her. Like the *Plan* figure, the *Matrix* figure is foreshortened—the thighs appear massive, the genitalia outsized. Volcano's sex is thrust forward and painted in saturated hues. It's the first thing you see. But, unlike in *Plan*, his head is in no way diminished—neither in size nor in force of character. By defining the contours of the head using planes of color, Saville gives it an appearance of strength. There's a hint of a sneer on Volcano's lips. His eyebrows slightly raised, he lifts his head to gaze directly at viewers. In contrast to the submissive, lowered eyes of the figure in *Plan*, Volcano's glance is challenging.

In more ways than one, this figure defies "anatomical correctness." Inasmuch as this work portrays Volcano's self-styled, hormone-boosted, gender-abolitionist body, its subject is a body that has been deliberately manipulated to transgress corporeal norms. Saville's professed purpose in making this work (and *Passage*) is to represent "the idea of floating gender that is not fixed" (Schama 2005, 126). She sought out Volcano to model for her because "he/she is a mutational body with gender defying body parts" (Gayford 1999). To get across her vision of "floating gender," Saville distorts some somatic spatial relations. On the left side of the canvas is Volcano's masculine head perfectly framed by womanly breasts that are sited exceedingly high on his chest. On the right side of the canvas, Saville places the predominantly female genitalia so conspicuously far forward in the crotch that they encroach on the figure's abdomen. Despite the resulting emphasis on the seeming contradictions of Volcano's body, the figure does not look like a hodgepodge of mismatched body parts. On the contrary, the figure in *Matrix* fuses presumptively incompatible corporeal elements to constitute a new human form.

Certain corporeal anomalies are plain to see. The figure has a moustache and goatee plus breasts and minus a regulation penis and testicles. Why doesn't this image collapse into a biomedical collage—a pick-your-own-parts body composite? This figure doesn't look undone by incoherence because Saville adroitly merges or juxtaposes other compositional elements. An androgynous tattooed decorative band encircles the slim upper arm, which morphs into a mountain of a shoulder. Directly in front of the shoulder, a big, soft breast slumps to one side. Together they form a pair of hills, natural neighbors. Volcano's genital region is visually salient, both because Saville's facture in this section is especially lavish and because the figure's hips tilt forward to show off the genitalia. The paint here is layered on in thick swathes and dabs of color—shades of pink-tinged creams, tans, and browns. The drawing is not at all like an anatomy textbook image. It's impossible to distinguish the parts you studied in sex-education class. Chromatic brushstrokes blend into one another, blurring the genitalia and creating folds of delicate flesh. Volcano has made sure that his genitals aren't neatly classifiable, and Saville paints him that way.

I agree with Donald Kuspit that Saville "restores beauty to the primitive genital organ" (1999). However, I think that he errs in interpreting *Matrix* as a descendant of Gustave Courbet's *Origin of the World* (ca. 1866). *Matrix* doesn't resurrect the age-old metaphor tying female reproductive paraphernalia to creativity. Saville's pigment tones and paint application are so lush that the tissue she describes looks sensual, excitable, sexually engaged. Kuspit notwithstanding, *Matrix* depicts the seductiveness and vitality of erogenous tissue in a manner that conveys sexual agency. Though by no means pornographic, this bit is very sexy.

Still, *Matrix* is hardly a rapturous celebration of gender-bending, medically mediated corporeity. Volcano is well aware of the hazards of gender abolitionism, and Saville ensures that her rendering of his body incorporates this danger.[13] The *Matrix* figure perches precariously at the edge of the supporting platform with an arm hanging straight down and a thigh dangling off the edge. Tilted toward the viewer, the figure is a little off balance. Although Saville provides solid support below the figure, she has had him assume an uneasy pose—a pose that comports with Volcano's disequilibrated, disquieting stance regarding gendered embodiment, not to mention his vexed social status. Viewers of *Matrix* see a form that is at risk of falling, yet somehow holding steady.

Yet, they also encounter a figure who offers himself for viewing.[14] Commenting on his own photographic work, Volcano affirms his recently found artistic and sexual agency:

> I am using my body and body parts as source material in my photographic practice with increasing frequency.... To reach the point where I could become my own subject took twenty years. At last I was able to own my body enough to give it away visually. While producing these images I felt the power one can access when freed from conventional notions about what constitutes an attractive body. (Volcano 1999)

Saville grasps the agency Volcano gained by refining and augmenting his intersexed body and making images of himself. *Matrix* captures Volcano's agency of evolving and self-presenting as a well-nigh postgender, corporeal amalgam.[15]

At first, Saville's title, *Matrix*, seems antithetical to Volcano's express desire to spotlight his masculine identity and agency and to downplay his femininity, for one definition of "matrix" is "womb," and the prominent genitals of the *Matrix* figure appear to me to be closer to female organs than male ones.[16] Yet, other definitions of "matrix" align her title with his identity as a gender abolitionist. Clearly, Volcano aspires to spark "a situation within which something else originates, develops, or is contained" and perhaps to be something like the "principal metal in an alloy" or a brand-new "mold or die" (http://www.thefreedictionary.com/matrix).

Transgender, Corporeity, and Agency

In discussing the gender-medicine juncture, it may be tempting to focus exclusively on political analysis. However, this temptation must be resisted, for it leads to neglecting the diversity of individuals' needs, values, motivations, and strategies for negotiating interpersonal derogation and institutional subordination.[17] Nothing is gained by unconditionally condemning or endorsing biomedical gender interventions. Here I seek to balance political, interpersonal, and personal viewpoints in order to clarify disanalogies between the mass medical come-on to nontransgendered women and the heterosexual mating scene that supports it, on the one hand, and various sex-reassignment options and the social context in which they are considered, on the other.[18]

Volcano's body and "hermaphrodyké" self-presentation constitute a standing critique of normative gender binarism and an ongoing reproach to anyone who, in Indra Windh's words, can't "count past two" (Volcano and Windh 2003).[19] In contrast, a nontransgendered, female cosmetic surgery customer's postprocedure body complies with and helps to perpetuate this invidious ideology.[20] Not surprisingly, there are interpersonal and discursive pressures in transgender support groups to consolidate a transsexual identity (Mason-Schrock 1996).[21] Although quite a few advertisements for Asian clinics turn up in a Google search for sex-reassignment surgery, and anecdotal evidence indicates that some surgeons regale audiences at conferences for transgendered people with exaggerated claims about the need for and benefits of their services, the western medical profession is not selling sex-reassignment procedures to transgendered people in the aggressive and systematic way that it is selling femininity-perfecting procedures to nontransgendered women. Whatever pressures there may be to buy sex-reassignment technology, they certainly have not gained the juggernaut power and cultural omnipresence of the beauty business's marketing to nontransgendered women (and increasingly to nontransgendered men). Indeed, resistance within transgendered communities to availing yourself of medical technology is on the rise (Heyes 2007, 58).

In my view, then, Volcano is right to ascribe both progressive political agency and personal autonomy to his appropriation of hormone treatment. However, because neither political agency nor personal autonomy is an all-or-nothing achievement, I acknowledge, as does Volcano, that bigotry and other repressive forces unjustly limit the political impact of his dissident body and art, as well as the freedom with which he enacts and the satisfactions he derives from his transgendered, intersexed identity.

Whereas *Plan* proffers an ironic allegory of art and medicine as conjoint practices in virtue of gender norms and power relations, *Matrix* brackets medicine for the sake of exploring the positive agentic possibilities of transgendered embodiment. Obviously, lots of women who have undergone cosmetic procedures testify that submitting to the knife or needle enhances their agency. Now that they are more attractive, they feel better about themselves. Consequently, they act with more confidence in a wider range of social situations. No doubt, many of these claims are true, and I have no reason to believe that Saville would dispute this. But since *Matrix* depicts enhanced transgendered agency, I'll concentrate on this topic and ask what this portrait, in conjunction with Volcano's autobiographical texts and self-portraiture, implies for agency theory.

It is useful to recall Volcano's assertion that it took him twenty years to free himself from ideals of attractiveness grounded in gender dimorphism and to gain sufficient body-esteem to start photographing himself. Judith Butler concludes an essay on justice and the struggles of intersexed people by striking a similar chord. Rejecting modernist suggestions that either a universal human core or an ineffable individual core can legitimate an intersexed person's demands for biomedical treatment, Butler proposes that a conviction that standard issue genitalia are irrelevant to the "lovability" of a person does legitimate these demands (Butler 2004, 71–74). Following Butler, Volcano's recollection of his own history might be understood as a process of crediting his own lovability and developing a healthy form of self-love.

Because Jay Prosser contests Butler's rejection of the claim that agency presupposes an individualized self to direct action, his reliance on Didier Anzieu's account of the "skin ego" seems altogether incompatible with Butler's thought (Prosser 1998, 65 ff). In some respects, Prosser's and Butler's accounts are indeed irreconcilable.[22] However, Sandra Bartky's discussion of a somatic dimension of love provides a point of intersection between them. Reflecting on a six-month separation from her partner, Bartky writes, "I realized after several months that I was suffering from something I had never seen described: it was a *skin hunger*. It wasn't sex that I missed so much as the comfort of a warm body in bed, the feeling of being held and stroked—touched" (Bartky 2002, 102). Whereas Butler's suggestion about lovability make sense of the loneliness of skin hunger, Prosser's psychoanalytic account of the need for sex-reassignment procedures makes sense of the necessity of undergoing some or all of these interventions as a precondition of feeling worthy of a loving touch.

Prosser recognizes, as does Butler, the facility with which the medically mandated narrative template of transsexuality infests the personal life stories of transgendered individuals, yet he counterposes this worry with a psychoanalytic account that lends a bit of credence to that "master narrative." In my view, his use of Anzieu's theory of embodiment and subjectivity is helpful for purposes of grasping the agency of transgendered individuals who seek out medical body modifications.

According to Prosser, "the transsexual does not approach the body as an immaterial provisional surround, but, on the contrary, as the very 'seat' of the self" (Prosser 1998, 67). Following Anzieu, he holds that your awareness of the surface of your body together with your sense of ownership with respect to your material form are integral to your body image, which, in turn, is integral to your sense of selfhood and agency (68–73; see also Gallagher 2005, 24–25, 35, 38). Your body image is not simply an imaginary replication of your corporeal contours. It is an emotionally charged construal of your body. Consequently, your "authentic body"—your owned body image—may fail to coincide with your actual body (Prosser 1998, 70).

This disjuncture is familiar from studies of phantom limbs (Prosser 1998, 78–84; Grosz 1994, 41, 70–73; Gallagher 2005, 86–106). Prosser characterizes the way discrepancies between a stubbornly intact body image and a body that has undergone amputation register affectively as "nostalgia" for a missing bodily attribute (Prosser 1998, 84). Ballerina Tanaquil Le Clercq (1929–2000), who was stricken with polio and paralyzed from the waist down at the age of twenty-seven, describes a similar experience:

"I had dreams in the beginning, for years," she says, "of going to the theater and discovering I'd forgotten my toe shoes, or rushing from one ballet to another and not being able to get my hair up. Anxiety dreams about all the horrible things that could happen to you as a dancer—when I couldn't even dance anymore. I outgrew those dreams eventually. Well, it was a hundred years ago. But when I dream now, I'm still walking, never wheeling. I know." She rolls her eyes. "After all this time, you'd think I'd get the message." (Brubach 1998)

So does Ahuva Cohen, who had sex-reassignment surgery at the age of thirty-three:

I had experienced my first epiphany about my true sexual nature under rather sleazy circumstances. When my college roommate persuaded me to take the subway down to Forty-Second Street with him to see *The Devil in Miss Jones*, I became transfixed by the images of Georgina Spelvin copulating on the screen. My simple erotic fantasies of the images of female bodies began to evolve into more elaborate fantasies of possessing a female body myself. When I met a girl and began having sex with her in my dorm room, I would imagine that someone else was doing to me what I was doing to her....

I would argue, however, that the intense "nostalgia" that I had begun to feel for a feminized body had been more than skin deep. Becoming a woman for me was not about wanting to play with dolls, or about wanting to adorn myself with jewelry, or about wanting to avoid military service, or about wanting to feel comfortable in social interactions, or just about wanting to feel comfortable in my own skin, but rather about needing to be fucked like a woman. (Cohen n.d.)

Both Le Clercq and Cohen speak of ineradicable, emotional bonds that connect them to body images encoded in dreams or fantasies that are at odds with their actual anatomies.

Of signal importance for understanding posttreatment transgendered agency, Prosser points out that an amputee's experience of a phantom limb can jumpstart adjustment to a prosthetic device (Prosser 1998, 85). Likewise, a transgendered person's pretreatment emotional investment in and fantasized anticipation of a posttreatment anatomy facilitate posttreatment ownership of and agentic acclimation to a reconstructed body (85–89). Alas, Prosser does not theorize the agentic enhancement that hormonal or surgical treatment can underwrite for a transgendered person. Although Volcano does not write about this dimension of his life in any detail, his self-portraiture supplies abundant evidence of amplified agency.[23] Moreover, as I have argued, Saville's portrait trumpets his agentic transmutation.

Saville's whole-person approach to portraiture allows her to include dimensions of Volcano's identity and agency that would ordinarily be excluded from a portrait and to represent Volcano's identity and agency more fully than would ordinarily be possible. Two themes provide foci for *Matrix*'s composition, and they are key to interpreting this work: (1) Volcano's "throwing down the gauntlet" attitude, centering on but not confined to his head, and (2) the unabashed sexual agency of Volcano's body, centering on but not confined to his genitalia. I note, as well, the tender image of Volcano's breasts framing his face. Saville conjures up a "Madonna with Child" synthesized in a single person—a mischievous, you might say "devilish," metaphor for Volcano's self-love and lovability.

If *Matrix* does not egregiously misrepresent Volcano, it sets a challenging agenda for philosophy of action. In what follows, I consider why the structure of many theories of identity and agency precludes explicating *Matrix*'s depiction of Volcano's agentic enhancement, and I suggest a criterion of adequacy that a theory of agency must satisfy if it is to accommodate the agentic advances that *Matrix* spotlights.

While differing in many details, a number of influential philosophical accounts of personal identity and agency rely on one of two versions of a top-down model, both of which position the mind as the supervisor of the body. The basic idea of the identity construction model is that the mind deliberates and decides which of your qualities and desires to endorse, tolerate, or try to acquire.[24] When you act on accepted attributes, you act autonomously. The basic idea of the action production model is that the mind deliberates and decides what to do.[25] Autonomous action issues from these determinations. I cannot review all of these accounts here, but, in my view, Saville's representation of Volcano is incompatible with top-down views of identity and agency. Nothing in *Matrix* warrants the inference that Volcano's mind has a monopoly on governing his conduct. What is missing in these theories, central to Prosser's view and memorably described in *Matrix*, is intelligent corporeity. To be sure, Volcano knows his own mind and acts accordingly, but *Matrix* foregounds his agentic body.

In some philosophical quarters, Kantian insistence on pure reason as the ruling faculty of an autonomous agent is losing favor. More and more, philosophers are acknowledging the contributions of affect to discerning what sort of person to aspire to be or what would be best to do. Basal affective states, such as self-trust, have gained entrée into some theories as necessary conditions for autonomy (e.g., Govier 1993; Benson 2000). Harry Frankfurt's contention that love demarcates the boundaries of the will further underscores the role of affect in identity and agency (Frankfurt 1988, ch. 7; Frankfurt 1998, chs. 11, 14). This salubrious trend opens the possibility that more philosophers of action will recognize the link between affect and embodiment and realize how crucial embodiment is to identity and agency. Purely mental affect is the exception rather than the rule, and somatically situated feelings are indispensable to intelligent agency.[26]

The most promising philosophical antecedent for a theory of corporeal practical intelligence is Maurice Merleau-Ponty's account of embodied habit. For Merleau-Ponty, habit is "the [body's] power to respond with a certain type of solution to situations of a certain general form" (Merleau-Ponty 1962/2004, 164–65). By virtue of habit, you corporeally apprehend the possibilities for action that an environment presents; select movement that comports with your needs, values, and aims; and rally your fund of know-how to act appropriately and meaningfully (129, 151–52, 161, 165). Although the term "habit" colloquially connotes mindless routines, such as smoking cigarettes or watching hours of escapist television, Merleau-Ponty's conception of habit references a flexible capability that is attuned to new information and responsive to it. As he puts it, habit constitutes "our power of dilating our being-in-the-world, or changing our existence by appropriating fresh instruments" (166). Your know-how expands as you put it to use. Although culturally mediated, your body is agentic—that is, capable of improvisation and innovation.[27]

In my view, one of Merleau-Ponty's examples of the workings of habit presciently anticipates key problems in theorizing transgendered agency. Consider a fashionable woman wearing a hat adorned with a long feather who effortlessly adjusts her movements to accommodate the feather's extension of her height (Merleau-Ponty 1962/2004, 165). According to Merleau-Ponty, she temporarily incorporates her apparel into her body image. Armed with this preconscious self-knowledge, she navigates the world without poking nearby people in the eye or crushing her feather in a cab door. Of course, she consciously donned this hat when she left home. Still, she didn't consciously revise her body image or consciously alter her behavior to take the plume into account. Merleau-Ponty maintains that people expand and contract their sense of their own spatial boundaries with surprising ease and frequency and that habit enables them to adjust their movement patterns accordingly.

Artist Rebecca Horn's prosthetic inventions and her films of performances in which individuals wear them demonstrate the human body's agentic malleability and versatility. For *Finger Gloves* (*Handschuhfingers* 1972), Horn constructed black hand attachments with straight, rigid "fingers" about three feet long. In the film, the performer uses her prostheticly elongated digits to feel her way around what appears to be a patio or balcony paved in stone. Through her artificial fingers, she finds her way around, encountering the surfaces of a low boundary wall and making contact with the back of a nude male body lying face-down on the stone paving. Horn never gives viewers a wide-angle look at the setting. Allowed to see only what the "gloved" performer comes across, viewers are vouchsafed a glimpse of the lived experience of an alternative embodiment.

Horn's artistic method for her *Personal Art* series is collaborative. The device she creates for each performer reflects her understanding of that individual's agentic identity. She describes her process as follows:

> The actual performance is preceded by a process of development in which the chosen performer participates. The performer's desires and projections determine the manner in which he presents himself. The "garment" is constructed and made to fit the body of the wearer. Through the act of fitting it and wearing it time after time, a process of identification begins to evolve, an essential factor for the performance. During the performance, the person is isolated, separated from his everyday environment, in order to find extended forms of self-perception. (Horn et al. 2000, 24)

What Merleau-Ponty invites you to imagine and Horn's films demonstrate is practically intelligent corporeity—affectively inflected proprioceptive and sensory awareness together with conatively triggered corporeal competencies. Your repertoire of know-how not only indexes your agentic identity but also functions as a vehicle of self-reimaging and self-direction.

Still, passé headgear and trendy artistic conceits might seem irrelevant to transgendered agency. After all, transgendered agentic identities and uses of medical technology do not concern appurtenances to be put on or taken off at will. They concern a person's experienced and experiencing flesh and the option of tampering with it. While acknowledging this disparity, I submit that the continuities are more philosophically significant.

Horn, recall, did not dream up costumes and then recruit volunteers to try them out. She designed garments to "fit" her performers psychocorporeally—to echo their yearnings, fantasies, and emotionally fueled body images. Likewise, Merleau-Ponty's lady of fashion dresses as she does because the figure-plus-hat gestalt she sees in her mirror pleases her. By her reckoning, it successfully synthesizes social standards of accessorization, her personal style, and her body image. She, too, is guided by affect and desire, and, like Horn's performers who developed strong identifications with their couture prostheses, she identifies with her mirror image.[28]

In my view, Volcano's experience of gendered embodiment, as portrayed in *Matrix*, is analogous. Whatever role rational calculation may have played in his decisions about ingesting hormones and posing for Saville, *Matrix* takes no notice of it. Urgent desires, compelling feelings, and vivid fantasies centering on a radically unorthodox body image underwrite the bodily configuration Volcano engineered for himself and the self-presentation Saville ascribes to Volcano. Neither *Plan* nor *Matrix* etiolates gendered subjectivity. In both works, libidinized gender saturates the models' bodies. The *Plan* figure is a victim of the clash between her body and feminine beauty ideals. Because her body image of gendered inferiority subdues her agency, she challenges philosophers of action to explicate corporeal agentic dysfunction—anomic, numbed, deskilled, immiserated embodiment. In contrast, *Matrix* represents corporeal agentic competence—attuned, versatile, confident, intelligent embodiment. In *Matrix*, the figure embraces his "mutant" body image, and the coordination of his feelings, desires, and body image quickens his agency. Paralleling Merleau-Ponty's philosophy and Horn's performance art, *Matrix* features Volcano's vibrant embodied subjectivity and credits his visceral experience as an arbiter of his agency.[29]

NOTES

1. Volcano makes a similar statement in a 1999 essay: "I no longer identify as 'woman,' and feel uncomfortable being read as female. I am intersex by design, an intentional mutation and need to have my gender specified as existing outside of the binary gender system, rather than an abomination of it."

2. I am not suggesting that Saville's work is unprecedented in western portraiture. For example, her work is often compared with Lucien Freud's nude portraits. Although I don't have space to make the case for this claim here, I believe that her work constitutes a significant advance in this genre in virtue of its evocation of psychocorporeality—the inextricability of selfhood, personal identity, and individual agency from the enculturated and intelligent human body.

3. For additional discussion of agentic bodies in Saville's oeuvre, see Meyers forthcoming, "Jenny Saville Remakes the Female Nude."

4. For relevant discussion, see Meagher 2003.

5. For discussion of the relevance of nontransgendered women's body issues to the topic of transgendered identity and agency, see Heyes 2003, 1097–98, and Heyes 2007, 40–42.

6. For a related reading of the geometry of *Plan*, see Rowley 1996, 93–96.

7. She also holds her left arm rigidly straight and pulls it tightly against her left side. For relevant discussion of women's need to make themselves as small as possible and to take up as little room as possible, see Bordo 1993, 185–212, and Bordo 1997, 127–33.

8. In addition to Saville's generous painterly treatment of the figure in *Plan*, the fact that she herself modeled for this painting provides evidence of her sympathy for the figure she portrays—indeed, her identification with this figure.

9. For my views about Orlan's work, see Meyers 2002, 133–37.

10. For further discussion of my views regarding feminine beauty ideals, personal identity, and agency, see Meyers 2002, chs. 5 and 6, and Meyers 2004, ch. 4.

11. Volcano says that a physician told him there's a 90 percent probability that he has a genetic mutation called "46XX true hermaphroditism" (Volcano 2000, 99). Recounting Volcano's intertwined personal and artistic development, Prosser reports that he first let his beard grow and then took male hormones and identified as a "Hermaphrodyké," a "queer-identified intersexual" (Prosser 2000, 10).

12. Although Saville uses bi-gendered pronouns to refer to Volcano, I'll use the masculine pronoun because Volcano affirms that he valorizes his "mutant maleness" and doesn't want to be read as female (Volcano 1999). I do this with misgivings, however, because Volcano characterizes himself as a gender abolitionist. Given the existing English framework of gendered or neuter pronouns, I suspect that far-reaching cultural changes would need to occur before language could be established that would neither gender nor thingify (I think I'm borrowing this term from Catherine MacKinnon) gender abolitionists who live their beliefs as Volcano does. As things are, we can have a third gender or an in-between gender, but we don't have the linguistic resources to refer to a nongender that isn't an "it."

13. Volcano outlines how he copes with the dominant gender regime: "Out on the street I often feel the need to pass (as male). But in my own queer community I don't want to pass as male or female. I want to be seen for what I am: a chimera, a hybrid, a herm" (Volcano and Windh 2003). Elsewhere he describes being assaulted on a London bus (Volcano 2004).

14. In this connection, it is worth noting that Saville inspires confidence in her models partly by taking risks herself. Volcano recalls: "She had photographed herself in the positions she wanted me to attempt, before I arrived. The fact that she exposed her own crevice impressed me and produced in me a desire to do whatever was required no matter how undignified or painful" (Volcano 1999).

15. For an interpretation of *Matrix* as a "study in body dysphoria" and an articulation of the thesis that you can't really choose to become the "opposite sex," see Halberstam 2005, 111. I find this view of *Matrix* dubious because Volcano assimilates his experience posing for Saville to what subjects have told him about their experiences posing for him and praises Saville's work (Volcano 1999).

16. I emphasize that this passage of *Matrix* looks this way to me because I take seriously Prosser's comment about the visual effect of Volcano's close-up perspective and enlargement of the images in his *Transcock* suite. Prosser claims that the size of these artistic manipulations enable many viewers who would not otherwise see these former clitorises as penises to grasp the "felt reality of this part as a penis" for the transsexual man who posed for the photograph (Prosser 2000, 9).

17. I discuss the interplay of individual autonomy, cultural norms, and political critique in a number of other essays—for example, Meyers 2002, chs. 1, 2, and 6, and Meyers 2004, chs. 2, 4, 10, and 13.

18. In contrast, Heyes underscores the analogies and continuities between the experience of women and transsexuals in order to make a case for feminist solidarity with transgendered people (Heyes 2007, 45).

19. Here is the context in which Windh uses this expression: "INDRA: The lenses through which I perceive the world allow me to see more than double. In fact I take in a beautifully shifting kaleidoscopic reality, an amazing mosaic of gender variance and norm deviance. Luckily, I have learnt to count past two and deliberately trained my eyes, and other senses, to detect a multiplicity of gendered possibilities all around and within me. I appreciate, value, respect, desire, admire and love what I see" (Volcano and Windh 2003).

20. It is worth bearing in mind that feminist dieters are also complicit in perpetuating oppressive norms of feminine heterosexual attractiveness (Heyes 2007, 59; see also Bartky 1990, 71–78).

21. For commentary on pernicious coercion that paradoxically enforces sex reassignment surgery as an exit route from the stigma of homosexuality in Iran, see Ireland 2007.

22. I do not have space to engage Prosser's critique of poststructuralist accounts of the subject, nor can I take up problems in psychoanalytic accounts, such as Anzieu's. In this essay, I isolate what I consider insightful in each position.

23. For reproductions of the self-portraits I refer to, see Volcano 2000, 88–98, 168–79.

24. The views of Harry Frankfurt (1988), Marilyn Friedman (2003), and John Christman (2005) exemplify this approach.

25. David Velleman's work (2000a; 2000b; 2002) exemplifies this approach.

26. For defense of these claims about embodied affectivity, see Meyers "Affect, Corporeity, and Practical Intelligence." Unpublished manuscript.

27. For complementary work in this area, see Dreyfus 1998; Dreyfus and Dreyfus 1999; Grimshaw 1999; Sheets-Johnstone 1999; and Sullivan 2000.

28. Prosser underscores the prominence of "mirror scenes" in transsexual autobiographies (Prosser 1998, 99 ff).

29. When Laurie Shrage first proposed that I write for this volume, I shrank from the task. I questioned whether I had any right to talk about life situations so different from my own. But Laurie persisted, and Ahuva B. Cohen, who underwent sex-reassignment surgery twenty years ago, permitted me to read and quote from parts of her memoire. Her text evidences such extraordinary candor, introspective insight, and skepticism about theories that I decided to try, with all due self-doubt, to take a first step toward understanding transgendered and transsexual agency. I want to take this opportunity to express my gratitude to both Laurie Shrage and Ahuva Cohen. I would not have attempted this essay, were it not for their help. I also thank Maureen Bray, director of the Sean Kelly Gallery for refreshing and correcting my memory of Rebecca Horn's *Finger Gloves*.

REFERENCES

Bartky, Sandra Lee. 1990. *Femininity and Domination*. New York: Routledge.
———. 2002. *"Sympathy and Solidarity" and Other Essays*. Lanham, Md.: Rowman and Littlefield.
Benson, Paul. 2000. "Feeling Crazy: Self-Worth and the Social Character of Responsibility." In *Relational Autonomy*, ed. Catriona Mackenzie and Natalie Stoljar. New York: Oxford University Press.
Boodman, Sandra G. 2004. "For More Teenage Girls, Adult Plastic Surgery: Rise in Breast Implants, Other Procedures Raises Doubts about Long-Term Effects." *Washington Post*. October 26, 2004, p. A01.

Bordo, Susan. 1993. *Unbearable Weight*. Berkeley: University of California Press.

———. 1997. *Twilight Zones*. Berkeley: University of California Press.

Brubach, Holly. 1998. "Muse, Interrupted." *New York Times*, November 22, 1998, sec. 6, p. 60.

Butler, Judith. 2004. *Undoing Gender*. New York: Routledge.

Cohen, Ahuva B. n.d. "The Road to Jerusalem." In *Testimony*. Unpublished ms.

Christman, John. 2005. "Autonomy, Self-Knowledge, and Liberal Legitimacy." In *Autonomy and the Challenges to Liberalism*, ed. Joel Anderson and John Christman. New York: Cambridge University Press.

Davis, Kathy. 1991. "Remaking the She-Devil: A Critical Look at Feminist Approaches to Beauty." *Hypatia* 6, no. 2 (1991): 21–43.

Dreyfus, Hubert L. 1998. "Intelligence without Representation." At www.hfac.uh.edu/cogsci/dreyfus.html.

Dreyfus, Hubert L., and Stuart E. Dreyfus. 1999. "The Challenge of Merleau-Ponty's Phenomenology of Embodiment for Cognitive Science." In *Perspectives on Embodiment*, ed. Gail Weiss and Honi Fern Haber. New York: Routledge.

Frankfurt, Harry. 1988. *The Importance of What We Care About*. Cambridge: Cambridge University Press.

———. 1998. *Necessity, Volition, and Love*. Cambridge: Cambridge University Press.

Friedman, Marilyn. 2003. *Autonomy, Gender, Politics*. New York: Oxford University Press.

Gallagher, Shaun. 2005. *How the Body Shapes the Mind*. New York: Oxford University Press.

Gayford, Martin. 1999. "A Conversation with Jenny Saville." In *Jenny Saville: Territories*, ed. Mollie Dent-Brocklehurst. New York: Gagosian Gallery.

Govier, Trudy. 1993. "Self-Trust, Autonomy, and Self-Esteem." *Hypatia* 8: 99–120.

Grimshaw. Jean. 1999. "Working Out with Merleau-Ponty." In *Women's Bodies: Discipline and Transgression*, ed. Jane Arthurs and Jean Grimshaw. London: Cassell.

Grosz, Elizabeth. 1994. *Volatile Bodies: Toward a Corporeal Feminism*. Bloomington: Indiana University Press.

Halberstam, Judith. 2005. *In a Queer Time and Place: Transgender Bodies, Subcultural Lives*. New York: New York University Press.

Heyes, Cressida J. 2003. "Feminist Solidarity after Queer Theory." *Signs* 28: 1093–1120.

———. 2007. *Self-Transformations: Foucault, Ethics, and Normalized Bodies*. New York: Oxford University Press.

Horn, Rebecca, et al. 2000. *Rebecca Horn*. Trans. Matthew Partridge. Stuttgart: Institut für Auslandsbeziehungen.

Ireland, Doug. 2007. "Change Sex or Die." *Gay City News*. At http://gaycitynews.com/site/news.cfm?newsid=18324930&BRD=2729&PAG=461&dept_id=569346&rfi=6. 05/10/2007 (accessed June 1, 2008).

Kuspit, Donald. 1999. "Jenny Saville: Gagosian Gallery, New York City, New York." *ArtForum* December.

Mackenzie, Suzie. 2005. "Under the Skin." *Guardian,y* October 22, 2005.

Mason-Schrock, Douglas. 1996. "Transsexuals' Narrative Construction of the 'True Self.'" *Social Psychology Quarterly* 59, no. 3: 176–92.

Meagher, Michelle. 2003. "Jenny Saville and a Feminist Aesthetics of Disgust." *Hypatia* 18, no. 4: 23–41.

Merleau-Ponty, Maurice. 1962, reprinted in 2004. *Phenomenology of Perception*. Trans. Colin Smith. New York: Routledge.

Meyers, Diana Tietjens. 2002. *Gender in the Mirror: Cultural Imagery and Women's Agency*. New York: Oxford University Press.

———. 2004. *Being Yourself: Essays on Identity, Action, and Social Life*. New York: Rowman and Littlefield.

———. "Affect, Corporeity, and Practical Intelligence." Unpublished ms.

———. Forthcoming. "Jenny Saville Remakes the Female Nude: Feminist Reflections on the State of the Art." In *Beauty Revisited*, ed. Peg Zeglin Brand. Bloomington: Indiana University Press.

Nead, Lynda. 1992. *The Female Nude: Art, Obscenity, and Sexuality*. New York: Routledge.

Nelson, Hilde Lindemann. 2001. *Damaged Identities: Narrative Repair*. Ithaca, N.Y.: Cornell University Press.

Prosser, Jay. 1998. *Second Skins: The Body Narratives of Transsexuality*. New York: Columbia University Press.

———. 2000. "The Art of Ph/Autography: Del LaGrace Volcano." In *Sublime Mutations*, ed. Del LaGrace Volcano. Tübingen: Konkursbuchverlag.

Rowley, Alison. 1996. "On Viewing Three Paintings by Jenny Saville: Rethinking a Feminist Practice of Painting." In *Generations and Geographies in the Visual Arts: Feminist Readings*, ed. Griselda Pollock. New York: Routledge.

Schama, Simon. 2005. "Interview with Jenny Saville." In *Jenny Saville*. New York: Rizzoli.

Sheets-Johnstone, Maxine. 1999. *The Primacy of Movement*. Amsterdam: John Benjamins.

Singer, Natasha. 2007. "Is the 'Mom Job' Really Necessary?" *New York Times*, October 4, 2007, at http://www.nytimes.com/2007/10/04/fashion/04skin.html?pagewanted=1 (accessed June 3, 2008).

Sullivan, Shannon. 2000. "Reconfiguring Gender with John Dewey: Habit, Bodies, and Cultural Change." *Hypatia* 15, no. 1: 23–42.

Velleman, J. David. 2000a. "From Self Psychology to Moral Philosophy." *Philosophical Perspectives: Action and Freedom* 14: 349–77.

———. 2000b. *The Possibility of Practical Reason*. New York: Oxford University Press.

———. 2002. "Identification and Identity." In *Contours of Agency*, ed. Sarah Buss and Lee Overton. Cambridge, Mass.: MIT Press.

Volcano, Del LaGrace. 1999. "On Being a Jenny Saville Painting." In *Jenny Saville: Territories*, ed. Mollie Dent-Brocklehurst. New York: Gagosian Gallery.

———. ed. 2000. *Sublime Mutations*. Tübingen: Konkursbuchverlag.

———. 2004. "Leap Day." At http://www.dellagracevolcano.com/text3.html (accessed May 21, 2008).

———. 2005. Statement, at http://www.dellagracevolcano.com/statement.html (accessed May 7, 2008).

Volcano, Del LaGrace, and Indra Windh. 2003 "Hermlove." At http://www.dellagracevolcano.com/text2.html (accessed May 21, 2008).

10

Sex and Miscibility

Laurie J. Shrage

Folk Sex

Several years ago in my son's bedroom, a leopard gecko laid some eggs. Fortunately, my son and I were prepared for this event, and so we quickly grabbed his leopard gecko manual and the incubator, which we had purchased along with his lizards. I turned to the chapter on "Egg-Laying and Incubation" and read the following:

> Recent studies have confirmed that the sex of leopard geckos is temperature determined within the first two weeks of incubation. If the eggs are incubated at a temperature of 79°F (26°C), most of the offspring will be female. At a temperature of 85–87°F (29–31°C), one can expect more or less equal ratios of males and females. At 90°F (32°C), the great majority of the hatchlings will be males. Herpetoculturists, depending on their goals, will have to determine the preferred incubation temperature(s) for their specific purposes.[1]

After deliberating a bit, my son decided to generate female geckos, primarily because adult males cannot be kept in the same enclosure. So we set the incubator temperature at 79°.

That the sexes of my son's expected baby geckos could be controlled by manipulating certain features of their gestational environment caused some surprise among our friends and family members. Our female gecko cohabitates with a male gecko, and my son enjoys giving unsolicited reports about the reptile sexual activity taking place in his bedroom. For this reason, we were operating under the assumption that our lizard eggs were fertile. We also assumed that the process of conception of the embryonic geckos had determined their sex. But the latter assumption was incorrect. So, in a moment of confusion, my son accepted his additional generative power and responsibility and then chose the sex of his possible gecko offspring.

The multiplicity of biological mechanisms for producing the bodily characteristics that we recognize as male and female are familiar to biologists, physicians, and animal hobbyists more experienced than my son and me. Chromosomal triggers of sex differentiation developed in the human species over millions of years. According to one report, "Millions of years ago sex was probably determined not by sex chromosomes, but by some environmental factor, like the temperature of the water at which the egg incubated. (Sex determination still occurs this way in some animals like crocodiles and sea turtles.) Over the years, a pair of autosomes differentiated into two distinct chromosomes, the X and the Y."[2] Because sex groupings have a genetic basis (unlike race), those aware of this fact tend to think that sex identities are biologically real and are not just social categories. In this essay, I consider whether the biological mechanisms of sex differentiation render our cultural distinctions real and empirically justified, and what aspects of sex identification are culturally and socially relative.

More generally, I compare our ordinary "folk" conceptions of sex identity with information we currently have from the sciences regarding sex determination in various organisms. My project is much like that of philosophers who have been exploring the relationship between folk concepts of race and the science of race.[3] A number of theorists have shown that outdated and discredited scientific concepts of race still permeate our ordinary understandings of race. I investigate how the partial scientific information that the average person receives about sex development informs our folk ideas of sex difference. In exploring the cognitive distance between current scientific and ordinary notions of sex identity, I consider the problems our ordinary understandings pose for people who appear to be abnormally sexed or sex-identified. Because our ordinary concepts of female and male draw from both current and outdated science, our folk concepts are overly simplistic and rigid, and in some ways they are erroneous.

Given that our folk concepts fail to recognize the diversity of bodies and the complexity of sex identification—especially bodies and identities that mix male and female traits—and given that these notions can render the bodies and identities of many individuals incomprehensible or even freakish, I explore alternatives for enriching, altering, or replacing common terms for a person's sex identity. In particular, I consider whether the introduction of terms such as "transsexual," "transgender," "transman," "transwoman," "trans," and "intersex" can transform our folk concepts in ways that render nonstandard bodies and identifying practices comprehensible and "normal." Because merely transforming or proliferating our folk categories of sex (and race) does not always challenge erroneous ideas, I also explore the potential advantages of eliminating some amount of "sex talk" or the practice of using sex (or race) to define, both informally and legally, who a person really is.

From the point of view of humans, reptile sex development is weird. Having learned that sex is inscribed deep in our chromosomes and genes, we find the relative malleability of lizard sex development to be odd. But it might offer some comfort to know that the sex traits of geckos, once developed, are relatively stable. This is apparently not so in other species. For example, the Florida Museum of Natural History includes the following item in the "Fish News" section of its website:

> What the movie "Finding Nemo" doesn't tell you about clownfish is that they're all transsexuals. In a study published in the journal *Nature*, evolutionary biologist Peter Buston and colleagues report that clownfish in Papua New Guinea reefs can change their sex at will for social reasons. Clownfish live in strict hierarchical communities. Each neighborhood is dominated by a top-ranking female breeder. Her male partner is next, followed by up to four progressively smaller, non-breeding fish. When the dominant female dies, her mate changes sex and becomes female. The top-ranking non-breeder becomes a sexually active male, and all the other fish shift up a rank.[4]

What do visitors to this website or museum make of sex changes in clownfish? How does the apparent "transsexuality" in fish help us understand sex changes or transsexuality in humans? This news release implies that transsexuals are individuals who "change their sex at will for social reasons." Yet many humans who identify as transsexuals believe that being male or female is beyond a person's control; persons can only control or modify aspects of their bodies to be congruent with their inner sex.[5] It is also doubtful that clownfish exercise much agency and autonomy over their sex identity, contrary to the suggestion in this glib report. Nevertheless, I am interested in how good scientific reporting and education could shape, restrict, and potentially alter contemporary ideas about sex identities in humans. How is knowledge of sex differentiation in other species, or over the long evolutionary stretch in humans, relevant to our contemporary sex identities?

In the first part of this chapter, I compare ordinary sex distinctions with common race classifications. In particular, I consider how we sort bodies into the categories "female," "male," "black," and "white." More specifically, I consider the bodily components and traits that enable the sexing and racing of bodies. I then investigate whether the standard configurations of bodily components indicative of each sex are as arbitrary as those indicative of different races.[6] I argue that our race and sex terms and categories impose greater unity and meaning onto certain common patterns of traits. I then consider and defend various linguistic and social practices that challenge current conceptions of sex identity.

Real Sex

About ten years ago, I was discussing with my students the asymmetry of the "one-drop rule" for classifying people according to race. I noted how this rule reflects concerns with the racial purity of so-called whites, "the darkening" of future generations, and the "mongrelization" (a rather hateful concept) of humankind. I then provided some anecdotes to show how attentive most people are to the lightness or darkness of children in relation to their parents, and how intrigued and surprised we become when we notice differences, especially if the children are perceived as lighter. One of my students offered the observation that people are typically surprised when a black child is born with light hair or blue eyes, and, before she could finish her comment, several students asked how a black person could have blue eyes. Their naive question suggested that this was not possible. At this point, my student opened her eyes widely and indicated that she was black and that she had blue eyes. Before the class ended, several students made sure they got close enough to her to see for themselves a blue-eyed black woman.[7]

I remember asking my students to just think for a moment about why this combination of bodily traits is possible, if somewhat uncommon. It didn't take my students very long to figure out that this woman must have ancestors on both sides of her family who carried the recessive trait for blue eye coloring. Yet, the incident demonstrated rather well how our racial classificatory scheme rendered certain facts invisible, such as the ancestry of people we call "black." Moreover, because we associate blue eyes with the whitest of white people—their badge of racial purity—it was confusing and perhaps disturbing to some of my students that a black person's eyes could be blue. A body like this blurred the boundary between black and white people and called into question our ideas about the results of racial mixing.

Our rules for sexing bodies can be similarly thrown off. We have certain notions about what separates the boys from the girls, and then we find it difficult to comprehend girl bodies with an XY karyotype and boy bodies that are XX—or lizard bodies in which sex is not in the genes. But chromosomes and genes are only one among several mechanisms in nature that determine an organism's sex and sex characteristics and, in perhaps two percent of humans, sex differentiation and development differ from the norm.[8] Indeed, the genes on the Y chromosome now appear to be disappearing,[9] and there seems to be some dispute in the scientific community about how significant the remaining genes are for generating sex differences in humans.[10] According to Joanne Meyerowitz:

> In the late nineteenth century scientists had relied on gonads as the determinants of "true" sex...; but by the end of the century they had begun to include other physical markers, especially hormones. Scientists discovered sex hormones in the late nineteenth century and soon identified them as either male or female. In studying sex differentiation, they focused increasingly on the impact of internal secretions rather than on the gonads themselves or on the morphology of genitals and reproductive organs. In the early twentieth century, scientists acknowledged chromosomes as the initial determinants of sex, but they turned to hormones, as the fluid carriers of sex, to help explain sexual development and the many variations and gradations they saw in the intermediate conditions.[11]

Historically, different features have served as definitive markers of sex, including gonads, hormone levels, chromosomes, external and internal morphological features, and phenotype (secondary sex characteristics). Yet, some bodies have a combination of male and female markers, and some markers are ambiguous, such as chromosomal patterns other than XX and XY (XXY, XO, etc.), or ovotestes.[12] How do we determine the true sex of such bodies? Are the components of sex miscible or immiscible; that is, can they dissolve into each other, yielding a male-female solution or blend, or do the components react and bond so that we end up with a new sex compound? And, if this use of terms seems to be stretching the chemistry metaphor too far, what other metaphors or models are available to describe bodies and minds that are "impure" with respect to sex?

The presence or absence of particular genitalia, reproductive parts, gonads, and secondary characteristics appears to be neither necessary nor sufficient to assign someone to one of the two standard sexes, when mixtures of various kinds appear. Castrated men can still be men, women without ovaries or uteruses can still be women, men with protruding breasts can be men, women on steroids can be women, short men with soft skin and little facial hair can be men, and women with beards and developed muscles can be women. Although some argue that brains can be sexed and may provide a more reliable predictor of gender identity, studies about sex differences in the brain are highly disputed and inconclusive at this point.[13] Mixed bodies are often socially invisible because people born with allegedly inconsistent reproductive or primary sex components typically live as either men or women (and not both), such as XY girls who may have Androgen Insensitivity Syndrome. Some might argue that the bodies described here are exceptions that prove the rule, yet when do enough exceptions accumulate for us to distrust the rule? Because our current classificatory practices often lead us to treat blended or compound bodies as abnormal, defective, and even freakish, perhaps the marginalizing and stigmatizing effects of our "folk" concepts of sex should lead us to question their utility and empirical justification.

The situation is similar in regard to race. Although the Human Genome Project has confirmed that there is no genetic basis for the racial distinctions we make, we still persist in sorting bodies by race.[14] We do this by classifying bodies primarily according to skin color, hair texture, and facial features. Certain bodily traits are treated as indicative of a person's race, while other bodily traits have little or no racial meaning. We then racialize the paradigmatic bodily components themselves, and recognize such things as "black hair," "white skin," and "Asian eyes." So black people are black in virtue of having black hair and black skin, and hair and skin are black by virtue of being associated with the bodies of people we call "black." That is, our concepts of race are logically circular and reflect socially, and not biologically, significant distinctions. There is nothing about skin color, hair texture, or eye, nose, and mouth shape that make them "racial" properties other than social conventions. And we can easily imagine alternative social conventions that would render racially significant such bodily features as buttock size, skull shape, cheekbone structure, arched feet, detached ear lobes, eyebrow density, gumline exposure when smiling, body height, overall hairiness, wrist or ankle width, and so on (some of these body parts have had, at other historical moments, more racial significance). It's true that certain combinations of skin color, hair texture, and facial features occur more frequently than others, but this is the result of mating practices that have taken place over millions of years, not some inner coherence or unity among certain traits. In sum, the fact that there are family resemblances among people with similar bodily features, and who may have ancestors who once shared a geographical region and therefore swapped genes for certain bodily traits, does not make such people a "race." As Anthony Appiah states, "No coherent system of biological classification of people—no classification, that is, that serves explanatory purposes central to biological theory—corresponds to the folk-theoretical classifications of people into Caucasian, Negro, and such. This is not, of course, to deny that there are differences in morphology among humans: people's skins do differ in color."[15] Yet, according to Appiah, folk sex classifications do correspond to biological kinds and serve explanatory purposes.

Humans reproduce sexually, and each organism generally possesses some subset of the anatomy necessary for procreation—that is, the possession of both "male" and "female" procreative parts is rare in human beings, unlike some other species. But is there a coherence or unity in each subset of procreative components so that it makes sense to divide people into sex kinds in accordance with their sexed body parts (male, female, mostly male, mostly female, equally male and female, neither male nor female, etc.)? Do people who have similar configurations of parts share a sex or only a reproductive potential that may or may not be realized? As a social concept, a person's sex identity carries a lot of meaning, but what relationship does this social concept have to the bodily components of sex? Are we all just the same underneath or behind our sexed parts, or are there fundamental differences between people with different configurations of sexed parts?

Sexed body parts are usually related to the body's reproductive functions, while raced body parts appear to have little physiological functionality. We know that skin pigment protects the skin from burning, premature aging, and cancers caused by exposure to sunlight, but most other differences that we racialize, such as hair color and texture, have little to do with physiological functionality. Are sex and race, then, disanalogous with respect to their biological basis, as Appiah suggests? Are sex kinds not quite as arbitrary (with respect to nature) as race kinds? This would seem to be the case if sex distinctions are really about reproductive parts and capacities. But when we classify people as female and male, are we really classifying them as egg and sperm producers, gestators and inseminators, and lactators and nonlactators? If female and male truly correlate with these functions, then we would need to have more sex categories than we currently do to describe the variety of bodies according to their reproductive components and capacities. For where do the infertile and postfertile fall in this classificatory scheme? Where do we place women who can produce viable eggs but cannot gestate? Where do we place men who cannot inseminate or impregnate? And given that new reproductive technologies can give people reproductive capacities not provided by nature, how do we classify people who make use of in vitro fertilization, medically assisted gestation or lactation, Viagra, and so on? In exploring why sex identities are treated as more primary or fundamental than other identities, Georgia Warnke makes similar observations:

> The idea of eliminating our categories of sex seems to shipwreck on the needs of reproduction. We need to interpret and divide human beings according to sex because doing so serves the requirements of reproduction. Yet how often do we want to reproduce? Given the limited number of times individuals in post-industrial societies do so, it seems odd to define human beings in terms of this capacity. More importantly, obviously not all those categorized as female actually have the capacity to reproduce; they are too young, too old, or infertile. Finally, with the present and future birth technologies of sperm banks, artificial insemination, artificial wombs, and cloning, and with the availability of these to "men" as well as "women," our current identities as male or female, as well as heterosexual or homosexual, seem at the very least unnecessary.[16]

Is it imperative that we classify bodies by their reproductive capacities and treat this as a basic way of ordering social life? Alternatively, just as reproduction is not the entire truth about sexuality, perhaps reproductive potential is not the most important truth about sex and gender expression or the social roles we assume.

In our sex classificatory system, not only do bodies have a sex but also the body parts indicative of a person's sex are regarded as sexed. Females are female in virtue of having female genitalia, and genitalia are female by virtue of being associated with the bodies of people we call females. Like our racial concepts, our sex concepts are logically circular. Sexed body parts generally serve reproductive functions, but are they male or female? Are breasts female, even though both male and female bodies have them? Are estrogens female, even though they are present in the bodies of men and women and they control bodily functions other than reproduction? (Are blue eyes racially white when they appear in bodies with dark skin?) Are androgens male, even though they have similar effects on male and female bodies? Are eggs female until fertilized by a Y sperm? Are sperm male when they carry an X chromosome? Are ovaries female and testes male, or are they simply organs (gonads) for producing "sex cells" (gametes): eggs (ova) and sperm (spermatozoon)? Is an XY karyotype male when it occurs in a body unresponsive to androgens (CAIS)? Is an XX karyotype female when it occurs in a fetus that produces and is responsive to androgens (CAH)?[17] Is gestational anatomy female even though male seahorses carry their young?[18] Are penises male when they appear on XX bodies, and are vaginas female when they appear on XY bodies, or can each of these parts belong to the bodies of both males and females?

In commenting on women's needs for testosterone and men's needs for estrogen, Anne Fausto-Sterling writes:

> Why, then, have hormones always been strongly associated with the idea of sex, when, in fact, "sex hormones" apparently affect organs throughout the entire body and are not specific to either gender? The brain, lungs, bones, blood vessels, intestine, and liver (to give a partial list) all use estrogen to maintain proper growth and development....Over this century, scientists have integrated the signs of gender—from genitalia, to the anatomy of gonads and brains, then to our very body chemistry—more thoroughly than ever into our bodies. In the case of the body's chemistry, researchers accomplished this feat by defining as sex hormones what are, in effect, multi-site chemical growth regulators, thus rendering their far-reaching, non-sexual roles in both male and female development nearly invisible. Now that the label of sex hormone seems attached with epoxy to these steroid molecules, any rediscovery of their role in tissues such as bones or intestines has a strange result. By virtue of the fact that so-called sex hormones affect their physiology, these organs, so clearly *not* involved in reproduction, come to be seen as sex organs. Chemicals infuse the body, from head to toe, with gender meanings.[19]

Fausto-Sterling here points out the logical circularity or regression embedded in the way that we project femaleness and maleness onto bodies and their parts. First we dub certain chemicals "female" and "male" as a convenient way to describe their involvement in certain sexual reproductive processes, and then we overlook the nonreproductive, and thus nonsexual, functions they direct. Bodies then become female and male by virtue of the presence of their respective female and male chemicals, and chemicals take on female and male properties by virtue of their presence in bodies we read as female and male. We then have the problem of explaining the presence of "female" hormones in male bodies and "male" hormones in female bodies. In other words, what starts out as one difference—different contributions to the generation of offspring—projects meaning onto every other bodily part and system so that the latter's properties are understood in terms of the former's. Bodies and their parts (including growth chemicals, genitals, brains, and psyches) are understood to have a coherent and exclusive sex in the way that certain generative roles in sexually reproducing organisms have a sex. But while it may make sense to describe certain components, roles, and contributions in the sexual generation of offspring as female and male, it makes less sense to describe other components, roles, and systems that have little to do with sexual generation as female and male. In short, sexual generation is only one of many things we do with our bodies, and it isn't the whole truth about our bodies, despite its evolutionary importance.

In linguistic terms, the use of the terms "male" and "female" for both persons and their parts is an instance of synecdoche, in which the whole stands for the part and the part stands for the whole. When we describe nonliving entities, such as electrical plugs, as "male" and "female," most people understand that these terms are being used metaphorically: that is, we are stretching or narrowing the meaning of these terms to extend their use. When we differentiate plugs that have prongs from those that have sockets by calling them male and female, respectively, the metaphor works by virtue of the insertive act attributed to male-female sex and to electrical connections. That is, the metaphor works because of sexual roles and anatomical parts that we stereotypically associate with males and females. But when we describe human bodies and their parts as "male" and "female," we fail to see that these designations are similarly based on stereotypical notions, simplifications, and conflations about biological processes and social or sexual roles.

We see both vaginas and bodies with vaginas as female because, stereotypically, vaginas and females are penetrated during sex, including nonreproductive sex, even though there are other orifices on the bodies of men and women that are commonly sexually penetrated. We see bodies with vaginas as female, whether the bodies belong to ftms (female to male), dominatrixes, or stone butch lesbians—that is, sexual actors who do not generally play the stereotypical female role in sex or in reproduction. Bodies lacking ovaries, uteruses, and breasts but equipped with vaginas are seen as female, despite the fact that such bodies do not produce eggs, gestate, or lactate. Because the vagina is the quintessential orifice for penetrative sex, and because being penetrated is stereotypically female, when other parts of the body are penetrated, they are viewed as analogous to a vagina. Thus men who are sexually penetrated are regarded as effeminate on two counts: for being sexually penetrated and for transforming some part of their body into a female receptor. Should we try to contest the conflation of genitals, sexual acts, and sex identities by sometimes referring to receiving parts—electrical and human—as male, this would probably suggest some kind of sexual and gender queerness rather than call attention to the somewhat arbitrary way that we stereotype and normalize bodies.[20]

If vaginas do not have a sex, but like breasts can occur on bodies that are differently sexed, then having or lacking a vagina is not indicative of one's sex. Yet because we define sex in logically circular ways, we see vaginas as female by virtue of being associated with female bodies, and we see female bodies as female by virtue of having vaginas. We cannot escape our sex concepts, just as we cannot escape our race concepts, because, indeed, bodies do have the parts we sex and race, even when the sexing and racing of these parts is logically circular. Social activists who would like to contest the alleged coherence of our sex and race concepts often deploy new sex and race terminology in order to call into question some aspect of the old terms. For example, some gender dissidents use the expressions "female-bodied men," "transmen," "bois," and "born males" to distinguish men with different configurations of sexed parts. But the new terms often combine or redeploy the old sex and gender ideas and probably would not be comprehensible if they did not incorporate some aspects of the old terminology. And because the new terms and categories often retain core elements of the old, they generally fail to alter old classificatory schemes. For example, "female-bodied man" implies that one's body can have a sex identity that differs from one's overall sex or gender identity, which may suggest that the truth about sex still resides in the body. Perhaps it would be better to talk of men who have nonstereotypical bodies rather than men with female bodies. Transmen who have had some stereotypical female parts removed and male ones added are at most "previously female-bodied men." Of these terms, I like "boi" the best because it merely signals, for social purposes, that the person so described has a dissident or nonstandard sex identity, without biologizing or essentializing this identity in a simplistic way.

As a menopausal, posthysterectomy woman, I tend to view female embodiment as a stage of life. At my present stage, my body is less feminized than previously in terms of reproductive capacity and parts, hormone levels, and secondary sex characteristics. Maintaining a feminized appearance takes more effort than previously, and I find that, in this respect, I identify more with the practices of transwomen than with younger stereotypical females. If I were to stop making various efforts to feminize my body, my appearance would be more ambiguous or masculine. In one significant respect I differ from transwomen, in that I don't necessarily value being socially recognized as a woman, perhaps because I take this for granted, or perhaps because I associate such recognition with sexist treatment. I politically value my identity as a woman because it makes it easier to demonstrate my solidarity with a group of people who have been socially oppressed. Despite the disappearance of feminized body traits, I belong to the category "woman," a culturally shaped category that includes people with my history, degree of feminization, and manner of sex presentation. To some extent, I choose to remain in the category that I was assigned from birth, though were I to change my sex identification, I would face much social resistance and disdain, and it would likely cause a great deal of turmoil in my personal life. A successful social transformation might also require taking hormone supplements or undergoing surgeries, and, as a person who values health and longevity over aesthetics, I would worry about the medical risks and side-effects of these. Another way to put this, perhaps, is that since I am still comfortable living within the boundaries of my assigned sex, the risks would not be worth taking for me.

The idea that some bodies are purely male or female exaggerates the degree to which male and female bodies are genetically, anatomically, and hormonally distinct. For instance, we see "true" female bodies as large-breasted, soft and smooth, abundant head hair but little body hair, petite and slight, but curvy, and able to perform stereotypical female sexual and reproductive functions. But such bodies are typically cosmetic and social achievements rather than expressions of natural womanhood. By treating sex assignments as objective and immutable facts, we are led to see those who resist their assigned sex, and the culturally valued bodily and behavioral traits associated with it, as perverts, freaks, or frauds.[21]

Sex identities are "socially real" and are important for expressing our social solidarities, sexual orientations, personalities, tastes, future and past reproductive roles, and community memberships. Many people find that their sex and race identities provide avenues for forming social networks, for achieving forms of cultural recognition and respect, and for guiding our erotic and intimate relationships. These are important aspects of life. But can we form social solidarities, gain respect from our communities, and negotiate erotic relationships without imagining that these identities are immutable and biologically determined?

In the next section, I explore whether the proliferation of sex and gender categories can draw attention to the diversity of bodies and the complexity of sex identities, or whether this just perpetuates the belief that bodies and people have a true sex and, once we get the correct categories, we can sort them properly.[22] I also consider whether we need to categorize people by sex in all contexts, and why we feel compelled to do so. Moreover, why are we obsessed with sexing bodies rather than recognizing the sexed and gendered social identities of people? If sex, like race, is a socially meaningful but invented grouping, much like one's religion, ethnicity, nationality, or sexual orientation, why don't we sex and race people in terms of their personal and interpersonal histories, social solidarities, and cultural inheritance?

Sex Talk

In the past half-century, gender dissidents and health professionals have introduced new terminology to describe nonstandard sex identities. Medical practitioners and sex researchers introduced the term "transsexual" to refer to those who desire to change their sex, through surgery and other means.[23] This term has been criticized by gender dissidents for treating cross-gender identity as a type of psychopathology and for reinforcing conventional gender categories.[24] The term has also been criticized for suggesting that the persons so described desire to change their sex rather than change their bodies to match their psychological sex. Social critics and activists later introduced the term "transgender" to refer to people who do not fit one of the conventional binary sex categories and who live in ways that contest the category they were assigned at birth or assigned because of their anatomy.[25] This term represents a socio-political rather than a medical or pathological understanding of cross-gender identity. Some use "transgender" as an umbrella term to cover a variety of ways of transgressing gender norms, including sexual norms associated with gender, and some use it more narrowly to refer to those who resist the sex categories to which they have been assigned, or resist conventional binary sex categories. On the broad understanding, "transgender" can include the entire GLBT (gay, lesbian, bi, trans) spectrum; on the narrow understanding, "transgender" includes only those who live outside conventional sex categories or assignments, but who are not necessarily seeking to bring their bodies into conformity with a particular category.

Some trans activists treat sex, gender, and sexuality as discrete, though related, identity categories, and some treat these categories as theoretical abstractions and tools for analyzing social behavior and expression. Shannon Price Minter has examined how gay activists in the twentieth century separated sexual orientation from gender nonconformity and thereby marginalized cross-gendered individuals within the gay movement.[26] Gay activists promoted the idea of gayness as a form of sexual difference rather than gender deviance in order to distance themselves from stigmatizing stereotypes of gay men as effeminate, psychologically confused about gender roles, or unable to demonstrate culturally valued masculine traits. Today, some transgender activists are promoting the idea that cross-gender identification is not about sexuality but only about gender. In part, they seem to be responding to the ways that cross-gender identification has been stigmatized as a psychosexual disorder, a paraphilia, or form of fetishism. For example, psychologist Ray Blanchard divides transsexuals into two types: homosexuals (especially those attracted to heterosexual men) and fetishists suffering from autogynephilia (heterosexual men who are sexually aroused by and attracted to themselves when they are transformed into women).[27] In both cases for Blanchard, the desire to change sex and one's body is motivated by strong and abnormal sexual desires. In response, some self-identified transsexuals contend that the desire to reconstruct their bodies derives from a desire to make their bodies match their psychological sex, which is discernable from hormonal influences on the brain, childhood interests, and other knowledge about themselves and personalities. On this account, transsexuality is not about sexuality but about gender orientation.

The gay and trans activists who want to separate sexual orientation from gender expression seem to reflect that, at present, one can have a transgressive sexual orientation *or* gender identity, but not both, and still be socially acceptable. Gay men who are manly and transsexuals with conventional erotic desires are okay, but effeminate gay men and transsexuals with kinky erotic desires are not. Moreover, if gay men can be cross-gendered to some degree and transmen can be gay, then it's somewhat unclear what it means to be attracted to someone of the same or opposite gender or sex. Neither queer nor nonqueer communities are happy with this outcome. The separation of sexual orientation from gender expression is similar to the separation of gender from sex. This separation allowed feminists to challenge restrictive cultural gender norms without challenging an important part of gender normalization—the idea that the division of men and women has a simple biological basis and is not also culturally determined from a set of biological facts. These conceptual separations may make gender and sexual deviance more palatable, but they do so by containing the radical and potentially liberatory implications of gender and sexual variation.

Will the introduction of new and independent categories of gender and sexuality permit us to recognize and accept a greater diversity of bodies, as well as forms of gender and sexual expression? Again, it can be instructive to think about how race works. In the United States, "black" people are now commonly referred to as "African Americans" in order to emphasize the social rather than the biological origins of race. Nevertheless, we usually classify people as African American according to how their bodies look rather than their family backgrounds. Moreover, such sorting still follows the one-drop rule. Instead of classifying people as black when they have "one drop of black blood," we classify people as African American when they have one (black) African ancestor. It generally does not matter how many generations back that ancestor is located, as long as the fact of ancestry is still evident in some way on their body. Although claiming an African American identity may, for an individual, be a claim of social and political solidarity, this claim is only regarded as authentic by others if the individual has certain bodily looks. That is, regardless of a person's family history or political sympathies, inclusion and exclusion from this category is based on skin color, hair texture, and so on. In short, "African American" is basically synonymous with "black" and operates according to the same logic. Moreover, because "African American" (or "Asian American" and "Native American") implicitly mark racial status, they function differently than do terms that appear to be parallel, such as "Italian American," "Jewish American," "Irish American," and so on. The latter mark ethnic or cultural distinctions and therefore can, to some degree, be chosen or cast off according to one's experiences and practices. So Madeleine Albright and John Kerry can be Roman Catholic rather than Jewish, and only those who see Jewishness as a racial identity will regard them as inauthentic.

In the past decade, more U.S. citizens are identifying as "multiracial" or "biracial" rather than as African American or black. But such identities are often regarded as politically progressive only when they call attention to one's multiple minority racial statuses; for example, if one has African and Asian ancestors, or African and Native American ancestors. When people use the biracial label to call attention to their European as well as African ancestry, they are often accused of trying to claim an undeserved or inauthentic racial status. In this way, "multiracial" and "biracial" follow the logic of the one-drop rule—if one has a drop of "black blood" and a drop of "Asian blood," their racial status is ambiguous; but if one has only a drop of "black blood" and the rest is "white," then they're simply black, not bi. Moreover, the sorting of bodies into mixed and unmixed categories may perpetuate the historically dangerous idea that some bodies are racially "impure" while others are racially unmixed and "pure" ("white"). In other words, the new practices of racial sorting suggested by these new identity terms may leave existing categories of race undisturbed while perpetuating the idea that one's racial group, whether mixed or unmixed, reflects a genetic or biological inheritance rather than a sociocultural one.

If the introduction of labels that pick out geographic origins and racial mixing has not dislodged biological notions of race, are there better terms? Some have begun to use terms such as "black-identified," "white status," "of the male persuasion," and "female class" to suggest that race and sex are social groupings rather than natural ones.[28] A recent cartoon depicts a confused person in front of two bathroom doors marked "female identified" and "male identified."[29] The confused character in the cartoon probably regards his sex assignment as a natural fact, while the signage on the door treats it as a social fact. Although the cartoonist appears to be making fun of new forms of political correctness, the labeling of the restroom doors in the cartoon offers some improvement over what currently exists. The cartoon could be used to highlight the incongruity between our ordinary ideas about sex and what we are learning from scientists, historians, and persons who have been oppressed because of their sex identities. If the person standing before the bathroom doors had a non-standard sex identity, he or she might not be confused by the signage and could find it somewhat liberating.

Whether such new terminology will be useful could depend on how we use it. For example, when we identify others by a race category merely on the basis of visual inspection, we suggest that their race can be read from their bodily features. Alternatively, if we apply these terms to people on the basis of their self-reports, social and political commitments, family histories, cultural knowledge, clothing, or speech styles, then our deployment of such terms better reflects the social and cultural dimensions of these groupings. It would also help if people were more willing to apply these terms transgressively—for example, by using the term "black-identified" of someone with a stereotypical "white" body when their family histories or social commitments warranted this. It would also be helpful if single-sex institutions, such as colleges and clubs, applied the terms "woman," "female," and "female-identified" to include transwomen and anyone living as a woman, regardless of their anatomy.

The Sex(ing) Drive

Several years ago I had a woman colleague whose body seemed to be sex ambiguous to my other colleagues. Periodically, one of the latter would ask me, in private, if my female colleague was really a woman. I'm not sure why they would ask me, possibly because they thought I knew her better or possibly because they know I research and teach about gender issues. In any event, I was not sure how to respond to such inquiries. Sometimes I resorted to joking: "I don't know, should I look up her skirt?" At other times, I replied with mock naiveté, "Why do you ask?" My answers were intended to get my colleagues to recognize the inappropriateness of their question—inappropriate because her gender expression was unambiguously female and because they were trying to force out what they thought might be secret. Unfortunately, my mocking answers did not always succeed in making my interrogators a bit more self-conscious, and sometimes a colleague would persist, as if they had a right to know. Sometimes their responses implied that my humor about their efforts to sex our colleague was inappropriate, and it was important that they know. I have no idea whether the woman in question was trans or not, and I really didn't see why it was important that my other colleagues should know this.

What this example suggests is that, when we find that we can't classify a person, we should question whether it really matters. Some of my female colleagues thought they needed to know our colleague's "true" sex because she used the women's rest-room. I asked them if all women should have to verify their status before entering. None of my male colleagues gave coherent answers about why they needed to know.

I've witnessed people similarly frustrated when they are unable to come up with a person's race identity. In these situations, we need to develop responses that make people more self-conscious about their classifying techniques and genuine needs.

After observing how much gender distinctions structure social life, Sharon Preves poses the following thought experiment: "Try—for just one hour—to stop yourself from classifying others' gender as you encounter them. Doing so is nearly impossible and will most likely heighten your awareness of the gender attribution process we go through every day to sort people into one category or another."[30] Nevertheless, Preves concludes that "in order to improve the quality of life not just for those labeled inter-sexed, but for us all, we must remove or reduce the importance of gender categoriza-tion and the need for gender categories, including the category of intersex itself."[31] Judith Lorber has recently argued for "degendering" our social institutions in order to address gender discrimination and inequality. She writes: "Degendering doesn't mean not thinking about gender; rather, it starts with the recognition that gender is a binary system of social organization that creates inequality. Therefore, degendering attacks the structure and process of gender—the division of people into two social statuses and the social construction of what we call the opposites."[32] Her work explores how to restructure social institutions and roles without employing stereotypical gender categories. Lorber's suggestions go beyond merely eliminating gender segregation and gendered divisions of labor in the family and the workplace. She advocates that we eliminate gender from the way we recognize people and define public spaces (e.g., eliminating "mothers" and "fathers" in favor of "parents," women's and men's restrooms, and so on). Both Preves and Lorber recognize that, in many contemporary societies, there has been some progress in removing gender barriers to social partici-pation. Nevertheless, gender still structures social life in profound ways and limits the social participation of those with nonconforming bodies and identities.

When we identify a person using a sex or race category, we often imply that their sex or race is one of the most salient and defining features they possess. Alternatively, by refusing to cooperate with the practices of proper sex and race sorting, we force people to reflect on their needs to have the apparent facts of sex and race acknowl-edged. Are we trying to assess someone's social "rank," as we understand bodies to be ranked by sex and race, or are we interested in their social histories and affilia-tions? Do we need to establish a person's sex or race before we know how to interact with them? Do we need to know whether they are of the same sex or race as us to know how intimate we should be, physically and socially, or how to interpret their gestures and speech? For me, personally, I often need to know someone's age, educa-tion level, cultural background, social titles, and so on before I know how to behave around them. And although I probably don't need to know a person's sex or race in most situations, I find that I have a very ingrained habit of classifying everyone I encounter by their sex and race.

Resisting, at times, sex and race classification has some affinity with the "elimi-nativist" approaches advocated by several philosophers of race. Given the contro-versies that eliminativism has caused, let me clarify the form of eliminativism I am promoting. First, eliminativist approaches to sex and race should not be confused with the promotion of sex and race "blindness" or ignorance. The latter presupposes that there are unquestionable facts about sex and race but that we should just ignore them. The eliminativism or degendering of the sort I've outlined questions whether there is a single, objective, or fully rational sex classificatory scheme. Given that sex and race assignments involve complicated judgments about evolving processes, we need to be comfortable with, and handle respectfully, situations in which a person's sex or race is indeterminate. Second, an eliminativist approach is not committed to eliminating all uses of sex and race categories but only those uses that perpetuate erroneous and pernicious ideas about sex and race. If one can find ways to use these categories that highlight their social and biological complexity, this would be helpful. There may be medical contexts in which it is helpful to know a patient's sex or race, though such "knowledge" merely represents a set of assumptions about their chromosomes, anatomy, or the geographic locations of the person's ancestors. Nevertheless, eliminativism should be committed to eliminating uses of sex designations that deny people the right to use public facilities, such as bathrooms, or the right to identify as they wish, such as restrictions on changing one's legal sex identity.[33] Third, eliminativism with respect to sex does not entail the imposition of androgynous identities or the elimination of butch lesbians, macho guys, or femme fatales. People will continue to fit themselves and others into available cultural categories, such as "male" and "female." However, by changing the way we fit people into these categories, we may change the meaning of the categories themselves. For example, by changing the way we assign people to the categories "black" or "female"—by using criteria other than bodily features—we change the meaning and social ramifications of those categories.

A (partial or modified) eliminativist approach offers a way to call attention to our ingrained habits of racing and sexing bodies and the corresponding social rankings that accompany these practices. People who inhabit bodies that do not fit our categories have much to teach us about the perniciousness of our linguistic and conceptual practices. Indeed, a primary reason for changing our practices of sorting and identifying bodies is so that people who inhabit bodies now regarded as incongruent, anomalous, or even frightening in terms of our race and sex concepts do not feel compelled to alter their bodies in order to be normal and socially acceptable. Moreover, doctors and parents should not feel compelled to impose painful and disfiguring surgeries on babies and children in order to render their bodies "normal."[34] While some surgical and hormonal body alterations may be appropriate for adults who want them and understand their risks, we should question a system that compels people to make huge personal sacrifices of their future health and financial resources in order to obtain bodies that conform to rigid cultural stereotypes.

Although there are important differences between the way that sex and race operate to oppress people, I've relied on numerous analogies in this essay in order to demonstrate how our thinking and talking can be, and has already, changed. Knowledge of human genetics has changed the way we understand the racing of bodies, and it is changing how we understand the sexing of bodies. New terms for race and sex identities reflect new scientific and historical knowledge about these concepts and should allow us to continue tracking race and sex injustices that persist, while encouraging a rethinking of the meaning of race and sex identities. Recently, more attention has been paid to the way that the discriminatory and hostile effects of race and sex sorting are experienced unequally by members of the same group. Light-skinned people who are classified as African American may suffer less racism than dark-skinned people. Women who are perceived as appropriately feminine may suffer less sexism than women who are perceived as masculine. Middle-class persons may suffer less discrimination by race and sex than working-class persons. Our current race and sex categories are not always adequate for tracking different degrees and intensities of racism and sexism directed toward people of ostensibly the same group. In other words, if blacks and women were to achieve equal representation and opportunity in our society, but all the successful blacks were light-skinned and all the successful women were conventionally gendered, pernicious forms of racism and sexism would still be present. Perhaps by attending to how we build unifying identities from the superficial components of skin pigment, facial features, body hair, and other body parts, we will recognize the need to build these identities in new ways.

NOTES

1. Vosjoli et al. 1998: 41.

2. At http://www.wi.mit.edu/news/archives/1999/dp_1029.html.

3. For example, see Zack 1993, 1998, and 2002; Boxill 2001; and Bernasconi 2003.

4. At http://www.flmnh.ufl.edu/fish/innews/clownfish2003.html (accessed June 31, 2003)

5. The websites of many trans activists promote the idea that sex and gender identity are not subject to individual choice or social manipulation, whereas the physical body can be modified to fit an inner gender identity. See, for example, http://ai.eecs.umich.edu/people/conway/TS/TS.html; http://www.transgendercare.com/guidance/what_is_gender.htm; http://transsexual.org/What.html ; http://www.gendertrust.org.uk/showarticle.php?aid=8; and http://www.transfamily.org/gendr101.htm.

6. By "arbitrary," I mean that these categories are not forced on us by nature but are cultural categories or interpretations of what is naturally given. For the history of the two-sex view, see Laqueur 1990. On the difference between social constructionist and interpretive (hermeneutic) conceptions of "sex," see Warnke 2001: 126–37.

7. Numerous online film bios of the South Asian star of *Bride and Prejudice*, Aishwarya Rai, comment on her blue eyes in ways that assume that this is an unusual but attractive feature.

8. Greenberg 2006: 51 and Preves 2005: 2–3.

9. "The End of Men," National Public Radio (NPR), December 13–15, 2004, at http://www.npr.org/templates/story/story.php?storyId=4229557, and "Scientists Decipher Y Chromosome," National Public Radio (NPR), June 19, 2003, at http://www.npr.org/templates/story/story.php?storyId=1303260.

10. Vernon Rosario writes: "The notion that the Y chromosome determines male sex now appears to be grossly simplistic. The identification of the SRY gene (i.e., the sex-determining region of Y) in the 1990s was quickly followed by the discovery of six other genes critical to male sex determination that are on the X chromosome as well as the autosomes (nonsex chromosomes)" (Rosario 2004: 284).

11. Meyerowitz 2002: 27.

12. Greenberg 2006: 56. Preves states that some individuals "have chromosomes that vary throughout the cells of their bodies, changing from XX to XY from cell to cell" (Preves 2005: 3).

13. Fausto-Sterling 2000: 115–43 (ch. 5: "Sexing the Brain").

14. For example, http://www.genomecenter.howard.edu/article.htm; http://www.sciam.com/article.cfm?articleID=0002A353-C027–1E1C-8B3B809EC588EEDF; http://www.lipmagazine .org/articles/feattalvi_123.shtml; and http://www.pbs.org/wgbh/nova/first/race.html.

15. Appiah 1990: 496.

16. Warnke 2001: 134; see also Warnke 2007: 120–52.

17. At http://www.pbs.org/wgbh/nova/gender/spectrum.html.

18. At http://www.sciam.com/article.cfm?articleID=000214BD-E52F-1EB7-BDC0809 EC588EEDF.

19. Fausto-Sterling 2000: 147.

20. Ladelle McWhorter states that, for Foucault, "The concept of 'sex' groups together 'anatomical elements, biological functions, conducts, sensations, and pleasures' into a 'fictitious unity' that can be cited 'as a causal principle, an omnipresent meaning, a secret to be discovered everywhere'" (McWhorter 2004: 40). Foucault is, of course, not claiming that the apparent unity between anatomy and behavior constitutive of sex is fictitious in a social sense, rather that these groupings represent only social conventions, albeit meaningful and efficacious ones. But the apparent unity is fictitious in the sense that it is not inscribed in nature. In this regard, it's interesting to think about why the decision of Thomas Beatie (an ftm) to go public with his pregnancy caused a media storm. When readers see beyond the "pregnant man" headlines that this man was assigned female at birth, by virtue of possessing female reproductive organs, is the usual grouping of pregnancy with female bodies reaffirmed, or does Beatie's male gender identity transcend his anatomy so that the story remains a story about a pregnant man? If the latter occurs, is this a sign that one long-standing fictitious unity is beginning to come apart or just an example of the appeal of media sensationalism?

21. For a discussion of the violent dynamics that often ensue from such perceptions, see Bettcher 2007.

22. Ruth Hubbard writes, "Major scientific distortions have resulted from ignoring similarities and overlaps in the effort to group differences by sex or gender" (Hubbard 1996: 164).

23. Meyerowitz 2002: 44.

24. Stone 1993.

25. Currah 2006: 3.

26. Minter 2006.

27. The recent controversy in the trans community over the book by Michael Bailey that promotes Blanchard's theory reflects how such theories uncritically legitimize and circulate stigmatizing ideas about trans identities. For a useful and well-researched history of the controversy that attempts to be balanced and fair, but is surprisingly gentle to a sexologist who is politically naive and irresponsible, see Dreger 2008. Also see Roughgarden 2004.

28. Naomi Zack has suggested something like this as an intermediate step toward the elimination of erroneous race and sex distinctions. (From private email correspondence with Zack.)

29. I am grateful to Adam Handwork for sharing this cartoon with me.

30. Preves 2005: 13.

31. Ibid. 154.

32. Lorber 2005: 7.

33. For a short history of the oppressive consequences of government efforts (in the United States) to police citizens' gender identities, see Shafiqullah 2004. In Shrage 2008, I argue that, when states are allowed nonconsensual access to hospital and medical records to determine a citizen's sex status, and when they make that status unchangeable, governments violate their citizens' rights to privacy and equal treatment.

34. For more on the imposition of medically risky and irreversible treatments on intersex infants and children, see Dreger 1999.

REFERENCES

Appiah, A. (1990) "'But Would That Still Be Me?' Notes on Gender, 'Race,' Ethnicity, as Sources of 'Identity.'" *Journal of Philosophy* 87, no. 10 (October): 493–99.

Bernasconi, R., ed. (2003) *Race and Racism in Continental Philosophy*. Bloomington: Indiana University Press.

Bettcher, T. (2007) "Evil Deceivers and Make-Believers: On Transphobic Violence and the Politics of Illusion." *Hypatia* 22, no. 3 (Summer 2007): 43–65.

Boxill, B., ed. (2001) *Race and Racism*. New York: Oxford University Press.

Currah, P. (2006) "Gender Pluralisms under the Transgender Umbrella." In *Transgender Rights*, ed. P. Currah, R. Juang, and S. Price Minter. Minneapolis: University of Minnesota Press.

Dreger, A. D. (1999) *Intersex in the Age of Ethics*. Hagerstown, Md.: University Publishing Group.

———. (2008) "The Controversy Surrounding *The Man Who Would Be Queen*: A Case History of the Politics of Science, Identity, and Sex in the Internet Age." *Archives of Sexual Behavior* 37, no. 3: 366–421.

Fausto-Sterling, A. (2000) *Sexing the Body*. New York: Basic.

Greenberg, J. A. (2006) "The Roads Less Traveled: The Problem with Binary Sex Categories." In *Transgender Rights*, ed. P. Currah, R. Juang, and S. Price Minter. Minneapolis: University of Minnesota Press, 2006.

Hubbard, R. (1996) "Gender and Genitals: Constructs of Sex and Gender," *Social Text* 46/47 (Spring/Summer): 157–65.

Laqueur, T. (1990) *Making Sex: Body and Gender from the Greeks to Freud*. Cambridge: Harvard University Press.

Lorber, J. (2005) *Breaking the Bowls: Degendering and Feminist Change*. New York: Norton.

McWhorter, L. (2004) "Sex, Race, and Biopower: A Foucauldian Genealogy," *Hypatia* 19, no. 3: 38–62.

Meyerowitz, J. (2002) *How Sex Changed: A History of Transsexuality in the United States*. Cambridge: Harvard University Press.

Minter, S. P. (2006) "Do Transsexuals Dream of Gay Rights?" In *Transgender Rights*, ed. P. Currah, R. Juang, and S. Price Minter. Minneapolis: University of Minnesota Press.

Preves, S. E. (2005) *Intersex and Identity*. New Brunswick, N.J.: Rutgers University Press.

Rosario, V. (2004) "The Biology of Gender and the Construction of Sex?" *GLQ: Journal of Lesbian and Gay Studies* 10, no. 2: 280–87.

Roughgarden, J. (2004) "The Bailey Affair: Psychology Perverted." At http://ai.eecs.umich.edu/people/conway/TS/Reviews/Psychology%20Perverted%20-%20by%20Joan%20Roughgarden.htm.

Shafiqullah, H. (2004) "Transgender and Gender Impersonation Law and Policy." In *Encyclopedia of Lesbian, Gay, Bisexual, and Transgender History in America*, ed. M. Stein. New York: Scribner's.

Shrage, L. (2008) "Does the Government Need to Know Your Sex?" At http://publicreason.net/wp-content/PPPS/Fall2008/LShrage2.pdf.

Stone, S. (1993) "The 'Empire' Strikes Back: A Posttranssexual Manifesto." At http://sandystone.com/empire-strikes-back.

Vosjoli, P. de, B. Viets, and R. Tremper (1998) *The Leopard Gecko Manual*. Mission Viejo, Calif.: Advanced Vivarium Systems.

Warnke, G. (2001) "Intersexuality and the Categories of Sex," *Hypatia* 16, no. 3: 126–37.

———. (2007) *After Identity: Rethinking Race, Sex, and Gender*. Cambridge: Cambridge University Press.

Zack, N. (1993) *Race and Mixed Race*. Philadelphia: Temple University Press.

———. (1998) *Thinking About Race*. Belmont, Calif.: Wadsworth.

———. (2002) *Philosophy and the Science of Race*. New York: Routledge.

11

Who Do You Think You Are?

When Should the Law Let You Be Who You Want to Be?

Graham Mayeda

In "You're Not in Kansas Anymore," Canadian author Ivan E. Coyote prepares to change her legal name and writes about the anxieties that this creates:

> So, you stand in line, you fill out some forms, take out a couple of ads in the paper, no big deal, right? You just change your name if they got it all wrong.
>
> I'll tell you what I'm worried about: do they make you explain yourself? Does the form make you say why you feel you must change your name? State reason below. Choose one of the following. Provide documents. Use a separate sheet of unlined paper if necessary. Please print in black or blue ink only.
>
> I can see myself, palms sweaty and stammering.
>
> "My legal name doesn't fit the rest of me. It never has, Your Honour. See, here, how I was born with no hips at all, and how my t-shirt hides my tits? I have hair on my chest, too, and well, everyone makes mistakes. I just need one more chance to get it right, if you will just allow me to write Ivan down on this form, if it pleases the court, I would be much obliged. I just turned thirty, Your Honour, and it's time something about me matched."[1]

This passage illustrates a number of things about interactions between the state and the individual that involve gender. First, it is clear that Coyote experiences the interaction as threatening and infantilizing; she is treated as a child who must justify her actions rather than as an adult who is simply asserting her identity. Second, it demonstrates the way in which the state conflates sex and gender by giving automatic legal status to a name given to us at birth based on our biological sex. By conferring legal status to the birth name in this way, the state fails to recognize how a name is also an expression of gender identity. Third, the anxiety created by the procedure for changing one's legal name gives a small taste of the much greater anxiety caused by the state in the case of a change in legal gender identity, which often requires medical certification and a guarantee that the change will be permanent and stable. Finally, the story demonstrates that the law, like most of our systems of social control, has too much invested in the existence of only two genders to admit the possibility that gender can be lived and expressed in many forms that go beyond the male/female dichotomy. In my view, the law is in bad faith in this regard: it shuts its eyes to the lived experience of many people that should be both recognized and affirmed.

In this chapter, I argue that the law should permit individuals to identify their own gender for legal purposes without requiring medical certification or a guarantee that their gender identity will remain stable throughout their life. Nevertheless, there will still be situations in which the state is justified in recognizing another's perception of a person's gender. The clash of legal rights between two people arising from a conflict between one person's self-identified gender identity and another's perception of that identity may require the state to legitimize a gender identity with which a person does not identify.

As part of the articulation of these two views, I address some of the common concerns that arise from allowing individuals to identify their own gender. The first is that people must have a stable gender identity, because social programs depend on the predictability and stability of gender identity. The second arises from the fact that gender has been and continues to be a basis for discrimination. Women have been marginalized in most societies, and the promotion of women's equality through state-based social programs and policies and civil society–based movements (women's political organizations, nongovernmental organizations, etc.) depends to varying degrees on the ability to clearly demarcate who is and is not a woman. Margaret Denike, Sal Renshaw, and cj Rowe express the concern of some women that allowing a person to identify their own gender identity will undermine women's search for equality:

> In some circles…women may speak as though extending rights to transsexual women could pose a "threat" to the integrity of "women-only" spaces—or as [though] the rights and needs of these groups are antagonistic or mutually exclusive. Of particular concern is the question of whether self-identification can be definitive of gender identity, and whether, for example, women's groups, spaces and services should be fully accessible to anyone who identifies themselves as female; and more generally, when recognition should be sanctioned in law.[2]

In this chapter, I (a) describe the challenges to permitting self-identification of gender and (b) provide a theoretical framework to address two of these challenges: namely, law's requirement of a stable and predictable gender identity and the potential problems that arise for the promotion of women's equality if self-identity is permitted.

The Challenges to Self-Identification of Gender

Predictability

Like most legal traditions, the common law depends on predictability. For example, the law of contract is concerned, among other things, with ensuring that the expectations of parties to a contract are respected.[3] To achieve this, judges have developed many rules to ensure that promises are kept and that, in general, the law of contract remains consistent enough that businesses can plan within a relatively constant set of legal rules. Indeed, the whole principle of precedent aims at ensuring that legal rules remain constant.[4] It is difficult for courts to go against their own precedents or against the precedents set by higher courts. The principles of precedent ensure that many judicial eyes scrutinize novel legal rules before they are introduced.[5]

In contrast to the common law, which mostly deals with private law matters, public law is theoretically less conservative. After all, a new government can repeal all existing laws and enact new ones if it wishes. However, many conservative forces exist to prevent this. For instance, the constitution (either written or unwritten) sets the general framework of legal principles within which lower-order laws and regulations are made. Moreover, in practice, it is difficult for legislators to radically change an established legal scheme, because subsequent schemes are frequently interpreted in light of prior schemes.[6] Also, stakeholders may have accrued vested rights through earlier legislation, and these rights are often recognized by courts.[7] Furthermore, new enactments are generally presumed to not have retroactive application.[8] When added to the political mechanisms that ensure consistency in legislation,[9] these and other legal mechanisms ensure that legal and social policy transforms only gradually and in a stable and predictable fashion.

The conservative forces within the law that favor predictability and stability have had a significant effect on how the law treats gender identity. One of these effects is that the law only recognizes two gender identities—man and woman—because it follows established cultural norms.[10] Another effect is that the law has conflated gender identity with biological sex, or perhaps it has even ignored gender identity altogether, preferring instead to make sex and not gender a legal category.[11] There are two reasons for this. The first is that biological sex, unlike gender identity, can more readily be determined through an examination of physical characteristics of a person's body. This means that there is a predictable test for establishing sexual identity for legal persons.[12] Furthermore, the use of biological sex as a legal category has been reinforced by the development of medicine as a science. The law, which has always deferred to experts in areas outside of its immediate sphere of knowledge, now has a science—medicine—on which it can rely for the categorization of men and women.

Second, the law in western European countries and their former colonies has emphasized the reproductive purpose of sexual intercourse, thereby reinforcing the importance of biological sex rather than gender. This is clear from the law's traditional treatment of marriage. Historically, the common law permitted the dissolution of a marriage if the partners could not or did not consummate the marriage by having "natural sexual intercourse," by which was meant vaginal penetration with the purpose of and potential for reproduction.[13] The law permitted marriages involving one or more transgender individuals to be dissolved on the basis that sexual intercourse between a biological male and a person with a surgically constructed vagina, or with another biological male, is not "natural sexual intercourse." Hidden behind this legal rule is the moral view that expressing nontraditional gender identities is a sign of sexual deviance.[14]

The conflation of gender identity with biological sex has also had the effect of ensuring the continued marginalization of women. The law has been used to perpetuate a sexist social system in which men exploit the sexual hierarchy to dominate and control women.[15] To perpetuate this marginalization, there must be some stable and predictable way of determining who belongs to the superior and who to the inferior group. Gender, which is highly variable and partly under control of the individual, is not a reliable basis for domination, since its variability too easily allows for passage from the group of the marginalized to the group of the oppressors. As a result, the law has relied on biological sex to ensure that the borders between the dominant and the marginalized are clear.[16]

While using biological sex as a legal category leads to predictability and the stability of existing social hierarchies, gender identity undermines this predictability and stability. This is clear from the way that Ivan Coyote describes the reactions of her family to her childhood (trans)gender identity. Trans identities are unpredictable, and they lead the characters in her stories to be constantly surprised by her identity. For instance, Coyote's grandmother is shocked by the way that Coyote's "tomboy" antics and appearance do not conform to the social expectations of girls.[17] Strangers, too, are "fooled" into thinking that Coyote is a young man or else a "butch" woman rather than accepting her trans identity. Indeed, Coyote affirms the potency of these social expectations when she wonders whether, in not disabusing an older woman of her idea that Coyote is a young man, Coyote has actually lied to her.[18] The complexity of gender identity is thus always liable to betray another's (un)reasonable expectations about norms of behavior and appearance.

As we can see, one of the main challenges facing self-identification of gender is the conservative nature of the law, which reinforces and is reinforced by the social hierarchies to which we have become accustomed. Challenging the binary of male/female surprises, and the law, like society, does not like surprises.

Access to Public and Private Markets, Services and Programs

Many public and private services (including markets for consumer goods and services) are provided to individuals of only one gender, or else they are provided differently to members of different genders.[19] Some might argue that because services are provided in this gendered way, we need stable legal categories of gender that are reliable indicators of who is entitled to what service.

In the market for private goods and services, we frequently use gender identification to distinguish who is entitled to purchase a particular good or have access to a particular service. The need to provide personal identification that states a person's sex, or that includes a photo that has certain gender markers that do not correspond to the current gender expression of that individual, gives rise to some of the most basic challenges that face people with a trans identity. An illustration of such a challenge is *Sheridan v. Sanctuary Investments Ltd.*,[20] which involved a preoperative male-to-female transsexual who, aware that she would have to live as a woman for two years before having sex-reassignment surgery, wanted to use the women's washroom in a gay and lesbian bar. She was denied use of the washroom, and on another occasion, was also denied entry to the bar, because her gender identity as a preoperative male-to-female transsexual did not match her sex on her driver's license.

Beyond identification, both the state and private organizations often demand a stable gender identity when providing services to the public to ensure that services targeted at one gender are not accessed by a person of a different gender "falsely masquerading" as the opposite gender in order to receive services to which he or she is not entitled. This issue becomes more complicated when the services in question (both private and public) are provided for the purpose of relieving or attenuating existing inequalities between the two genders.[21] An example might be social assistance, employment, or counseling programs that are targeted at single mothers or women more generally,[22] or programs and policies intended to prevent violence against women or help women recover from such violence. It would appear to defeat the purpose of programs that aim to ameliorate inequality to allow individuals to access social services by identifying as a particular gender while not suffering from the inequality at which the program is aimed.

As well, some government functions are carried out in different ways for men and women. Many obvious examples are in the area of law enforcement. For instance, women and men are incarcerated in separate correctional facilities. This gives rise to two, sometimes conflicting, issues. First is the failure of the state to meet the different needs of women and men in prison. Louise Arbour, former judge of the Supreme Court of Canada and recent U.N. High Commissioner for Human Rights, documented such failures in her inquiry into events at the prison for women in Kingston, Ontario. She said:

> [The] reports confirmed, each in its own way, that women prisoners, by virtue of their offences, experiences and needs, present different security and classification concerns from male offenders. Each report concludes that these issues have not been adequately considered by past correctional administrations. There is therefore no lack of documentation that correctional programs and accommodations for women have been largely unsatisfactory and inferior in quantity, quality and variety to those for male offenders; and, that women prisoners have been denied equal treatment. Historically, female offenders have also been largely neglected by criminological researchers, and by correctional planners, who have focused their research money and program initiatives on male offenders.[23]

The second issue arises from the failure of the state to recognize trans identities and to accept self-identification of gender in correctional facilities. For instance, in *Kavanagh v. Attorney General of Canada*, the Canadian Human Rights Tribunal dealt with the case of Kavanagh, a male-to-female transsexual convicted of second-degree murder whose request to be detained in a women's prison until she obtained sex-reassignment surgery had been refused. In another case of conflating sex and gender, the tribunal held that while the policy of Correctional Services of Canada was discriminatory, the practice of placing inmates in facilities based on their biological sex was rationally connected to its objective of properly caring for inmates.[24]

Another example from the area of law enforcement involves police searches and investigations. The Supreme Court of Canada has held that the Canadian Charter of Rights and Freedoms requires arrestees to be strip searched by officers of the same sex as the person being detained.[25] As a result, state officials must be able to identify an individual's sex to determine the appropriate manner for violating his or her privacy. Although the law requires that searches be performed differently for women and men, law enforcement officers continue to have difficulty with searches of transgender individuals. For instance, in *R. v. Hornick*, five male police officers entered a women's bathhouse identified as a women-only space open to "women and transgendered people." Despite the fact that Canadian law requires women to be searched by women in most circumstances, the Crown Attorney argued that because the event was transpositive, men must be present at the event.[26] As a result, it was not reasonable for the event organizers to maintain that it was a "women-only" event. As one of the organizers pointed out, the effect of this argument was to "define trans people as outside of the community [of women] without even a rudimentary idea of who they are or how they're part of our community."[27]

Outside of the domain of law enforcement, services are also provided in a gendered way. Medical services represent one such area; abortions are the quintessential example of a service provided only to biological women. Services are also provided in a gendered way in the area of employment. For instance, in Canada, while parents are entitled to thirty-five weeks of paid parental leave, to be divided between the parents as they wish, an additional fifteen weeks of paid leave is available only to women. Of course, employment itself is provided on a gendered basis, and employment-related requirements such as dress and behavior are gendered. *Doe by Doe v. City of Belleville* is just one example of a case involving gender expression at work. The plaintiff sued when employees harassed him because his gender expression "did not conform to his coworkers' view of appropriate masculine behavior."[28]

A further problem occurs if public or private programs depend on the creation of a gender-based group identity to promote the equality of that gender. An example of this might be a group for female survivors of male violence or a group intended to support those with a particular sexual identity. The success of such gender-based groups might depend on the exclusion of individuals perceived as men. For instance, in *Mamela v. Vancouver Lesbian Connection*, the Vancouver Lesbian Connection was found to be in violation of the B.C. Human Rights Act when members of its board confronted a preoperative male-to-female transsexual who identified as a lesbian but not a woman. The board members' claimed that Mamela's public avowal of her identity "would erase women's experience of themselves."[29]

Kimberly Nixon v. Vancouver Rape Relief Society also illustrates the perceived need for exclusive sex-based groups to ameliorate the situation of women. The case involves a postoperative male-to-female transsexual named Kimberly Nixon. She had experienced male violence and had benefited from rape-counseling services. Out of a desire to give back to the community that had helped her, she signed up to train as a rape counselor at the Vancouver Rape Relief Society. Although she passed the initial screening interview, Nixon was denied access to the training because one of the facilitators identified her as having been born a man. Rape Relief justified excluding Nixon on the basis that "only a woman, born so, and who grew up understanding what it means to be a girl and a woman in an oppressive society, could understand Rape Relief's political view of male violence and, therefore qualify as a 'peer' for Rape Relief's purposes."[30] Nixon filed a complaint with the British Columbia Human Rights Commission, which ruled that she had been discriminated against on the basis of sex. The British Columbia Superior Court disagreed, and its decision in favor of the society was upheld by the British Columbia Court of Appeal.[31] The case is illustrative of the potential problems that exist when trans identities complicate the provision of gender-based services aimed at ameliorating the situation of equality-seeking groups.

The gendered manner in which both private and public services are provided poses a serious problem for my view that individuals should be able to identify their gender for legal purposes without resorting to less-changeable markers such as biological sex. First, it will be difficult to determine who is entitled to services that are provided in a gendered manner. Second, many services are provided in a gendered way in order to alleviate the disadvantage of women or to deal with the privacy and safety issues that are particular to women, whether due to social convention or the historical and ongoing oppression of women. I address both of these concerns next.

Addressing the Challenges in Theory and Practice

The Social Construction of Gender

While I maintain that in most cases individuals should be able to identify their own gender, there appear to be legitimate situations in which others' perceptions of a person's gender are relevant for determining access to certain public and private services and programs. To identify the cases in which a person should be able to impose a gender identity on another, it is first necessary to determine how this is even possible—that is, it is necessary to briefly explain how gender identities are constructed in the space between people rather than being solely created through self-identification. In my view, gender is constructed through the interactions of individuals because of its socially constructed nature. Gender identity is not simply something that we can choose.[32] In this section, I briefly explain how this is the case. In the subsequent sections, I explain that, despite the socially constructed nature of gender, we have an ethical obligation to accept the gender identity that individuals adopt.

Many feminist and queer scholars have argued that gender identity is socially constructed.[33] It is not always clear what scholars mean by "socially constructed." What I mean by "socially constructed" has two aspects. First, I mean that an individual's gender identity is the result of a process of socialization into the signs and symbols that identify a man and a woman, along with the performance of these signs and symbols in the individual's life.[34] Second, I mean that the signs and symbols that identify men and women are the result of a historical process of construction.[35] There is also a third meaning to "social construction" that I do not discuss here. That is the construction of people as individuals whose gender can be studied scientifically—gender dysphoria, transvestism, and so on have all become objects of sociological, anthropological, psychological, and medical study.[36]

Gender is socially constructed because it arises through social interactions rather than simply through isolated acts of individuals. This means that gender identity is determined through the interaction between a person and those who perceive her. Individuals may choose to adopt the signs and symbols current in our society for expressing particular gender identities. But individuals cannot change their identity by adopting signs and symbols that are not part of our social vocabulary for identifying particular genders. For instance, it is easier for an individual to become a blacksmith to express his identity as a man or to become a nurse to express her identity as a woman, because these professions have traditional (exclusionary and discriminatory) gender associations. It would be useless to become the owner of a grocery store, however, to express gender identity since there is not a strong historically established social link between a particular gender identity and the ownership of grocery stores.[37] Gender identity is *socially* constructed in the sense that it is not purely up to the individual. Instead, it is constructed in the interactions between the individual and others when faced with certain combinations of physical features that symbolize male and female in our society. The individual must use the signs and symbols of society to construct a gender identity, and because these signs and symbols are social, they are open to interpretation by others.

The observation that gender identity is socially constructed does not lead to the conclusion that we cannot change the norms for identifying a person's gender; the criteria for identifying gender is not in the hands of a faceless society over which we have no control. As Ian Hacking points out in *The Social Construction of What?*, new categories for understanding our experience are constantly emerging, and these categories have significant repercussions for social policy (on the macro scale) and how individuals view themselves (on the micro scale).[38] Thus socially constructed categories are constantly changing and have real effects on people. But more than this, the recognition of the social construction of gender does not lead to moral relativism; we can still make a moral argument about how we ought to recognize a person's gender identity—for instance, by accepting her own description of her identity. In other words, the fact that gender identity is constructed from historically emergent signs and symbols does not mean that a person's gender identity must be recognized in accordance with these signs and symbols. Instead, we can argue that a person is free to identify as a man if she chooses while at the same time agreeing that a person's physical appearance would, when observed through traditional signs of masculinity and femininity, be consistent with her being a woman. In fact, as I argue in the next section, we have an ethical responsibility to acknowledge a person's self-stated gender identity.

Legal and Ethical Obligations

The fact that gender identity is socially constructed means that it is constructed in the space between two or more individuals. One person performs or speaks her gender identity, and the other experiences and interprets the signs and symbols of gender that are manifest to her. But gender identity is not solely defined by these physical processes of performance and reception. In what follows, I explain how the ethical and legal relations differ from the relation of pure perception and what the state's ethical and legal responsibilities are for recognizing socially constructed gender identity.

Ethics

An encounter with another person is not limited to our perception of his physical presence. In addition to perceiving a person's physical characteristics, we also encounter his subjectivity—the subject who acts and reacts in ways that we do not control. This recognition of the subjectivity of the other is the beginning of ethics. In fact, as Emmanuel Levinas has demonstrated, ethics is the recognition of the subjectivity or "otherness" of the other and taking responsibility for the inviolability of this otherness. The paradigm for recognizing the subjectivity of another is the "face-to-face." When we come face-to-face with someone, listen to what they say, and really look at who they are rather than perceiving them through the veil of our own sclerotic patterns of thought and ideas, we begin to recognize how we should treat others. Levinas describes the face-to-face relation that is the origin of ethics as follows:

> The way in which the other presents himself, exceeding *the idea of the other in me*, we here name face. This *mode* does not consist in figuring as a theme under my gaze, in spreading itself forth as a set of qualities forming an image. The face of the Other at each moment destroys and overflows the plastic image it leaves me, the idea existing to my own measure and to the measure of its *ideatum*—the adequate idea....
>
> The notion of the face...brings us to a notion of meaning prior to my *Sinngebung* and thus independent of my initiative and my power. It signifies the philosophical priority of the existent over Being, an exteriority that does not call for power or possession, an exteriority that is not reducible, as with Plato, to the interiority of memory, and yet maintains the I who welcomes it. It finally makes possible the description of the notion of the immediate.[39]

In the first passage, Levinas articulates the idea that coming face-to-face with another is an opportunity to see through my ideas and preconceived images of that person. When I am in a genuine encounter with another, how I perceive her is not based on an image that conforms to my own idea of her. In the second passage, Levinas explains that in this face-to-face interaction, we discover a meaning "before *Sinngebung*," by which he means that we discover certain basic aspects of an ethical relationship that exist before our rational concepts of ethical behavior. For example, when we genuinely encounter another and do not objectify him, we realize that we cannot kill him or harm him. It is only when we objectify and eliminate the subjectivity of the other that we can cause this kind of harm.

What kind of ethics arises from the face-to-face interaction? In *Otherwise Than Being*, Levinas explains the nature of the responsibility that arises from this face-to-face encounter as being a kind of utter passivity, as if one is accused by the other. When one is accused, one is passive, because one is forced to respond or take responsibility even though one has not chosen to do so.[40] In Levinas's words:

The responsibility for another, an unlimited responsibility which the strict book-keeping of the free and non-free does not measure, requires subjectivity as an irreplaceable hostage. This subjectivity it denudes under the ego in a passivity of persecution, repression and expulsion outside of essence into oneself.... In the accusative form, which his a modification of no nominative form, in which I approach the neighbor for whom, without having wished it, I have to answer, the irreplaceable one is brought out (*s'accuse*). This finite freedom is not primary, is not initial; but it lies in an infinite responsibility where the other is not other because he strikes up against and limits my freedom, but where he can accuse me to the point of persecution, because the other, absolutely other, is another one (*autrui*).[41]

When I stand before another without preconceived ideas about who she is, the other does not address me in the nominative as simply an object. Instead, she addresses me in the accusative, asking me to take responsibility for the subjectivity that I recognize in the face-to-face. This responsibility is a form of passivity, because it involves abandoning my own projects and living my life bound by the responsibility that arises from my experience of truly coming face-to-face with the other. I am transformed from a "free" subject whose freedom consists in pursuing my own plans into someone who is affected and limited by acknowledging for the first time the subjectivity of the other. Asher Horowitz describes the nature of the limitation that responsibility imposes on me: the "ethical relation...signifies the unlimited responsibility of a singular sensibility to the height of the other, a responsibility and desire that can never be fulfilled and that increases as it is assumed."[42]

What does this imply for gender identity? The imperatives of ethics derive from coming face-to-face with another and recognizing the other's subjectivity. In recognizing this subjectivity, I recognize her freedom from my own projections on to her—from my ideas and plans that objectify her—and I, passively accused by her, take responsibility for this subjectivity. The recognition that I cannot speak as another person or know what she is thinking or perceiving requires that I accept her gender identity and take responsibility for it by ensuring that she has a voice to announce and articulate it without myself appropriating her voice.[43]

To illustrate this ethical relationship, let us return briefly to Coyote's short stories. In "Walks Like," the story described earlier that deals with the author's grandmother's reaction to her tomboy ways, Coyote's grandmother has the opportunity to act ethically in the Levinasian sense. An ethical response on the part of Coyote's grandmother would be, upon being surprised by her granddaughter's nonconforming gender behavior, to recognize this behavior as an expression of Coyote's identity rather than to appropriate it by understanding it in relation to her preconceived gender norms. In another story, "No Bikini," Coyote relates how, as a young girl with no physical signs of her femininity, she slipped off her bikini top every day during swimming lessons. She discovered that "[it] was easier not to be afraid of things, like diving boards and cannonballs and backstrokes, when nobody expected you to be afraid."[44] In other words, if we recognize another's self-identified gender identity, we have the possibility of freeing them from restrictive social norms, and thereby we take responsibility for both the subjectivity of the other and the way in which these norms exclude her.

Justice and the Law

Like ethics, justice describes a relationship between two individuals but mediated by a third—the judge. As discussed, for Levinas, ethics is about the face-to-face relationship between two (or more) individuals. It is about the responsibility that arises from being confronted by another whom I cannot ever completely understand and whose subjectivity would be denied through the appropriative act of knowing.[45] In contrast, law is about appearing face-to-face with another before a third person. How does the judge change the legal relationship? The judge represents community.[46] The judge demands that I take responsibility for the ways in which I objectify others, since this objectification leads to the infringement of the other's rights. Unlike the accusation that the other levels at me in a face-to-face relation, the judge does not only accuse, she also sets out a community standard of behavior and demands compliance.

The law does violence to our identities. This is because the appearance before a third has two important constituent elements: justification and objectification. Justification requires that parties explain to each other in language acceptable to all why it is justified to limit the freedom of the other party. As Levinas points out, when one appears before a third, there is a "copresence on an equal footing."[47] In the ethical relation, one recognizes one's responsibility because one is accused by the other, and so one takes responsibility before any question thematizes the other.[48] However, when appearing before the third, there is thematization—I must describe my actions and allow them to be described by another from that person's perspective.[49] This necessarily involves objectification of myself by the other, because the thematization does not occur from my own standpoint alone.[50] In other words, when appearing before a judge, we become a "theme" or an "object" for the judge, because we are not free to explain who we are and how we behave. Instead, the judge also considers another's account of our identity and our actions to resolve the conflict between the individuals.

Once we have appeared before the judge and the dispute is resolved, the state uses violence or the threat of violence to enforce the legal decision. The most famous statement of this view is by Immanuel Kant, who explains in the *Metaphysics of Morals* that "the *rightful* effect of what is culpable is *punishment* (*poena*)."[51] Similarly, Moses Mendelssohn, another influential Enlightenment philosopher, in his distinction between a person's perfect and imperfect duties, defines perfect duties as those which, if they are not performed, the state has the right to enforce performance.[52] Finally, Theodor Adorno and Max Horkheimer identify the use of state violence as one of the characteristics of law in *Negative Dialectics*:

> Law is the primal phenomenon of irrational rationality.... In its extant forms its destructiveness shows undiminished, thanks to the destructive principal [*sic*] of violence. While a lawless society will succumb to pure license, the law in society is a preservative or terror, always ready to resort to terror with the aid of quotable statutes.[53]

What Adorno and Horkheimer mean by "irrational rationality" is that the law uses the threat of state violence to prevent violence between citizens. It promises peace through violence.[54]

Three aspects of this brief characterization of the law and the relation of justice are relevant for the recognition of gender identity. First, justice involves the mediation of the relation between two individuals by a third—the judge—who represents community standards. The judge does not meet the parties in an ethical face-to-face relationship but sees them through the lens of the community. Second, this mediation involves resolving a potential conflict of rights, because the plaintiff (or victim in the case of criminal law) claims that the defendant has objectified her and failed to recognize her subjectivity. Thus the judge may not accept a person's self-identified gender. Instead, she may consider the other party's characterization of it, because she must acknowledge the way in which the plaintiff or victim claims that her rights have been violated. Third, once the rights of the two individuals are established, the state may use violence to enforce justice. This means that to vindicate the rights of one party, it may use force or the threat of force to impose a gender identity on an individual. This is the source of the anxiety that animates Coyote when she goes to change her legal name.

The Different Relations between State and Individual

In this chapter, I am dealing with the legal recognition of gender identity. By "legal recognition," I mean recognition by the state. What is confusing about calling this "legal recognition" is that the state is not always in a legal relation with its members. Sometimes it is in an ethical relationship, as is the case when an individual is asking the state to recognize her self-declared gender identity for the purpose of accessing public and private services, and sometimes it is in a legal relationship, as is the case when the state is adjudicating a dispute about the conflicting rights of citizens that arises because of different perceptions of a person's gender identity. For instance, the state is in an ethical relation with a person who is seeking a publicly provided identity document such as a driver's license. The state is giving that person a legal means of identifying himself and is not using state-sanctioned force to impose an identity on him. The determination of the applicant's gender does not involve the balancing of rights or the prevention of harm to others, and so there is no question of using force to limit the applicant's rights. Moreover, the state is standing in the place of other private individuals. By issuing an identity document, the state is not just saying that the state recognizes that this document describes you. It is also saying that others ought to recognize you as the state has. In this case, I argue, the state has an ethical duty to recognize a person's self-identified gender.

However, there will be times when the state is in a legal relation with the individual: the state may have to restrict an individual's rights through the use of state-sanctioned force. The state is in a legal relation with a person when the relation between individual and state is mediated by a third (a judge, a magistrate, or justice of the peace or members of an adjudicative tribunal, etc.). The ethical and legal relations differ, because in the case of an ethical relationship, the state is establishing the gender identity of an individual for the purpose of determining the services to which he or she is entitled, but in the case of the legal relation, there are competing rights or entitlements that must be resolved. In other words, in a legal relation, the determination of the rights and entitlements of one individual (or group) depends in part on the determination of the rights and entitlements of another individual (or group). As discussed in the next section, in these cases, B's perception of A's gender may be relevant for determining how to balance the rights and entitlements of A and B. In such a case, the state may legitimately betray its ethical duty and refuse to accept A's self-identified gender, since it may result in harm to B or to an unjustifiable infringement of B's rights and entitlements.

In what follows, I explain how the nature of the state's relation to an individual— be it ethical or legal—affects the recognition of gender identity.

The State's Ethical Obligation to Recognize a Person's Self-Identified Gender

Basic questions of gender identity should be determined through self-identification.[55] When individuals obtain publicly provided identification documents (driver's licenses, social assistance cards, passports, health cards, etc.), they should be given the choice to identify as a man or a woman.[56] This follows from the fact that in an ethical relationship, one is precluded from imposing one's own categories and concepts on another. Recognition of the subjectivity of the other demands that the state not use preconceived notions of "man" and "woman" to categorize individuals against their will. Furthermore, the state must take responsibility for the subjectivity of the other by facilitating public recognition of her identity. The ethical obligation to respect a person's own identity has been recognized in the case of race. The state no longer uses physical criteria where it asks individuals to identify their race: it is up to the individual to self-identify. Similarly, the state should not use physical criteria for identifying legal gender. To do so confuses sex with gender and fails to respect the individual's self-expressed identity.

Further, the state has an ethical obligation to accept a person's gender identity without requiring a medical opinion. First, requiring a medical opinion conflates sex with gender. It presumes that the medical category of sex is determinative of gender identity. Second, this violates the state's ethical obligation to respect the other's subjectivity. The U.K.'s *Gender Recognition Act 2004* is an example of unethical legislation in this regard. In order for a person to change his official gender, the act requires that the request be evaluated by a Gender Recognition Panel. The panel will only approve the application if the applicant has or has had gender dysphoria, has lived in the acquired gender throughout the preceding two years, and intends to continue to live in the acquired gender until death.[57] Though the U.K. legislation is progressive in many ways, it prioritizes gender stability over the state's ethical responsibility to accept self-identification.[58]

Of course, if the state fulfills its ethical obligation to accept a person's self-identified gender, this will make personal identification documents less useful for the provision of state or private services that aim at ameliorating the disadvantaged position of women. However, this will not be as problematic as it seems. Few services exist that are provided differentially purely based on gender. Health insurance is perhaps one of the few such services, since there are statistically significant differences between men and women in terms of longevity and mortality due to certain medical conditions, and therefore there are different insurance rates for the two genders.[59] Most other ameliorative services are based on the intersection of various identities (gender and status as primary child caregiver, gender and marital status, etc.) and are provided in a gender-neutral way, even if they are targeted primarily at a particular gender.[60] Thus, although these services are provided in a gendered manner, gender identity is usually not the only criterion for determining a person's entitlement to the service; other aspects of a person's identity (income, marital status, etc.) can still serve to ensure that services are reaching their intended target.

Finally, it is hard to accept that in order to promote stability, the state in its ethical relation with an individual must only recognize sex rather than gender identity. When we are dealing with a conflict of rights, stability is a legitimate concern. But in most cases in which an individual asks the state to recognize her gender identity, no conflict exists. In such cases, the state should permit changes in gender identity because an individual's gender identity is not itself stable. Requiring a stable gender identity is based on convenience and social convention, and these concerns cannot be reconciled with the obligation to recognize another's subjectivity.

The Legal Relation between the State and an Individual: Dealing with the Competing Rights of Marginalized Groups

In the case of legal relations, a third party—the representative of the public interest—is present.[61] Here, ethical obligations are not sufficient to determine how gender identity should be recognized because what is at issue are competing rights that the state has undertaken to promote and protect.[62] In these cases, the legal face of the state is engaged because its enforcement mechanisms can be employed to limit the rights of one or more parties to a conflict.

Why is the state justified in imposing a particular gender identity on an individual in these cases? As I discuss in the preceding section, gender is socially constructed. This means that it is determined both by the subject and by others who perceive her. In an ethical relation, respect for the subjectivity and absolute autonomy of the subject requires me to accept the gender identity that an individual expresses. However, in the legal relation in which there are competing rights and interests, the acceptance of person A's gender identity may result in the state limiting some other right of person B. For instance, in the case of Kimberly Nixon, if the court recognizes that Nixon is a woman rather than a biological man who identifies as a woman, the result will be the limiting of the Vancouver Rape Relief Society's ability to serve a group that believes that only women born as and having lived their lives as women are suitable rape counselors for women who have experienced violence by men. Or put another way, if the Court forces the Rape Relief Society to train Kimberly Nixon as a rape crisis counselor, some women's right to be free of the fear of male violence will be violated (or else those women will not have access to rape counseling services).

In such a case of competing rights, courts and other adjudicators must take into account B's perception of A's gender identity as a relevant factor in assessing which rights and interests are to be promoted and protected by the state. The reason for this is the presence of the third party—the judge. In an ethical relationship, the subject cannot be asked to justify his subjectivity; responsibility arises before thematization. In a legal relationship, however, each party must justify the limitation of the other party's rights in publicly acceptable language. To put this more concretely, the law requires the Rape Relief Society to justify in language that respects the equal rights of all why Kimberly Nixon ought to be denied a service generally available to the public on the basis of her birth sex.

But at the same time that the law requires justification, it also demands objectification. The law requires us to do two things: to reduce the complexity of our identity to a few characteristics (e.g., "I am a man" or "I am a woman" rather than "biologically I am a man but I live as a woman") and to take into account another's characterization of me. What this objectification means for transgender identity in the law is that self-identity cannot always be the standard when there are conflicting rights at issue.[63] There are occasions in which the law must either force an identity on a person ("you have a mental disorder because you meet the legal definition for having a 'disease of the mind'" or "you are gay because you were assaulted in a gay neighborhood"[64]) or permit a person's identity to be constructed through the constitutive perspectives of multiple individuals. This is what occurred in *Nixon v. Vancouver Rape Relief Society*. Kimberly Nixon's self-identity as a woman was not the only relevant identity. Rather, her identity from the perspective of the Rape Relief Society, or more specifically, from the perspective of women who had been assaulted by men, was also considered to be relevant.

There are a number of possible responses to this characterization of a person's gender identity in law. One possible response is that it is unjust—it is not only a betrayal of the state's ethical responsibility to recognize a person's self-identified gender, it is also a conflation of sex and gender and, consequently, a failure to recognize the diversity of gender identities. This is probably true. The primary purpose of my distinction between ethics and the law has been to justify why there are limits to self-identification of gender. These limits arise when another person's rights will be limited due to her perception of my gender, and they result from the fact that the adjudicative process for resolving these conflicts necessarily involves objectification. However, I have not argued that the normative content of the law is justifiable. Elsewhere, I have expressed the opinion that the law conflates sex and gender and that this is a category mistake with profound negative consequences for the trans community.[65] I also argued that our current human rights legislation is inadequate because it does not allow tribunals and courts to address whether a group's beliefs are unacceptably discriminatory. For instance, in *Nixon*, the higher courts did not consider whether it was legitimate for the society to believe that only a woman born as a woman would be a suitable rape counselor. It is hard to imagine that this proposition is true[66]—violence against trans men and women is severe,[67] and women, both trans and not, might feel more comfortable with a trans rape counselor. However, this issue was not canvassed in the legal cases because the *B.C. Human Rights Act* permits groups to exclude others if the group is characterized by, among other things, a common sex. The act does not require an inquiry into the legitimacy of the basis for the exclusion. Perhaps this is justified, because courts are not a suitable forum for debating whether a group's discriminatory views violate public policy.

A second possible response is that the legal relation is fundamentally unethical because it does not respect the individual's subjectivity—that is, her right to identify her own gender and to have that identity change in different situations. I think that this is a valid criticism. The question then becomes whether we should require an ethical legal system or whether an ethical legal system is even possible. As Asher Horowitz points out, it seems that an ethical legal system is not possible. As long as the law claims the right to enforce compliance with the law through force, it will always betray its ethical aspirations.[68]

Although I have expressed the view that courts may legitimately consider one litigant's perception of the other litigant's gender identity to determine that person's rights and entitlements, I do not think that there are many practical circumstances in which another's perception would be relevant to or should be determinative of the outcome. Margaret Denike points out that while it might be acceptable to exclude a postoperative male-to-female transsexual from being a rape counselor, it does not seem reasonable to bar such a person from a women-only space whose purpose is to gather women together to listen to music, as is the case with the Michigan Womyn's Music Festival.[69] I agree entirely with this view. It is hard to see how the ability to listen to music in the company of people of the same sex is a fundamental right like access to rape crisis counseling. Protecting a person's bodily integrity and autonomy is of an entirely different order from cultural experiences.[70]

Conclusion

In this chapter, I argue that we all have an ethical obligation to accept a person's self-identified gender. In most interactions with the state, the state likewise has an ethical obligation to accept a person's identity. However, there are circumstances in which the state's relation to an individual is a "legal" relation in the technical sense discussed here: the state is represented through a "third person" (a judge) before whom two or more parties are disputing their rights and entitlements. In such situations, there may be cases in which a conflict arises because of one person's perception of another's gender, regardless of the latter's self-identified gender. If this occurs, the necessity of justifying the infringement of another's rights or entitlements may require a judge to take into account one of the litigant's perceptions of the other litigant's gender. However, this failure to accept a person's self-identified gender is not ethically justifiable. It is unethical and violent in two senses. First, it does violence to an individual's autonomy—her freedom to express who she is through her gender expression. The state objectifies the individual rather than accepting her as a free, autonomous individual. As I note, failure to recognize a person's self-identified identity goes far beyond the infringement of human dignity inherent in equality claims. In an equality claim, we generally do not challenge a person's identity as part of a marginalized group, whereas in the cases discussed here, a person's identity is in issue. Second, having objectified a person, the state does violence to her by limiting her rights and entitlements and backing this limitation with the threat of state-sanctioned force.

In this chapter, I have by no means addressed all of the concrete legal issues that face transgendered people. Some discrimination against trans individuals raises pure equality issues rather than identity issues. For instance, if a person quits her job while transitioning in order to avoid discrimination, but is then denied access to employment insurance on the basis that she does not have a legitimate reason for having quit her job, it is clear that this is not a question of identity but of a denial of equality to a person who is transitioning.[71] However, I leave the discussion of these and other issues for another time.

NOTES

1. Ivan E. Coyote, "You're Not in Kansas Anymore," in *Close to Spider Man* (Vancouver: Arsenal Pulp, 2000), 79–81, at 80–81.

2. Margaret Denike, Sal Renshaw, and cj Rowe, "Transgender Human Rights and Women's Substantive Equality," National Association of Women and the Law (NAWL), 2003, at http://www.nawl.ca/ns/en/index.html, at 5. For another statement of potential conflicts between feminism and transgender identity, see Shannon E. Wyss, "Sometimes Boy, Sometimes Girl: Learning to Be GenderQueer through a Child's Eyes," in *Trans/forming Feminisms: Trans-Feminist Voices Speak Out*, ed. Krista Scott-Dixon (Toronto: Sumach, 2006), 58–64, at 61.

3. It is a basic rule of the construction of contracts that they are to be interpreted in the context of the intention of the parties to the contract. See, for instance, Kim Lewison, *The Interpretation of Contracts* (London: Sweet and Maxwell, 1989), at 124; Joseph Chitty, *Chitty on Contracts*, 26th ed., vol. 1 (London: Sweet and Maxwell, 1989), at 520.

4. As Justice Brandeis of the U.S. Supreme Court stated: "It is usually more important that a rule of law be settled, than that it be settled right" (*Di Santo v. Pennsylvania*, 273 U.S. 34, 47 S. Ct. 267 (1927), at 270 S. Ct.). See also Justice Benjamin Cardozo's words in *The Nature of the Judicial Process* (New Haven, Conn.: Yale University Press, 1960), at 149. On departure from precedent being the exception, not the rule, see *R. v. Bernard*, [1988] 2 S.C.R. 833, [1988] S.C.J. No. 96, at 849; *R. v. Chaulk*, [1990] 3 S.C.R. 1303, [1990] S.C.J. No. 139, 1352; *R. v. Salituro*, [1991] 3 S.C.R. 654, [1991] S.C.J. No. 97; and *David Polowin Real Estate Ltd. v. The Dominion of Canada General Insurance Co.* (2005), 76 O.R. (3d) 161, at para. 118 ff.

5. Of course, the rule serves many other less noble principles, such as judicial economy (Cardozo, *Judicial Process, supra* note 4, at 149).

6. For instance, in *R. v. Jobidon*, [1991] 2 S.C.R. 714, 66 C.C.C. (3d) 454, Justice Gonthier, writing for a majority of the Supreme Court of Canada, interpreted the new provisions on assault in line with the case law interpreting the old provisions, stating:

> Parliament could have taken the opportunity to specify whether the common law, which already had had much to say about assault and the requirement of consent, was being emptied of relevance. But it did not do these things. Nor did it have to.
>
> Just as the common law has built up a rich jurisprudence around the concepts of agreement in contract law, and *volenti no fit injuria* in the law of negligence, it has also generated a body of law to illuminate the meaning of consent and to lace certain limitations on its legal effectiveness in the criminal law.

7. The definitive statement on vested rights in Canadian law is *Spooner Oils Ltd. v. Turner Valley Gas Conservation Board*, [1933] S.C.R. 629 at 638. See also *Dikranian v. Quebec (Attorney General)*, 2005 SCC 73, [2005] 3 S.C.R. 530 at para. 32 ff.

8. On the distinction between the principle of nonretroactivity and vested rights, see *Dikranian*, at paras. 30–31. See also Pierre-André Côté, *The Interpretation of Legislation in Canada*, 3rd ed. (Scarborough, Ont.: Carswell, 2000) at 156.

9. Generally speaking, the legislative platforms of various political parties in a mature democracy do not vary all that widely.

10. "There is perhaps nothing so firmly entrenched in the way that our society thinks about the world than that there are two and only two-genders [*sic*], and that those genders never change" (barbara findlay, Sandra Lafrarnboise, Deborah Brady, Christine Burnharn, and Septima (Ron) Skolney-Elverson, *Finding Our Place: Transgendered Law Reform Project* [Vancouver: High Risk Project Society, 1996], at 14). finlay points out that "because the law reflects the society of which it is a part, the law, too, can only 'see' two genders, male and female" (quoted in Margaret Denike, Introduction to Section III, "Inclusion and Exclusion," in *Trans/forming Feminisms: Trans-Feminist Voices Speak Out*, ed. Krista Scott-Dixon [Toronto: Sumach, 2006], 136–44, at 137). reese simpkins points out how North American culture's "hegemonic discourse" of sex requires rigid characterizations of what qualifies as "male" and "female" (reese simpkins, "Transmasculinities," in *Trans/forming Feminisms: Trans-Feminist Voices Speak Out*, ed. Krista Scott-Dixon [Toronto: Sumach, 2006], 79–85, at 80).

11. Graham Mayeda, "Re-imagining Feminist Theory: Transgender Identity and the Law," *Canadian Journal of Women and the Law* 17, no. 2 (2005): 423–72; Francisco Valdes, "Queers, Sissies, Dykes, and Tomboys: Deconstructing the Conflation of 'Sex,' 'Gender,' and 'Sexual Orientation' in Euro-American Law and Society," *California Law Review* 83 (1995): 1; Mary Anne C. Case, "Disaggregating Gender from Sex and Sexual Orientation: The Effeminate Man in the Law and Feminist Jurisprudence," *Yale Law Journal* 105 (1995): 1; and Katherine M. Franke, "The Central Mistake of Sex Discrimination Law: The Disaggregation of Sex from Gender" *University of Pennsylvania Law Review* 144 (1995): 1.

12. On the irony of this reliance on biology for a "reliable" indicator of sexual identity, see note 3.

13. *Corbett v. Corbett*, [1970] 2 All E.R. 33 at 107.

14. Caroline White and Joshua Goldberg point out that "Going outside prevailing gender norms, or loving someone who does, is a sign of sexual deviance" (Caroline White and Joshua Goldberg, "Expanding Our Understanding of Gendered Violence: Violence against Trans People and Their Loved Ones," *Canadian Woman Studies* 15, no. 1/2 [2006]: 124).

15. Catharine MacKinnon states: "The social relation between the sexes is organized so that men may dominate and women must submit and this relation is sexual—in fact is sex. Men in particular, if not men alone, sexualize inequality, especially the inequality of the sexes" (Catharine MacKinnon, *Feminism Unmodified: Discourses on Life and Law* [Cambridge: Harvard University Press, 1987], at 3).

16. Of course, this reliance on scientific categories of sex is ironic, since science recognizes that sexual identity is not confined to two simple categories (Julie A. Greenberg, "Defining Male and Female: Intersexuality and the Collision between Law and Biology," *Arizona Law Review* 41 [1999]: 265).

17. Ivan E. Coyote, "Walks Like," in *Close to Spider Man* (Vancouver: Arsenal Pulp, 2000), 17–19.

18. Ivan E. Coyote, "What If," in Coyote, *Loose End* (Vancouver: Arsenal Pulp, 2005), 167–69.

19. Maternity leave, for instance, is only provided to women who give birth to their children. Although many shelters now accommodate the trans community, some women's shelters for women who experience male violence provide services on a gendered basis. Toilets and change-rooms in athletic and other recreational facilities and in retail stores are frequently provided to one or the other gender, but rarely both (see *Sheridan v. Sanctuary Investments Ltd. (c.o.b. B.J.'s Lounge),* [1999] B.C.H.R.T.D. No. 43 (QL)). Some occupations have not been open to both genders, though this is slowly changing.

20. Ibid.

21. On the importance of adequate social assistance in the prevention of violence against women, see Jane Mosher and Pat Evans, "Welfare Policy: A Critical Site of Struggle for Women's Safety," *Canadian Woman Studies* 25, no. 1/2 (2006): 162.

22. The University of Ottawa where I am employed provides a grant for teaching release for women to help them prepare for tenure. In Ontario, women who have experienced violence can obtain a deferral from workfare programs if they have experienced domestic violence (Mosher and Evans, "Welfare Policy," *supra* note 21, at 164; Janet Mosher, Pat Evans, Margaret Little, Ontario Association of Interval and Transition Houses and Ontario Social Safety Network, "Walking on Eggshells: Abused Women's Experiences of Ontario's Welfare System," 2004, at http://osgoode.yorku.ca/osgmedia.nsf/research/mosher_janet, at 40). Note that the deferral is available to either gender if a person has experienced domestic violence. But the fact that most domestic violence is experienced by women and children indicates that, despite the neutral wording of Ontario Works Directive 6–16, this is a rule pertaining primarily to women.

23. Louise Arbour, *Commission of Inquiry into Certain Events at the Prison for Women in Kingston* (Ottawa: Public Works and Government Services Canada, 1996), at 241–42.

24. *Kavanagh v. Attorney General of Canada,* [2001] CHRD No. 21 (QL).

25. In Canada, see *R. v. Golden,* [2001] 3 S.C.R. 679, 2001 SCC 83, at para. 101. For the analogous policy in the U.K., see *Police and Criminal Evidence Act 1984* (U.K.), 1984, c. 60, Code A, para. 3.6.

26. *R. v. Hornick,* [2002] O.J, No, 1170 (QL) (Ontario Court of Justice) [Hornick]. For another interesting case involving a strip search of a transgender person, see *Forrester v. Peel (Regional Municipality) Police Services Board,* [2006] O.H.R.T.D. No. 13; 2006 HRTO 13. In the decision the Ontario Human Rights Tribunal sets out some guidelines—some positive and some problematic—for the police to follow when searching a transgender person.

27. Paul Gallant, "Got Booze, No Privacy," *XTRA!* (1 November 2001).

28. *Doe by Doe v. City of Belleville,* Ill., 119 F. 3d 563 (7th Cir. 1997) at 580. For other cases on harassment in similar circumstances, see *Rene v. MGM Grand Hotel, Inc.,* 305 F. 3d 1061 (9th Cir. 2002); *Nichols v. Azteca Restaurant Enterprises, Inc.,* 256 F. 3d 864 (9th Cir. 2001); and *Smith v. Salem, Ohio, et al.,* No. 03–3399 (6th Cir., filed 1 June 2004).

29. *Mamela v. Vancouver Lesbian Connection,* [1999] B.C.H.R.T.D. No. 51 (QL).

30. *Nixon v. Vancouver Rape Relief Society,* [2002] B.C.H.R.T.D. No. 1, 2002 BCHRT 1 (QL) at para. 44.

31. For the Superior Court decision, see *Vancouver Rape Relief Society v. Nixon,* [2003] B.C.J. No. 2899; 2003 B.C.S.C. 1936. For the Court of Appeal Decision, see *Vancouver Rape*

Relief Society v. Nixon (2005), 262 D.L.R. (4th) 360, 2005 BCCA 601. For a discussion of the case by Nixon's lawyer, see barbara findlay, "Acting Queerly: Lawyering for Trans People," in *Trans/forming Feminisms: Trans-Feminist Voices Speak Out*, ed. Krista Scott-Dixon (Toronto: Sumach, 2006), 145–53. See also Mayeda, "Re-imagining Feminist Theory," *supra* note 11 and Lori Chambers, "Unprincipled Exclusions: Feminist Theory, Transgender Jurisprudence, and Kimberly Nixon," *Canadian Journal of Women and the Law* 19:2 (2007): 305–334.

32. For a different view, see Darryl B. Hill, "On the Origins of Gender," in *Trans/forming Feminisms: Trans-Feminist Voices Speak Out*, ed. Krista Scott-Dixon (Toronto: Sumach, 2006), 39–45. Hill interviews a number of people who identify as trans and demonstrates that some hold an essentialist position—they were born with a particular gender identity—while others hold a constructionist view. For another essentialist view, see Lesley Carter, who states her identity as follows: "I firmly believe that I was born a woman but lived in an uncomfortable denial for many years" ("Female by Surgery," in ibid., at 56).

33. Susan Williams, "Feminist Legal Epistemologies" B*erkeley Women's Law Journal* 8 (1993): 63. See also Luce Irigaray, *The Ethics of Sexual Difference*, trans. Carolyn Burke and Gillian C. Gill (Ithaca, N.Y.: Cornell University Press, 1993).

34. This does not mean that I do not consider the physicality of a person's body as playing a role in the construction of his or her gender. However, the physical body only takes on the meanings assigned to it through language. On the conflict between social constructionist and physicalist views of gender, see Judith Butler, "Doing Justice to Someone: Sex Reassignment and Allegories of Transsexuality," *Undoing Gender* (New York: Routledge, 2004), at 62–67.

35. Here, I am following Judith Butler to some degree, who states that "gender is the apparatus by which the production and normalization of masculine and feminine take place along with the interstitial forms of hormonal, chromosomal, psychic, and performative that gender assumes" (Judith Butler, "Gender Regulations," *Undoing Gender* [New York: Routledge, 2004], at 42). On the distinction between construction as process and construction as product, see Ian Hacking, *The Social Construction of What?* (Cambridge: Harvard University Press, 1999), at 36–39.

36. Hacking discusses this type of construction by using the example of Kurt Danzinger's *Constructing the Subject* (1990). Hacking points out that the construction of the subject of psychological study has created "a kind of person who hardly existed a century and a half ago: fit subject for testing" (Hacking, *Social Construction of What? supra* note 35, at 52).

37. In the past, there may well have been such an association, given that the law of property often denied women the ability to own property.

38. Hacking, *Social Construction of What? supra* note 35, at 162.

39. Emmanuel Levinas, *Totality and Infinity: An Essay on Exteriority*, trans. Alphonso Lingis (Pittsburgh: Duquesne University Press, 1969), at 50–51 and 51–52.

40. Here, we are dealing with the phenomenon of accusation and reaction. Of course, in a social context, individuals can avoid answering an accusation because structures of ethical power betray ethical responsibility.

41. Emmanuel Levinas, *Otherwise Than Being or Beyond Essence*, trans. Alphonso Lingis (The Hague: Martinus Nijhoff, 1981), at 124.

42. Asher Horowitz, *Ethics at a Standstill* (Pittsburgh: Duquesne University Press, 2008), at 2.

43. Judith Butler questions whether recognition of the other's subjectivity can ever avoid destroying this recognition (Judith Butler, "Longing for Recognition," in *Undoing Gender* [New York: Routledge, 2004], at 144–46).

44. Ivan E. Coyote, "No Bikini," *Close to Spider Man* (Vancouver: Arsenal Pulp, 2000), at 23.

45. Levinas is clear that the other is not "unknown" as opposed to "known." He says, "The sense of our whole effort lies in affirming not that the Other forever escapes knowing, but that there is no meaning in speaking here of knowledge or ignorance" (Levinas, *Totality and Infinity, supra* note 39, at 89).

46. For instance, in the *Critique of Judgment*, Kant explains that judgment involves divorcing oneself from one's own proclivities and assessing a work of art from the point of view of community standards. Hannah Arendt, taking Kant as her starting point, applies Kant's theory of aesthetic judgment to political judgment and grounds this judgment in regard for the views of a concrete community rather than using the abstract approach that Kant advocates (see Hannah Arendt, *Lectures on Kant's Political Philosophy* [Chicago, IL: University of Chicago Press, 1982]).

47. Levinas, *Otherwise Than Being, supra* note 41, at 157.

48. If one thematized the other, one would be seeing the other through one's own categories and projections.

49. As Levinas says, "contiguity" with the other (i.e., appearing before a third with the other) "presupposes both thematizing thought and a locus and the cutting up of the continuity of space into discrete terms and the whole—out of justice" (Levinas, *Otherwise Than Being, supra* note 41, at 157).

50. Ibid., at 158.

51. Immanuel Kant, *The Metaphysics of Morals*, trans. Mary Gregor (Cambridge: Cambridge University Press, 1996), at 19 [6:227].

52. Moses Mendelssohn, *Jerusalem, or On Religious Power and Judaism*, trans. Allan Arkush (Hanover, N.H.: Brandeis University Press, 1983), at 46–47.

53. Theodor Adorno and Max Horkheimer, *Negative Dialectics*, trans. E. B. Ashton (New York: Seabury, 1979).

54. On the way in which the law betrays its goal of eliminating violence by threatening violence, see Horowitz, *Ethics at a Standstill, supra* note 42.

55. For a similar view on self-identification, see Lori Chambers, "Unprincipled Exclusions: Feminist Theory, Transgender Jurisprudence, and Kimberly Nixon," *Canadian Journal of Women and the Law* 19, no. 2 (2007): 305–334.

56. In my view, they should also be given the opportunity of not providing their gender identity or of providing some alternative to male or female if they wish. However, I do not discuss that possibility here.

57. *Gender Recognition Act 2004* (U.K.), 2004, c, 7.

58. Even more problematic are laws that require surgery before a change in gender can be registered. For instance, *Ontario's Vital Statistics Act*, R.S.O. 1990, ch. V.4, s. 36, permits a change of "sex" only if a person has undergone "transsexual surgery." For commentary on the medicalization of gender identity, see Denike, introduction to *Trans/forming Feminisms, supra* note 10, at 138.

59. It is not clear whether insurance companies collect data based on biological sex or gender, nor is it clear which is the causal factor—biological sex or gender. Are young transgendered men who have adopted traditional male forms of gender expression more likely to be involved in fatal traffic accidents than the women with whom they share more biological similarities?

60. For instance, the *Employment Standards Act*, 2000, S.O. 2000, c. 41, allows either parent to take "parental" leave, although statistically, more women than men take advantage of this provision.

61. On the relationship between the judge and the community, see Graham Mayeda, "Uncommonly Common: The Nature of Common Law Judgment," *Canadian Journal of Law and Jurisprudence* 19(1) (2006): 107–31, and Graham Mayeda, "Between a Rock and a Hard Place: Judging in the Space between Community and the Individual," on file with author. In my view, the issue of whom the judge represents is difficult to resolve.

62. As Neil MacCormick points out, one of the hallmarks of the liberal state is that it sometimes promotes inconsistent or conflicting rights (Neil MacCormick, "Natural Law and the Separation of Law and Morals," in *Natural Law Theory: Contemporary Essays*, ed. Robert P. George [Oxford: Clarendon, 1992], at 126–29).

63. A friend recently criticized my view that balancing rights might require a court to take into account a transgendered person's biological sex. He said that transgendered people always get the short end of the stick when rights are being balanced. This is an important point. If one were to imagine that Nixon had identified as a woman but had what are traditionally identified as male physical features and had been excluded from the training program on that basis, it seems unlikely that courts would balance the right to identify one's own gender with a rape victim's right to security and bodily integrity in the same way. In such a case, it is more obvious how the imposition of a gender identity on a person is objectionable. But as I have stated, the difficulty is that human rights legislation permits groups to hold what are arguably discriminatory views.

64. See the two cases *R. v. J.S.*, [2003] B.C.J. 2877 (QL), and *R. v. Cran*, [2005] B.C.S.C. 171 (QL). Both involve an attack on Aaron Webster, a man killed in a park in a notorious gay "cruising zone" in Vancouver. In *J.S.*, the judge accepted that the crime was a hate crime against a gay man although there was no direct evidence that Webster identified as being gay. This is a classic example of how the law imposes identities on individuals.

65. Mayeda, "Re-imagining Feminist Theory," *supra* note 11.

66. For a different view, see Christine Boyle, "The Anti-Discrimination Norm in Human Rights and Charter Law: *Nixon v. Vancouver Rape Relief*" *University of British Columbia Law Review* 37(1) (2004): 31; and Joanna Harris, "Competing Claims from Disadvantaged Groups: *Nixon v. Vancouver Rape Relief Society*," in *Trans/forming Feminisms: Trans-Feminist Voices Speak Out*, ed. Krista Scott-Dixon (Toronto: Sumach, 2006), at 170–81.

67. Kyle Scanlon, "Where's the Beef? Masculinity as Performed by Feminists," in *Trans/forming Feminisms: Trans-Feminist Voices Speak Out*, ed. Krista Scott-Dixon (Toronto: Sumach, 2006), 87–94, at 89; Joshua Goldberg and Carolien White, "Anti-Violence Work in Transition," in ibid., 217–26; Emilia L. Lombardi, Riki Anne Wilchins, Dana Priesing, and Diana Malouf, "Gender Violence: Transgender Experiences with Violence and Discrimination," *Journal of Homosexuality* 42 (2001): 89–101; FORGE, *Transgender Sexual Violence Project: Raw Data Graphs* (Milwaukee: FORGE, 2005).

68. On the one hand, a just state seems to be ethical, since it aims at achieving a peaceful society. However, the state betrays ethics by using force to achieve this society. This contradiction is expressed by Horowitz: "the ethical relation ethically demands the just State which both expresses an defeats the ethical relation" (Horowitz, *Ethics at a Standstill, supra* note 42, at 5). Emmanuel Levinas recognizes this in his later work. For instance, he writes that politics simply betrays ethics (*Otherwise Than Being, supra* note 41, at 177). On this point, see also Jacques Derrida, "The Force of Law: The Mystical Foundation of Authority" (1990) 11 *Cardozo Law Review* 920–1046.

69. Denike, introduction to *Trans/forming Feminisms, supra* note 10, at 140–42.

70. Cultural feminists might reach the opposite conclusion.

71. Scanlon, "Where's the Beef?" *supra* note 65, at 88.

Index

LaVergne, TN USA
10 September 2010
196596LV00002B/1/P